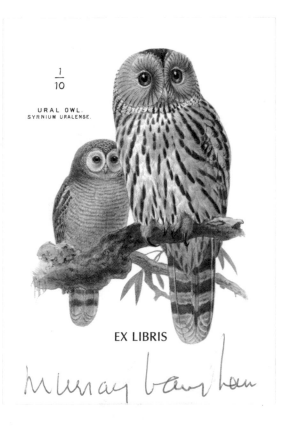

$\frac{1}{10}$

URAL OWL.
SYRNIUM URALENSE.

EX LIBRIS

# Maurice Collis
# Diaries: 1949–1969

# BY LOUISE COLLIS

### NOVELS:

*Without a Voice*
*A Year Passed*
*After the Holiday*
*The Angel's Name*
*The Great Flood*

### HISTORICAL ESSAYS:

*Seven in the Tower*

### BIOGRAPHIES:

*The Apprentice Saint*
*Soldier in Paradise*
*A Private View of Stanley Spencer*

# Maurice Collis
# Diaries: 1949–1969

*edited and introduced by Louise Collis*

HEINEMANN : LONDON

William Heinemann Ltd
15 Queen Street, Mayfair, London W1X 8BE

LONDON   MELBOURNE   TORONTO
JOHANNESBURG   AUCKLAND

First published 1977
© Louise Collis 1977

SBN: 434 14071 6

Printed in Great Britain
by W & J Mackay Limited, Chatham

# CONTENTS

Introduction                              1

The Diary 1949–1969                      15

Finis                                   204

Index                                   212

# ILLUSTRATIONS

*Facing page*

1  A manuscript page of the Diaries                                          56

2  Maurice Collis in his studio (*Gerti Deutsch*)                            56

3  Maurice Collis' mother aged 85, drawn by Feliks Topolski                  57

4  Maurice Collis' Burmese horoscope                                         57

5  L. S. Lowry (*Sports & General*)                                          88

6  U Nu, Maurice Collis and Sir Reginald Dorman-Smith                        88
   (*The Central Press Photos Ltd*)

7  Maurice Collis with Burmese officials and editors (*far left* U Thant)    89

8  Stanley Spencer in 1956 (*Radio Times Hulton Picture Library*)            89

9  Bill and Bronwen Astor                                                    120

10  Cliveden (*Fine Art Engravers Ltd*)                                      120

11  Henry Moore in his studio                                                121

12  Barbara Hepworth at work on *The Spirit of Discovery*                    121
   (*Radio Times Hulton Picture Library*)

13  Mervyn Peake                                                             152

14  Nancy Astor in 1957 (*Radio Times Hulton Picture Library*)              152

15  Maurice Collis sorting the Stanley Spencer papers (*Mark Gerson*)        153

16  Feliks Topolski, Louise Collis and Maurice Collis, 1972                  153

# INTRODUCTION

I

Maurice Collis was born in Dublin on 10 January 1889. His father was a solicitor whose firm, Collis & Ward, became successful, imprinting itself on the mind of the young James Joyce as he wandered the streets of the city, immersed in strange dreams. The seedy lawyer, Richie Goulding, in *Ulysses* is represented as a partner in Collis & Ward.

In the 1890s the family moved to Killiney, a pretty seaside place some miles south of Dublin. Here Maurice grew up with his four younger brothers and sisters. Though he remembered this period with affection, in actual fact family life was explosive, for Mrs Collis was of a tempestuous nature, lavishing a fierce possessive affection on some of her children and rejecting one utterly from the moment of his birth. The house resounded to the roar of battle daily and the servants left with a regularity that grew more frequent as the years went by. Mr Collis existed as peacefully as he could in this whirlpool, occupying his leisure with hunting, fishing, golf, billiards and Dickens.

After a conventional education in England, as was the custom, Maurice left Oxford in 1910 with a first-class degree in history, having already decided to go in for the Indian Civil Service. He had poetic leanings at this time, but they were slight and undeveloped, whereas the idea of travel to the other side of the world and an immediate good salary appealed strongly to the active and romantic part of his nature. There were also family connections with India. Some of his aunts were missionaries and his uncle, Sir George Grierson, was a famous orientalist who had been opium agent, a sinecure given to him by enlightened superiors so that he might complete his *Linguistic Survey*, eventually published in 18 volumes and covering 179 languages, mostly Indian, and 544 dialects.

In 1912, then, Maurice found himself posted to Burma as he had not passed the civil service examination well enough to secure a position in India which held out much better prospects of advancement. He was very ambitious: knowing himself to be clever and strong-willed, he had resolved to rise to the top of his profession. But his expectations were too simple. Although, in the end, he was to become curiously famous in Burma, it was not through the attainment of high office; he was destined to excel as an author, after his civil service career had more or less crashed.

These events, however, waited in the future as he set off for Rangoon with the girl he had recently married. Just before leaving, he had written a book on the Napoleonic legend as developed by the nineteenth-century poets, for which he had failed to secure a publisher. He had no further unconventional ideas. 'In 1912,' he wrote,* 'no one thought it strange that every year young Englishmen were posted five thousand miles into Asia to govern countries belonging to other races. What will our descendants think of us when they read that the British banished the King of Burma, annexed his country and proceeded to govern it by officials of their own race. Historians will add that we saw no harm in this, though we always resisted such a fate to the death whenever it threatened our own land.' The subjugation of the dark people had been embalmed in layers of secular missionary zeal, so that it was accepted by persons otherwise intelligent that the poor natives were incapable of managing their own affairs and that it was the duty of educated white men to help and guide them to a life more consonant with western ideals than that which they had led before.

Only gradually did Maurice Collis begin to think there was some fallacy in this. His first years were untroubled. He enjoyed learning the job, trying to speak Burmese, hunting, bathing and playing tennis at the club to which, of course, no coloured person was admitted except as a servant. He was not allowed to volunteer for the army in 1914, and only when a Burmese brigade was raised in 1917 did he serve for a short time in Palestine where he never was engaged in battle. When he arrived home in 1918, it was six years since he had seen Europe.

During this time, his marriage had ended and his romantic enthusiasm for the Orient had been tested against reality. In the loneliness of jungle creeks and villages, where he might be the only educated man for hundreds of miles, he had meditated on his situation, wondering whether he had made the right choice of a career.

* *The Journey Outward*, 1952.

Was he suited to an official life? Would it not be much more stimulating to find a job in England and become a writer? These questions agitated him during 1919 as he saw old friends, went to exhibitions and concerts and madly wrote poems in the manner of the Celtic revival.

By the end of 1919 he had discovered that he could not get a suitable job, that no one would publish his poems and that the oriental world had made a profound impression tending to cut him off from those of his acquaintance who, having survived the war, now inhabited literary London. He therefore returned to Burma. He was thirty and his hungry mind fastened on the literature of India, China, Burma: on Buddhism, Hinduism, Confucianism; on the history, ceramics, sculpture, painting of the entire East; on the village life he had before his eyes; on western art and writing as reflected in the stream of magazines and books he ordered from London and which, arriving six or eight weeks later up some tidal river, gave him many peaceful days. He wrote long poems in the Spenserian mode, chiefly on the subject of Druids.

He also became acquainted with a memorable holy man, a Buddhist monk, abbot of a small monastery in the forest who had the title Sayadaw, which may be translated Royal Teacher. By study of the scriptures and strenuous meditation, he had developed psychic powers. He spent part of his day working on astrology and magic which perhaps were connected with his metaphysical speculations. He ate only once in twenty-four hours, begging the food from house to house. His predictions were remarkable. On reading the horoscope which Maurice had had made by an official astrologer, last relic of the court of Mandalay, he said that Maurice had an extraordinary future in front of him, that he would die famous and that he would shortly leave his present post and marry again. The Sayadaw's method of arriving at his conclusions was to rise at dawn and sit with the horoscope, which was inscribed on a palm leaf, resting on his hands. After a while he would have a prophetic vision.

When the people of the district heard these things, certain manifestations began to occur. A pagoda emitted rays of light, an indication that the Buddha, or one of his emissaries, was visiting the place; and a spirit inhabiting a small mountain on an island intimated that it wished to see Maurice Collis when he came to check the treasury and investigate complaints.

Shortly afterwards, Maurice suddenly decided to take leave on half pay, dividing his time between London, Paris and Ireland. He would try to get his verses published and look again for a job. Soon he was in Paris, tearing round the art shows, the museums, the ballet, the theatre. It was 1921. The new art was in full swing. All the artists later so famous, now so incredibly expensive, were to be seen walking the streets. Lopokova danced. James Joyce had just finished *Ulysses*. The excitement was endless. One day on a tram he met Eleanor Bourke who was working at the British Embassy. He had known her slightly as a boy, for she had lived in Killiney not far fom his home. Now he fell in love with her and they married almost immediately.

He managed to get his poems printed in London, but the cruel things the critics said of them and the minuscule sales depressed him; nor could he find a job. In 1922 he returned to Burma. 'I had fifteen more years before I could get my pension,' he noted.* 'The prospect would have overcome me, I think, had I been going out alone, but now I set off believing it could be borne.'

Yet he was divided on this point. Sometimes he felt he could rise very high in the service and that he was really better fitted for an active executive career than the more contemplative life of a writer. Besides, he had not been able to think of anything to write except poems that were generally deplored by people qualified to judge them. He therefore applied himself busily to his work as an adminis- trator, keeping in touch meanwhile with the Sayadaw, who assured him that present dissatisfactions were due to adverse astrological in- fluences; these would be resolved in 1930–31 after a clash with people of his own nation. He was unable to give details, or to accept pay- ment for his advice.

'From a worldly point of view,' subsequently reflected Maurice,* 'it is not a good plan, if you belong to an organisation, to improve your general education.' The impetuosity of his mind was such that he could not prevent himself doing this continually. The width of his interests and the vigour with which he pursued them created a dis- tance between himself and his colleagues who, though all university men, had not, for the most part, kept up the intellectual life. He had a few friends, but the colonial round in small towns and hill stations of dinner and bridge parties, picnics, tennis and golf became less enjoy-

* *Into Hidden Burma*, 1953.

able. At no time was he tactful with those he considered bores.

He gave satisfaction, however, being promoted to a better country district in 1923,* where there were certain ruins guarded by the ghost of an old woman who had been sacrificed at the building of them and bound by magic to watch for ever. So she remained, a forlorn spirit wandering the precincts of a former palace, well known to the local inhabitants, though not to Maurice. One evening she decided to visit him. The house where he was sitting shook and he saw an old woman slowly climbing the verandah steps. She stared at him for an instant and went away.

Next morning he enquired of the people if there had been a slight earthquake the evening before, and whether one of them had come to ask him something. They said, no. In further conversation, they explained what had happened, expressing great pleasure that this renowned spirit had taken an interest in him. A guardian ghost always shook the house before appearing. It was a habit left over from the old days when the king and his ministers were thus warned of danger. It was very unusual for her to be bothered with a European.

Early in 1925, Maurice received orders to go to Rangoon on special duty. He was made deputy secretary to the Governor. This was a substantial move up and seemed in accordance with the Sayadaw's predictions of eventual fame and prosperity, but he found the work exacting. He had to remain in an office all day long with endless trays of papers brought in by Indian clerks, and files to be taken home in the evening. No curious gods or goddesses haunted these corridors. The Burmese were hardly to be seen amongst the multitude of Indians inhabiting the city, to which they were not foreigners in law because Burma was technically a province of India. The time for reading and reflection was much reduced, and there was less scope for the individualist, the dreamer, the consulter of oracles. The clubs appeared to be stuffed with bores and one was obliged to be a member of them all. Nevertheless, he worked hard and conscientiously until the end of 1926. He had been four years without leave.

In London again in 1927, he met Geoffrey Faber whom he had known since their schooldays together at Rugby. Faber was on the point of founding his publishing house and asked Maurice whether he

* The Sayadaw wrote to tell him this would happen some months before he received the official posting.

would like to join him. It was the sort of offer he had longed for in the jungle solitudes and from underneath the mountain of files and papers at the secretariat. When they went into the matter, however, it became clear that he could not raise anything like the amount of capital Geoffrey required. It was a cruel disappointment. He spent much of the rest of his leave in Paris studying Chinese ceramics.

The next posting in Burma turned out to be a country district. A change had come over the villages: Gandhi's ideas had arrived in a confused form. While educated Burmese in Rangoon agitated for national independence, or home rule, and had, indeed, obtained some changes in the constitution, the villagers were firmly of the opinion that a saviour king was about to appear who, attacking the invaders of their land with magic and the supernatural, would restore the ancient grandeur of the Burmese court.

After a few months, Maurice was made Deputy Commissioner and District Magistrate of Rangoon. Though technically not such a good job as a secretaryship to the governor, it suited him much better. The court cases were varied and sometimes entertaining. His other duties brought him in touch socially with the leading members of the Chinese, Indian and Burmese communities, very different in outlook and experience from the farmers of the villages.

Everything went smoothly until November 1929 when the Sayadaw suddenly appeared from his jungle fastness, saying that the time of tribulation was at hand. But it would be short and, in the end, beneficial. He brought a magical diagram which he advised Maurice to wear in order to ward off immediate dangers. He then retreated as mysteriously as he had come.

Three weeks later a European was brought to court accused of having caused the death of his servant by bullying him to such an extent that the wretched man jumped out of the window. He was acquitted, but Maurice lectured him from the bench on the inhumanity of his behaviour. This caused a furore in the English community. Never had a white man been humiliated in front of the Burmese like that. It was simply not done.

Within two months, the Mayor of Calcutta, Sen Gupta, was accused of making seditious speeches while passing through Rangoon. He was closely associated with Gandhi who was on the point of launching his civil disobedience campaign when thousands of his followers went to the seaside and made salt, thus infringing the law; and other thousands sat down on the streets of cities and refused to move. The government were afraid of the disturbances spreading to Burma and wished Sen Gupta to be convicted as a dangerous agitator. Unfortunately the evidence against him proved to be only technical and Maurice sentenced him to ten days' imprisonment, a judgment the higher court was unable to dispute.

The official community now began to look on Maurice with suspicion, calling him pro-Burman, bolshy, and other opprobrious names. He had also begun publishing cheerful little stories under a pseudonym in the *Rangoon Gazette*, a sign of unconventionality which must have increased their distrust. His judgments had, indeed, made him popular with the Asian community, for they knew from experience that although all were equal before the law, there were occasions when a European was either not prosecuted or else let off lightly in order that he should not lose his superior status. This would reflect on the whole structure of the Empire, which depended on the acceptance by the Indians and others of the idea that the British were by nature princes and great lords: there were no secret police, nor places of torture, nor even a large army to persuade the people against their inclination. Anyone who seemed to offer comfort to the new nationalist movements epitomized by Gandhi and the home rule party in Burma risked becoming an outcast.

Everyone could see that these were dangerous times and Europeans should stand together firmly lest their position be eroded, undermined, wrecked. You did not have to be a Sayadaw to read these omens. On the day of Gandhi's arrest, 5 May 1930, there was an earthquake in Burma. The ground opened, buildings toppled and many were killed. The people believed either that Gandhi himself had done this, or that it was an indication of divine displeasure at his imprisonment.

On 26 May, a Burmese mob suddenly massacred 200 Indian labourers, after a fight in the Rangoon docks. On 26 June a desperate mutiny occurred in the prison: 34 convicts were killed and 60 wounded before order could be restored. Maurice's official enquiry found that the riot was caused by the harshness of the Indian superintendent. No one could quarrel with that, yet, at the same time, he was observed to be dining with Chinese merchants, discoursing on

Oriental art and literature and arranging an exhibition by a young Burmese painter at Government House, which was temporarily occupied by a Burmese deputy as the Governor was on leave. He was a mere puppet, real power being reserved to his European advisers. The private view was multi-racial and quantities of people who had never been allowed to set foot in those august precincts were to be seen eating, drinking, looking at pictures and generally enjoying themselves.

A short time later, in September 1930, the cases for trial included that of a lieutenant of the Queen's Own Cameron Highlanders who was accused of having driven furiously over a crossing in defiance of the Indian policeman's signals and seriously injured two Burmese women. If the accused had been a native, everyone would have agreed that the correct penalty was imprisonment. But no Englishman had ever been sent to jail for such a small matter as criminal negligence while driving. Great pressure was put on Maurice to substitute a fine, on the grounds that the young man would be cashiered if he went to prison. He refused to do so. Although he knew the appeal court would vary the sentence, he gave the lieutenant two months and a moderate fine. The High Court judge did not dispute the facts of the case, nor the interpretation of the law, but said that under the particular circumstances, the maximum fine was appropriate rather than imprisonment.

It was now clear to his superiors that Maurice was not a man who could be promoted to the higher reaches of the Civil Service. He was removed from the bench and given a temporary job in the customs and excise, and would then be posted to remote country districts until he retired. His marriage was also in ruins. He and his wife had been romantically in love when they married and for some years afterwards, but they were fundamentally unsuited. She was of a timid nature, conventional, unintellectual, without interests beyond the domestic life. She could not understand a passion for art and literature, a liking for unusual company, the expression of unorthodox views. Such things at once frightened and outraged her. While his mind and character developed, hers shrank into itself like a snail seeking refuge in its shell from a rough world. She therefore felt, and said, that he had brought the crisis in his career on himself by quarrelling with everyone and making a spectacle of them both. His view was that he had been betrayed by the one person who, above all, should have supported him through a difficult time.

Although never formally separated, they were not able to close the gulf between them. The pattern was repeated again and again in small matters and in large, and caused a brooding tension in the home, like a perpetually unbroken thunderstorm. There might be lightning: for he had little patience with fools, a quick temper and a tendency to be arrogant and overbearing. Yet, with judicious management, so slight as to become instinctive with practice, these defects would hibernate and the essential generosity and kindness of his nature, the wit and vivacity of his conversation flourish unhindered. She could not learn even the rudiments of this most necessary art. It was not her fault. She was just like that.

Such, then, was his official and private position as he stood on the wharf at Rangoon, ready to embark for London on leave in April 1931. Among those gathered to see him off was the Sayadaw, now trembling with age in his yellow robe, an acolyte holding an umbrella over him as a sign of his high rank in the Church. The time of tribulation had been much more severe than expected. Was it really over? How could it be said to be beneficial? The Sayadaw replied that the adverse influences which had culminated in a final burst of malevolence in the past year had vanished, or dissolved, or departed. The way was now open and extraordinary good fortune would supervene. He was not able to describe the process exactly. He saw fame and happiness.

Maurice set sail on this dreamlike note. During his leave he visited Ireland, looked up old friends, and tried to advance the cause of a Burmese delegation which had arrived in London in the hope of negotiating some sort of moderate home rule for their country similar to the arrangements being made with India.

In the course of these peregrinations, it occurred to him for the first time that he might write about Burma. He had been studying the country, its language, history, inhabitants, drama, festivals, religion, art for twenty years. He had turned himself into an orientalist without noticing it. His learning was formidable, spread over east and west, fortunately prevented from overpowering friends and acquaintances by a characteristic gaiety, and by poetic fancies that were sometimes moving, sometimes ludicrous, always individual. His mind was

9

keen, tenacious and supported by a physique that made it impossible for him to understand the meaning of exhaustion until the age of seventy-seven, or thereabouts.

He began to feel that the Sayadaw had been perfectly correct as usual, if vague. In three years' time he would qualify for a reduced pension which would just keep the family going. There was no point in continuing his civil service career as it could not now lead anywhere except from one sleepy country district to another. Surely in three years he would find a suitable Burmese subject and launch himself in the new profession he had so long desired?

These ideas and questions were circulating in his head as he sailed for Burma once again in January 1932. He had been posted to the most southerly district in the country, 500 miles from Rangoon on the neck of the Malay Peninsula. The headquarters was the old port of Mergui which was on an ancient trade route between the Bay of Bengal and the further East. Arabs, Indians, Chinese, Portuguese and English freebooters had all established themselves there in the course of history. The innumerable islands of the archipelago surrounding the approach to the harbour had been the resort of a notable breed of pirates.

I remember the place well. Our house was on a ridge overlooking the quay and the islands spread across the water as far as the horizon. The one directly opposite the house had many pagodas and monasteries on it. Others were uninhabited, except by spirits to whom offerings were made on landing. One contained caves as large as a cathedral which could only be entered by boat at low tide. The descendants of the pirates, now called sea gypsies, used to climb the vertical walls with candles in their mouths to collect the nests made by strange birds that spun them, like spiders, with a substance from their own bodies. These were sold to the Chinese for that rare delicacy and aphrodisiac, birds' nest soup. All the islands, whether large or small, high or flat, occupied or solitary, were very beautiful.

Many processions used to pass along the street below our house. The sound of gongs and bells, of singing and the creak of bullock carts came plainly up to the verandah. A great white band was painted on the roof, on which the weekly steamer from Rangoon took a bearing at the harbour bar. One could hear the Indian seaman on the bows chanting the depths as he swung the lead. There was a flagstaff in the garden where the Union Jack was run up every day; and also several ancient cannon which were ceremonially fired on the Burmese new year.

Such was Mergui by day. The nights were often terrifying, for the place was infested with ghosts. They were especially numerous along the ridge above the town and were said by the local people to be the result of a massacre of Europeans in some previous era. These souls had, by the utterance of appropriate spells, been turned into guardian spirits, forever on the watch against pirates or other enemies. They may have constituted an effective system of defence, but they were certainly difficult to live with. Our house was on their beat. It was well known. Every deputy commissioner and his family had had the same experiences.

The visitations were frequent. They began mildly: the house started creaking everywhere; next there were bangs on the roof, walls, wardrobes, ceilings; the tempo increased, it seemed as if the place was invested by a thousand ghosts. Suddenly there was silence and the principal was heard coming up the stairs, wearing a certain sort of slippers of the country that made a characteristic slapping noise. Crossing the verandah, it made for the room where I slept with my brother and our nurse. It walked up and down four or five times, while the beds shook under us. At last it departed by the other stairs, occasionally whistling in the garden, to the consternation of the hens in their coop. Gradually we learnt that hurricane lamps were the answer: if these were kept burning all night the manifestations were much reduced.

Several times a year, we would set off in the government launch for a tour of the islands, so that Maurice could hear complaints and collect the revenue. Our Indian butler then had to move into the house as watchman. He did not trust entirely to lamps, nor yet to pagan incantations, for he was a Christian. He borrowed our gramophone and two records on which were four hymns. He played them continuously during the dark hours.

Maurice became excited as he gradually explored the history and geography of his district. He discovered that the massacre which was said to have provided the army of guardian ghosts had occurred on 14 July 1687. At that date, Mergui belonged to the King of Siam who had for years employed as governor a certain Samuel White of

Bristol, an adventurer and a most desperate and disreputable character. He enriched himself by extensive piracy in the Bay of Bengal until the East India Company, where he had once worked as a pilot, sent a man of war to arrest him and bring him to Madras for trial, unless he agreed to hand over Mergui to the Company. When the townspeople began to suspect that such might be their fate, they fell on the English and killed about sixty of them. White himself escaped.

Here at last was the subject Maurice had sought for so many years. He flung himself on it with enthusiasm, walking over the ground, rowing up tidal rivers, touring the islands. Wherever he went in the course of his duties, White had been before him. Mrs White's tombstone was to be seen in the town. Somebody found a seventeenth century wine bottle in a mangrove swamp; someone else a brass candlestick and an iron ladle. People were happy to sell him anything they discovered.

His other great interest was Chinese ceramics, of which he had now a wide knowledge. The ground round Mergui was sown with them, for here they had been loaded for the Indian market, after coming overland from the Gulf of Siam. The Burmese knew an antique when they saw one. Sometimes they used it until it got broken. The more pious, however, felt that these ancient plates and cups inhabiting the earth, the sandbanks and swamps were the property of spirits and often gave them to monasteries where they were ground to powder and used in medicines of various kinds.

When it was discovered that Maurice was mad not only about local history, but also antiques, people began to look out for them. He was willing to pay what they asked and it put him in a good mood: a subsequent humble petition for a gun licence, on the grounds that a tiger had eaten a couple of relatives, had a good chance of being granted. One might even obtain a remission of taxes because wild elephants had flattened the crops, or the seed had inexplicably failed to come up, in spite of every care and attention.

Matters continued in this agreeable way for the three years of his district commissionership. It came to be generally felt that the spirits wished him to have their Chinese and Siamese *objets d'art*. News of the way he had stood up for the principle of justice for everyone before the law percolated from Rangoon. It became known that the holy Sayadaw had prophesied greatly concerning his future. A monastery was rededicated and named after him, and also a pagoda. These things would not have been done unless the spirits had said they wanted it.

In November 1934, Maurice stood on the wharf saying goodbye to friends, colleagues and acquaintances of all sorts. The people of the town presented a farewell address in which they expressed their certainty that extraordinary good fortune awaited him. This they interpreted to mean high office in the Civil Service. But he knew that he would never see any of them again; the beauty, the strangeness and loneliness of their country would be perceived only with the eye of memory. He was going to start a new life at the age of forty-five and how could he say for certain that he would be better, happier, more contented? Perhaps Mergui was the nearest he would get to paradise on earth. At this point he burst into tears, to the consternation of the Commissioner of Police, his immediate subordinate.

II

As soon as he arrived in England he set to work with characteristic energy and singleness of mind and, within a few months, had written his first book, *Siamese White*. It was an instant success: the best critics praised it and the films made an offer. He was launched in his second career. Book followed book at the rate of two a year to begin with. He reviewed. He wrote art criticisms and film scripts. He lectured. Twice a week he would set out from Maidenhead (where he had rented a house) and spend the whole day in London rushing from one appointment to another, cultivating an army of friends and acquaintances, for his vitality and charm made him popular wherever he went. A certain insensitivity to other people's feelings, a tendency to be boastful and a bit of a bully, surfaced only during the days he spent at home working until midnight.

His wife took no part in the social whirl, having neither the requisite stamina nor the interest. She became increasingly isolated and lonely as the years went by, a sad faded presence with a bitter tongue. Nothing one did, or tried to do, had the smallest beneficial effect. It was as if she were lost in some gloomy wilderness from which it was impossible to rescue her for reasons that could not be explained.

13

Maurice, on the other hand, mellowed. The greatest happiness for an artist is in the practice of his art. Success improved him. There was also the very close friendship which he and I gradually established between us. We were both crazy about museums, art and books. We enjoyed the same sort of jokes. We loved standing for hours at parties and downing quantities of drink. In addition, I was able to exert that calming influence his temperament required, thus greatly reducing the number of explosions in the house. 'You manage me so tactfully,' he once remarked, 'that I don't know what's happening. I only realise afterwards that I've done what you wanted.' I think the true secret was that I never wanted him to do anything to which he had a reasonable objection.

Between 1934 and 1949 he published seventeen books. He did not keep a regular diary of his multitudinous activities until the latter date, when he bought the first of the seventeen foolscap volumes from which I have taken the extracts which follow. As the entries always record his days off, they give the impression that life was a perpetual party. But during this period he wrote twelve major books and five minor ones. He also conducted numerous love affairs of which his wife never suspected him; and as he did not wish these to become public property, he very wisely omitted to put them on paper.

The diaries are almost entirely in his own handwriting, the few exceptions being those parts he dictated to his secretary. He would write them within a few days of the events described, rapidly and without correction—the exact opposite of his method of composing his books, where he usually rewrote in the morning what he had done the evening before.

In 1949 he was sixty. His vigour was unimpaired; he never knew what it was to be depressed. Voracious reading and a retentive memory had made him widely and variously learned. He was interested in practically everything and his conversation was full of ingenious turns—fantastic, sarcastic, witty, prejudiced, gay; he was above all a stimulating companion.

# THE DIARY 1949–1969

## 13 January 1949

After being photographed by Elliot & Fry for Faber in all the attitudes of a writer, go to lunch with the Princess Fahrunissa.* I found her alone in the boudoir of her new residence, 15 Kensington Palace Gardens, a large quiet house until lately occupied by the young King of Iraq. She rose to receive me, pressing my hand. She was dressed in black and looked remarkably young, though she must be forty-seven or so. No one else had been invited and soon lunch was announced and we passed into the main dining-room. An elaborate meal of lobster and turkey was served on solid-silver plates. The Princess was extremely animated. She spoke of her youth in Istanbul, of her first marriage and how she sought to gather about her the artists and writers of that capital. After lunch I looked at her latest paintings. As a distraction she has been painting little stones of curious shape to bring out innate characteristics, such as faces. Before leaving she made me presents of dates and wine in a lavish and splendid manner that reminds of the fabled Orient. She came to the door and waved me farewell. Nothing could be warmer, franker, more high spirited than her manner. I found the occasion tremendously pleasant. One of the topics which the Princess spoke of was her surprise at finding that in England artists and writers were not regularly to be met with at society functions. The fact is that for long the English court and aristocracy have taken no interest in art or literature and, in fact, are no longer reflected in the arts.

## 20 January 1949

After luncheon to the B.B.C. to record a talk on how I became a writer, and went to the Princess Fahrunissa. Found her on a sofa with a tray of whisky and a plate of savouries. I brought her a present of

* H.R.H. Princess Fahrunissa Zeid el Hussein, wife of the Iraqi ambassador, H.R.H. Prince Zeid el Hussein.

flints, curiously shaped stones all of them, on which were the faces of men and animals, of ghosts, the grin of skulls, and shadowy figures enclosed in the stone. She was delighted with their strangeness and spent some time trying to divine the shapes, speaking with the utmost animation. Then she showed me four paintings she was sending to an exhibition in Bristol. The Prince had returned from abroad, and she took me upstairs to find him. He was in some room, perhaps dozing, and came out and in his plain Arab way thanked me for what I was doing to help his wife in the arts. She made me repeat to him what she had said of him in her last letter to me—*le meilleur et le seul ami que j'ai au monde*—and I repeated it as she kissed him violently on the cheek.

### 24 January 1949

Had a conversation today with Bob* on the phone to Dublin. My mother is sinking. She had a sort of stroke about a week ago and was unconscious. For a time she did not know Bob. Now she is clearer, but evidently very near her last day. She has got much thinner since I saw her two months ago. And she also has a temperature. In December when I was there the force of her character had hardly abated, and she was able to afflict those about her by the violent effect of her likes and dislikes. I gather that now she has passed into a more negative state. Bob will inform me at once if things take a final turn and I will hurry over. A message by lunch and I can be there by breakfast next morning.

### 26 February 1949

Read Aldous Huxley's *Ape and Essence*. It is exciting to read once, but is rubbish. Some critics seem to be taking it seriously, as if Huxley really was foretelling man's downfall. But its ideas throughout are essentially popular; they are scientific and other notions of the day put in a vulgar form for popular consumption. One has the impression that he has been associating with a lot of poor minds. It reflects badly on his alleged pursuit of transcendental wisdom. Had he had even a glimpse of the peace and happiness that passes understanding he would not want to write in that way.

* Dr W. R. F. Collis, Maurice's brother.

*22 March 1949*

Arrive at Korda's* office at 5 p.m. and find him and Zoltan.†
Zoltan immediately said how much he liked my script for the *Second
Jungle Book*, how everyone thought it excellent, but that unfortunately the Company was not able at the moment to get to work on it.
He apparently alluded to the difficulties which the film industry was
meeting with just now. Then Korda said he had asked me to come
because he wanted to put another proposition. Could I write him the
same sort of script on the subject of the Taj Mahal and the Emperor
Shah Jehan and Mumtaz Mahal. I said yes, but declared that a retaining fee for a year would be far more satisfactory than an *ad hoc* fee for
another piece. He asked what I would want and I said a thousand
pounds. He agreed. I will do the Taj Mahal script and after that
others, exploring the ground for an Indian film. If any of the scripts
are used I then get my share. This takes a load off my mind, because
book sales are very bad at present and the production of *The
Motherly and Auspicious*‡ at the Embassy has fallen through for the
time being. Without Korda's help I would be in a poor way. I am
told that London is full of impoverished Hungarians and that Korda
supports many of them out of film money, giving them retaining
fees to write scripts, though no one bothers to read the scripts.

*8 April 1949*

Drove up to London and called on the film Barons, Korda and his
brother. They are doing a film on Graham Greene's *Heart of the
Matter*. Zoltan asked me what I thought of it. He agreed that the end
would have to be changed, not only for film reasons but because it
was a weak ending. Zoltan is good at inventing plots and he has
thought of a new end and Graham Greene is writing it for him.
Instead of the main character taking poison, he does what is in-
directly suicide, attempting to use a revolver when his strength lay
in his only carrying a cane.

*12 April 1949*

Calling at my bank, I was informed by the cashier, a reader of my

* Sir Alexander Korda of London Films.
† Zoltan Korda, his brother.
‡ A play by Maurice, published 1943 but never produced.

books, that he knew Saw Po Min, the owner of the white elephant which about twenty years ago was brought here to the zoo by him and which I afterwards saw in Rangoon. An unlikely conversation with a cashier.

*16 May 1949*

At 7 p.m. I arrived at Topolski's* house in Regents Park and found the Earl of Darnley on the premises, fabulously tall, vague and without humour or sense, and convinced of his own importance as an artist, and yet strangely anxious for that to be confirmed. When I told him that I could not, owing to having no space left this month, write about his watercolour exhibition at the R.W.S. Gallery, he was deeply disappointed. He is clearly a nice man in many ways, but insufferably conceited and slow. How Topolski has been able to bear him, staying so long last summer at Cobham and listening to the Earl's conversation, I do not know. Darnley is the perfect example of the aristocratic amateur who wants to get flattery from professionals. All his work is cliché.

After changing at Topolski's into a dinner jacket I went to the reception given by the Polish Ambassador at Lancaster House, St James's, for the centenary of Chopin's performance at that place before Queen Victoria. The identical programme was played. The pianist, who played with enormous and vigorous competence but with little feeling, was the opposite of affected, being more like a stout business man manipulating a mechanism. He also looked as if he was not grown up, like the fat boy. So was the great Chopin impersonated after a hundred years. I was introduced to the Chinese Ambassador, Cheng Tien-Hsi. He seemed delighted and said how he had frequently read passages from *The First Holy One*† to lecture audiences. He went on in a most animated manner, quoting the Chinese poets on friendship and speaking of God. He was a little drunk. At midnight he asked me to come back with him to the Chinese embassy. On arrival Her Excellency went to bed and we sat in the dining-room which was laid for breakfast. He sent for Napoleon brandy and a variety of Chinese caviar. A special tea was made by the butler. 'I don't want to be vulgar, but I must tell you the price of it is

* Feliks Topolski, artist.
† On Confucius, by Maurice. Published 1948.

£6 a pound,' he declared. 'It comes from the hills beyond my home.' It had a subtle perfume and was a wonderful stomachic and invigorator. We sat talking till 1 a.m. The brandy was finished and many cups of tea. He was uproariously happy, shouting and laughing. In all my life I have never had exactly such an experience—and for an Ambassador, on first meeting, to take me into his home and there, in the middle of the night, as if speaking to an old friend, pour out his thoughts. It was modelled, I suppose, on the traditional Chinese picture of two scholars carousing. When I said, 'The Chinese surpass all nations because they treat men of letters with respect,' he was profoundly pleased. It was a very genuine, spontaneous occasion.

*22 May 1949*

Leave for Dublin by the night mail to see my mother who is reported by Bob to be sinking. She is believed to be about eighty-seven years of age.

*23 May 1949*

At 10.30 a.m. I went to the hospital and found my mother partially conscious. After a time she smiled, as an infant smiles when it recognises its mother or nurse or person well known to it, for she had recognised me. She could not speak, but in half articulation could repeat words put to her. She was emaciated, having lost perhaps six stone during the fast she had imposed upon herself. It seems that she came to believe that she could not swallow and that if she did attempt to do so she would choke. She therefore refused solid food and could with difficulty be persuaded to swallow liquid. In fact, there was nothing wrong with her throat. But it had not been that she was passively starving herself to death. Very frequently she screamed, shouted, resisted, abused her attendants. Her condition bordered on dementia and Bob, who had all this long time (a period of five months) devoted himself to alleviating her condition, used to quiet her with varieties of soporifics and sedatives. When I saw her today, however, her physical condition was so low that no drug was necessary to keep her quiet, and in fact none had been administered for over 24 hours. In appearance she was very strange. Her eyes were wide open and staring, as if she was terrified. Her complexion was very white, and unlike her natural complexion, which was brown and rather blotched in later years. Her mouth was drawn down at the corners, giving an expression of extreme bitterness. She looked very aged and in certain angles almost masculine, though again she would seem youthful from the intensity in her eyes. Her hair, which was not entirely white, was curled and waving on her head, its natural movement, as I suppose.

Bob gave it as his considered opinion that she could not live through the night. Leaving her room I went in to see my sister Joyce, whose room was adjacent. A confirmed invalid from long-standing consumption, which has deprived her of the use of the top of both her lungs, she is trying and embittered, the strain of her mother's last illness having added to her infirmities.

### 24 May 1949

No message came from the hospital during the night and on my presenting myself there I found my mother in what seemed more like sleep than unconscious. There was no indication of immediate death. But she had taken no nourishment or liquid of any kind for over twenty-four hours. Bob's opinion remained that she could not last into the following day.

I made three visits during the day. On the second I met the doctor attached to the home. Though he too had been emphatic that she must die on Monday night, he now said it was impossible to feel that there was any certainty when she would die. I may be detained in Dublin for some time with nothing to do but wait, and assailed by my usual feeling of claustrophobia when I am out of London or England, have decided to return home unless on the following day the event declares itself.

### 1 June 1949

On arrival in Dublin I rang up Bob. He reported that my mother's breathing stopped about 2.30 a.m. on May 31st, her heart, however, continuing to beat for some time longer. I went to see her body. She was lying in her bed at the St Vincent Home with wreaths of Kilmore* flowers which Bob had gathered immediately after her death in the first light of dawn. It seems that he was accompanied by his dog and that after he had gathered the flowers, which took two hours, he

* The family house at Killiney, Co. Dublin. It is on the sea.

went on to the beach and sat awhile on the White Rocks looking over the sea. When I saw him, however, this morning he was recovered, for he had taken a sleeping draught and had slept deeply all night. My mother in death was changed. Her face was more youthful, and resembled her sister Helen (FitzGibbon) as I remembered her, and also her mother (née Apjohn), judging from photographs. The bony structure of her face was pronounced. Her nose was very Roman and high, her chin powerful and there was a touch of nobility in her brows. Her mouth was turned down. All wrinkles and lines were smoothed out. They had arranged her hands clasped in front in a gesture of peace not characteristic of her, and had placed in them a crucifix. But indeed it was only her body. She herself was not there. The room was empty. I was suddenly overcome with emotion. But I did not want to stay long and went out.

We then drove to the cemetery where my father was buried. The same grave was opened, in which also was buried my grandfather Collis and grandmother Jameson. The actual interment was performed during a heavy shower. It was a melancholy occasion, but grief was not apparently felt, for my mother had given so much trouble during the interval of two-and-a-half years since my father's death. During those years she had become increasingly violent and difficult to manage. She made things very difficult for Bob and Joyce who had the duty of looking after her and persuading her attendants to remain. Some of Bob's letters, which I have preserved, give an idea of the scenes. She was frantic and largely demented, and her worst qualities, which were always quarrelsomeness, hatred of servants, extreme touchiness, secretiveness, a tendency to live in squalor, jealousy and suspiciousness, were dreadfully intensified. But later perhaps the memory of what she was like when younger will come uppermost and the other be forgot. Then she had great charm, vivacity and extraordinary warmth.

## 16 June 1949

I met Henry Moore at the Leicester Gallery. He was his old self, with that eager optimistic manner, serious yet humorous, giving a sense of purpose and hard work, and a resolve to be even more famous. He said that he had done a big bronze, a family group. This will be his first big bronze and shows that he is less insistent than he was that carving from the stone is the only kind of sculpture worth doing. Like all the modellers he made his clay and sent it to be cast, though as he said there would be a good deal of surface chiselling to do when he got it back. I spoke of making an excursion to see him in his remote country retreat during the summer, and would love to do so, if petrol allows, some wonderful day of high summer.

## 3 July 1949

(In Paris.) I called on Alice Toklas in 5 rue Christine, which is behind the Mint in an old-fashioned quarter of narrow streets. On entering the doorway of No. 5, I could see no concierge and had to look for Alice Toklas's flat. I passed into a small courtyard from which a staircase began. Following it I climbed up and up, past several possible doors, with no names on them. At the top I heard female voices and called out 'Madame'. At that the concierge, who was gossiping, appeared and led me downstairs again to a door on the first floor. She rang, opened the door, and I went in to find Alice Toklas and her dog, a large white poodle. It was barking furiously at me. 'Don't mind,' she said. 'It is his only exercise. He will stop after a bit.' She was a tiny woman, five feet high hardly, about seventy years of age or a bit more, with cropped hair, a pale little face with a great nose, and a trace of American accent. The walls of the hall were studded with pictures and the salon, in which she led me, equally so. 'The kettle is about to boil,' she declared, 'and I must go and make tea. You look at the paintings. Francis Rose's* are over there.' But in fact she hovered round me a while before going for the tea, showing me Rose's early work hanging among the Picassos. (The prime reason for the visit was that I should see the paintings by Rose which Gertrude Stein had acquired between 1930 and 1939, when Rose was her *protégé*, her discovery and hope, and it was he who had written to Alice Toklas to receive me.) Rose's paintings were unframed and stuck on the wall, one above the other. It was extremely difficult to perceive in what lay their charm for Gertrude Stein, the collector of Picassos, and who possessed also Matisse, Picabia and Cézanne, though with few if any others. Alice Toklas, as she dispensed tea, good china tea and 'tartines' of her own invention, described how Gertrude Stein first saw a Rose in some small *marchand de tableaux*,

* Sir Francis Rose. Maurice had written about his work.

22

when she was looking for youthful talent, and bought it; how she enquired for others and bought them; how she became infatuated with them and taking down her other paintings hung them with the Picassos. She did this hanging the day before she left for a holiday. On her return, before taking the luggage out of the car, she rushed upstairs to get the effect after an absence, and came down again radiant, exclaiming 'I was right.' She conceived the view from then on that Rose was the greatest English painter and would be acclaimed so one day. Alice Toklas, still the shadow and echo of her celebrated friend, fervently declared her own faith to be the same. She had little discrimination for as she turned out from a side room more of Rose's canvases (they must have had forty at least) she liked the bad ones as much as the good ones. All this, combined with the narrowness of the collection, made me wonder whether the two women really had the flair for painting with which they were credited.

Gertrude Stein bought from Picasso long before he was known. I saw the series of studies she had of heads for his *Demoiselles d'Avignon* (1907), and his pink and blue period nudes, and even a small work in the style of Lautrec. But did she like his work or like him? The visit to Alice Toklas raised all these questions in my mind. I could not answer them. After all Gertrude Stein was not there, she was dead. I was talking only to her faithful shadow. The shadow may always have been without aesthetic sense and had taken her views from Gertrude Stein. My instinctive feeling that she did not understand painting may have had no relevance to G.S.'s capabilities. So I talked on to Alice Toklas till 7.30 and she was reluctant to let me go. Indeed, I had difficulty in getting away at last, and made fervent promises to visit her again. If I do, perhaps I shall probe better into the mystery of Gertrude Stein, her collection and her relations with painters.

*17 July 1949*
Francis and Frederica Rose came down here to Maidenhead today and we paid a visit to Stanley Spencer at Cookham. Spencer has a small house just above Cookham station. It is a squalid little place, furnished with cheap furniture and without even the minor comfort of electric light. We went upstairs to Spencer's studio, a small room with a hard bed in it and a green oilcloth on the floor. Lining one wall completely was part of a huge unfinished picture of the resurrec-

tion of the dead. Along another wall was a smaller picture of another part of the churchyard in which the resurrection was taking place. He also unrolled a further large canvas on the floor, which was the other half of the large unfinished picture. These works* showed Stanley Spencer at his best. The design was bold, tense and highly original. The episodes were Spencer's own entirely. The faces were often very lovely. But like all his work, the actual painting itself lacked quality, though this lack consisted only in a lack of interest in beautiful textures and surface effects, such as impasto. This weakness in a painter would suffice to prevent Spencer from being held a great artist were it not that his vision and sense of design and his personal style were high enough to compensate, as it is in Blake. Stanley Spencer himself is a tiny little man, slight and boyish in figure, though he is over sixty. In manner he is bright and animated, with a frank air, essentially kind and fresh, without any sort of conceit or consciousness of his celebrity. After showing us his paintings he took us downstairs, where tea was ready, consisting of bread, butter and honey, large slices that he had cut. He knew that his painting was unlike any other's and that it did a lot of things which today painting is supposed not to do, such as telling a story and illustrating human feelings. 'I do not think of such criticisms but simply paint in the way that comes natural to me.' His unfinished canvas was squared up small and the picture was traced in pencil with enough shading to give the volumes. He also showed us some lovely pencil portrait drawings.

## 21 July 1949

I went to lunch with the Princess Fahrunissa. I found her seated in her closed verandah studio, surrounded by her paintings. On the table beside her was a tray of bottles. From one containing a strong liqueur whisky she poured me out a stiff glass. After some animated conversation the butler announced lunch. She made me sit at the head of the long table, and a lunch was served on the silver dishes of soup, lobster, chicken and fruit ices, with a sweet sauterne to drink. The Princess desired that the conversation be in French. She said that my French was so excellent and that moreover she understood it better than my English. My French is sometimes good but it does not stay good for more than half an hour. I was glad when she permitted me

* Known as the *Glasgow Resurrection* series.

to relapse into English, though it was one of my good days for French. After lunch she caused the butler to bring in her latest canvases. Some of them were very large and he toiled in placing them right, and was still inclined to get them upside down. They represented, in the form of abstractions, her sensations when crossing the Atlantic by aeroplane.

*9 August 1949*

At 1.15 p.m. I met Zoltan Korda. The most important thing for me was that he said he had read the Taj Mahal treatment and liked it enormously. I asked him some plain questions. Could I count on regular employment by London Films? Had I an aptitude for film work? He replied emphatically in the affirmative to both questions. 'All your anxieties will be at an end when Alex reads your Taj Mahal,' he said. 'I believe he will immediately want you to prepare a shooting script of the Taj Mahal on the enhanced salary covered by your contract. You will work with him or me.' And he repeated how wonderfully good the story was.*

*14 August 1949*

Stanley Spencer came to the house at 4 o'clock and stayed till 7.30. He was clearer than usual. He spoke of his methods. First he makes drawings of the subject which include everything that is to go in. Having selected a drawing or (in the case of a large canvas) a series of drawings, he squares them up, squares up the canvas, and copies the drawing exactly to the last line with no alterations. 'Before I start painting,' he said, 'I must know down to the last detail what I am going to paint. It must all be drawn on the canvas in pencil. For me doing the drawing again in paint is not mechanical or boring. I enjoy it all over again.' And he went on to explain that he was incapable of composing in paint as he went along, like Topolski. 'It seems wonderful to me,' he declared, 'that he can know how to shape the picture when composing with the brush.' Speaking of what was behind his painting, he said: 'I wanted to find an equivalent in paint for the extraordinary feeling I had of divine presence both in Cookham church and the Cookham scene.' He then spoke of his loss of inno-

* The film was never made. Maurice incorporated much of the material into *The Mystery of Dead Lovers*, published 1951.

25

cence with his first marriage. As he has now returned in his present paintings of resurrection to his earlier themes and is again painting Cookham as a place informed by divinity, he has left the period when, in the thirties onward, he saw it invaded by strange lusts. He spoke also of his first patron, the Duke of Westminster, who lived at Cliveden and wore side whiskers. It was he who paid for him at the Slade. He also spoke in glowing terms of his brother Gilbert, the artist. His opinion of his own landscapes was not high. 'I had to paint them to live,' he said. 'I know they are hard and metallic, though well disguised. Good drawing,' he added, with reference to his brother's landscapes, 'tells you things that you did not know.' He talked so much that he tired me somewhat. As I drove him home to Cookham, he said: 'I am miserably poor.'

### 10 October 1949

At 5.45 went to the Chinese Ambassador's reception commemorating the fall of the Ch'ing and founding of the republic thirty-eight years ago. Arthur Waley came up to me cordially, as if he had not abused me in public and was my sincere well-wisher. We talked in an animated way about his forthcoming books. He enquired of my next book. We seemed the best of friends, but unfortunately with Waley that does not mean that one will escape a nasty and unfair attack in the press, if he has the opportunity.

### 27 January 1950

Commander Taffy Rodd invited me to lunch at White's. After waiting some minutes and not seeing Rodd I went into the hall again to enquire from the porter. At that moment appeared a man with a naval beard and the face of a man of action who was also a man of thought. He said something to the porter about Rodd and I told him that I also was looking for the same person. He turned to introduce me to another of the Rodd brothers who was strolling by, rather drunk. A search was made for Commander Rodd and he was declared not to be in the club. Meanwhile the man with the beard took me to the bar, asking my name. When I said 'Collis,' he asked 'Burmese Collis?' and I assented, though it was the first time I had ever heard myself so described. I then asked him who he was, and he replied that he was Lord Stanley of Alderley. He said: 'I was in

Rangoon in 1947 and your name still stank at the Pegu club.' I was amazed that this could be so after seventeen years, but he assured me that the Pegu club had not moved, even though at that date the Republic of Burma was only a few months away. It seems that Lord Louis Mountbatten, as Viceroy of India, had asked Lord Stanley to negotiate privately with General Aung San,* begging him to keep Burma within the Empire, but that he arrived in Rangoon the same day as Aung San and his colleagues were assassinated. He followed this tale with another about how he smuggled some valuable rubies out of Burma by putting them in a tube up his anus and how he lost them in the Persian Gulf on his way back when his aeroplane ran into the sea.

Rodd being definitely *non est*, Lord Stanley invited me to lunch with him instead. The brother Rodd joined in, as did the Earl of Antrim, though he had already had lunch. During the meal Lord Stanley gradually revealed his buccaneering character. He related how he lived on a ship of 250 tons and went about the world looking for adventure. He had just failed, he said, in getting the job of taking off Chiang Kai-shek from Formosa with 20 millions in gold and carrying him to Mexico. And he went to the electric fire and taking out a bank note lit it and lit his cigarette with it, taking care however only to burn a fraction of the edge of it. Part of the conversation was directed by then into literary channels and part of it was the light and rather juvenile badinage in which that society indulges and which consists in veiled references to persons in their set and is unintelligible like any other patter. On my going Lord Stanley came to the hall door. In some curious way a bond was established between us. We had become suddenly intimates. Yet I may not see him again, for he starts at once in his boat for some secret destination.

### 7 February 1950

Went to Barbara Hepworth's private view, with cocktails, at the Lefevre. This was a bid by her for a premier place in British sculpture. She had still marine suggestions, but her sticks and stones were now rather ancestral presences of the land, emanations of the cliffs and headlands of Cornwall, which seen in their proper landscape and wind would have been hauntingly strange. One can imagine the wind

* First Prime Minister of independent Burma.

whistling through their holes in a melancholy song. In museums or private rooms they would seem emptied of content, like gods taken from their sacred groves and become ethnology.

### 29 June 1950

Found Scottie Wilson selling his pictures in Sloane Square. He had some of them propped up against the wall of the subway leading down to the gentlemen's lavatory, others in a portfolio. It was a bright morning with a fresh breeze. I selected a picture called *The Indian Temple* and he let me have it for a pound. When he sells at Gimpels he gets fifteen or more pounds. This represented one of those occasions when he wants cash in a hurry. He has always sold at give-away prices when the fancy took him, much to the annoyance of the dealers who have tried to put him on the market. I had a long talk with him. He is a plump little man, strongly built, with huge fists, a common face, like a man behind a counter in a small shop, but with curious eyes. He speaks with a cockney accent mixed with Scotch, and expresses his meaning with difficulty. He told me that he painted in the small hours of the morning and did so in a sort of trance. The ideas came to him without his knowing how they came. He did not consciously invent his pictures. In my view he is a genuine painter of the unconscious, who has evolved a style and symbols suited to express what comes up. He asked me to write something about him, which he could use as an introduction to his paintings, if he published a booklet about them. I agreed.

### 10 July 1950

Having heard from S. I. Hsiung\* that Carol Coombe, an actress who has taken the lead in *Lady Precious Stream*, wants to take an option on *The Motherly and Auspicious* and has sufficient financial backing to get it produced, I am to meet her and Hsiung tomorrow to discuss the matter. Having been disappointed so many times in this regard I go without any sort of conviction that what has been represented is true or that, if truly represented, it will eventuate. The actress will either have changed her mind, or she will want time to think it over when she will change her mind, or some difficulty will have

\* Author of *Lady Precious Stream* and collaborator with Maurice in *The Motherly and Auspicious*.

arisen which will make it impossible for her to carry out her design. Being naturally optimistic and sanguine I would not write this way, had not bitter experience, constantly repeated, forced me to view with extreme scepticism any proposition from the stage. Tomorrow will tell me whether negotiations, which have been going on for eight years, will succeed or not. Is this possibly a turning point in my fortunes? I cannot tell.★

*18 July 1950*

After lunch I went to the I.C.A.'s† exhibition at 17 Dover St of what are called the American symbolic realists. Osbert Sitwell opened it. He has got to look rather like Korda, but has no charm. He seemed very nervous as he read his speech, his hand shaking as he turned the pages. Besides him was sitting Edith Sitwell in a large black hat and black gown. She is a tall large woman with a pale complexion, a splendid nose and a look of calm disdain, and yet with a touch of softness. It is a face once seen never to be forgotten, with its serenity, beauty, aristocracy and depth. She was far more attractive-looking (at 62) than in any portraits of her which I have seen. The occasion was one when many persons connected with the arts were gathered. John Hayward‡ was wheeled into the room in his chair and as usual a little knot of people gathered round him. It is extraordinary how he maintains his authority, looking so really repulsive and being himself, in spite of his cleverness and learning, an unpleasant sort of man.

*1 August 1950*

London. Went to see Rosalie Mander§ at her flat in St Ermins and found there Edmund Blunden, the Georgian poet, a small man, fragile, very nervous with the trick of clutching his shabby coat with his left hand and pulling at it from inside the front. He was well informed and positive, a little like Stanley Spencer. Leaving Rosalie at 7.15, I went on to see Mervyn Peake, now living high up in a house, 12 Embankment Gardens, Chelsea. He looked out of the window and I climbed the stairs. He is a man of great imagination

★ It wasn't.
† Institute of Contemporary Arts.
‡ Literary critic. He was paralysed from youth.
§ R. Glynn Grylls, author.

and talent, frail, wild-eyed, dirty, laughing, agitated, bankrupt, incompetent in money matters and delightful to meet. He showed me some portraits and signed a volume of his poems, *The Glass-blowers*, which I had bought. I do hope that he will have a great success with *Gormenghast*, as vol II of *Titus Groan* is called, and long to read it.

### 8 October 1950

Sally Astor★ decided to take me over to Blenheim to see the palace. We drove to Woodstock, then through the Triumphal Gate into the first quadrangle and thence into the grand courtyard before the palace, which has a massive and sombre beauty. Leaving the car there, Sally led me through the side entrance to the private apartments. At the top of the stairs we saw a footman and asked for His Grace. He was not in his study, but Sally said we would wait there and sent the footman to find him. In his study I observed a late Corot, larger than usual, two immense Hubert Roberts, a McEvoy portrait of the Duchess and a painting I did not identify, but perhaps Fragonard. In a few minutes the 10th Duke came in, tall, reckless looking, with the Churchill face, something of the bully, yet now in excellent mood, for he likes Sally Astor. One felt he was a man one would have to stand up to. Sally kissed him and he shook hands with me pleasantly. Then we set out at once on a tour of the grand apartments. Sally had her little Charles II spaniel on leash. At first the Duke tended to draw our attention to his big game heads, fine horns, generally African. Here Sally was guilty of a solecism. The Duke pointed to a fine buffalo head. 'A water buffalo' said she, as if the Duke had potted a tame creature in a cart. 'No, no, a wild buffalo,' the Duke corrected her. It was shortly after this that the little spaniel sat down to make a mess on the carpet but was dragged on leaving only a spot which the Duke did not notice. We continued and saw the famous Reynolds group of the then Marlborough family with the Orpen opposite in which the present Duke figured as a child. We admired the battle tapestries, the finest things of the sort on earth and enormous historical documents. When the Duke was showing us a Roman bust from Herculaneum, the dog, taking it to be a real person, barked. In one of the rooms I saw at a distance a collection of ninth century Persian

★ Maurice was staying the weekend with William Waldorf, later 3rd Viscount Astor and his wife Sally at Bletchington Park near Oxford.

ceramics, blue self colour, and stopped to admire. The Duke was very pleased. 'I bought them myself,' he said. 'I didn't pay much. About a couple of hundred.' They were his chief addition to the collection. I was lucky. The Duke expanded after this. He told us of the flag that he paid to the King yearly in lieu of rent on the anniversary of the battle of Blenheim. We saw the dining table laid ready, the Grand Hall, the Chinese ceramics, his own portrait, which was abominable and should have been in an attic, and so came to the long gallery past the statue of Queen Anne to the huge polar-bear rugs, at which the spaniel barked furiously. By the main door of the Grand Hall the Duke gave me the palace guide book, an attractive publication fully illustrated. 'It costs half a crown,' he said, 'but you can have it.' The man in charge of the sale of these books objected. 'His Grace is always doing this,' he complained. We returned to the study. The Duke slumped into a chair, as if exhausted. Sally kissed him again and we prepared to leave. 'Come again,' he said to me, 'and bring your friends.' He saw us off to the head of the staris. We descended, passed through the passage and came to the door. The spaniel sat down on the mat and was dirty. As we got into the car we heard a roar behind and beheld the Duke emerging from the palace. Four people had entered the courtyard, though it was not a day when the palace was open to general visitors. The Duke advanced upon them in a menacing manner. He had a stick in his hand. 'Didn't you see the notice? he shouted. 'Back you go. I'll make you read it.' And he herded the four trespassers through the arch into the outer quadrangle and, confronting them with the notice, made them read it aloud. They were horribly discomforted and cowed.

*3 November 1950*

Had tea with Mervyn Peake at the Kardomah café, Piccadilly. Peake looked if possible wilder and more extraordinary. His mouth trembled, he seemed all sensibility. We spoke about the reception of his book, *Gormenghast*. He has had numerous and good reviews, and it would seem reasonable sales. But hardly that decisive applause which the immensity of the imaginative flight should have called out. However, it is so strange and powerful a book that it must have time to sink in. As he had not read my *Descent of the God*, I procured it from next door at Hatchards and gave it to him.

## 16 November 1950

Talked of John Hayward, who is one of London's characters with his paralysis, bath chair, fearful lip and rude manner. How had he managed to attain the position he holds in these circumstances, a man who has written nothing, whose culture is limited? It is a case of character, combined with his infirmity. His peremptory talk, malicious, overbearing, coarse, insolent, coming from a scarecrow in a wheelchair, seems extraordinary, I suppose, and enables him to impose himself. He is really one of the most curious men in London society.

## 5 December 1950

Met John Symonds at the Café Royal, the Symonds who I hope will become famous as the biographer of the sinister and extraordinary Aleister Crowley the satanist. Symonds came in rather late and flustered. I took him to Soho for lunch. He said that he hoped to make a name and a fortune over Crowley. It seems that another publisher has made an offer, which if implemented would put £5000 in his pocket. I besought him to let me know the issue. With his long hair (now streaked with grey though he is only thirty-five), the kindness of his expression and the strangeness of his eyes, he has a notable personality. Of Crowley, the most remarkable thing he said, besides speaking of his abominations, was that he believed that through him the gods had being. He said also that when he lay dying his last words were: 'I am perplexed'. Continuing on this subject, he recounted that he (Symonds) when writing the biography had occasion to consult Gerald Kelly, the present P.R.A. Anyhow Symonds was invited to Kelly's home, the latter declaring that he would give him an excellent dinner. Symonds, hungry and shabby, sets out for the famous artist's studio. On arrival, Kelly putting a bottle of Algerian wine in his pocket takes Symonds to a cheap foreign restaurant in Charlotte Street where they had a poor dinner, very moderately enlivened by the Algerian wine. Afterwards Kelly brings him back to the house, where the famous Jane (if indeed she is to be called famous because Kelly has exhibited portraits of her over thirty years) offered him a cigar, though he had the impression that Kelly hardly thought it necessary. He accepted the cigar, and, what with its strength on top of an unsatisfactory dinner, he felt unwell after a while and told

Kelly that he must have some fresh air. Kelly led him to the front door and hardly had he felt the night air on his face than he was sick down the steps. Kelly, it seems, had closed the door, though he was not in ignorance of what had occurred. Presently, half dead, Symonds re-enters and finds Kelly standing before the fireplace. 'I am afraid I have been sick down your steps,' confessed Symonds. Kelly had on the air of a senior and successful man of the world and did not make it easy for Symonds. 'So I observed,' he replied in the tone of a man delivering a rebuke. 'Nevertheless, he was very kind to me,' added Symonds in extenuation.

In the afternoon I went to see Scottie Wilson's exhibition. Scottie was looking out for me. His paintings were of particular excellence. I heard that John Rothenstein had asked for three to be sent to the Tate for the Committee to select one. Scottie himself, as much like a little city dealer as ever, was very vague about what was, after all, a decided step up towards his proper recognition. 'There was a man a while ago with big glasses and a face like a Chinaman,' he said. 'Was he the Director of the Tate?' He added that the Institute of Contemporary Arts was hanging his largest painting at their anniversay show next week, but had not invited him. It was amusing, too, to observe the British Council fussing over him. Only now, after it being drummed into them for two years, can they see that he is a unique artist.

*27 December 1950*

I saw today that James Stephens was dead. I recollect how when I was in Ireland in 1922 he was then Director of the Irish National Gallery. I had just published my execrable little book of verse called *Danse Macabre* and was full of literary ambitions, though I despaired of realising them. He talked to me in his animated way for an hour and declared that he found me ready to start a literary career then. But I could not believe him, though enormously encouraged, and fourteen years passed before I published my first book of prose, *Siamese White*. He perceived that I had it in me. What he could not know was that my time was not yet come; I would have to wrestle with an active and official life in Burma until 1934 before I could turn my mind away from the ambition of high office to that of writing well. The two ambitions were equal in my mind all those years, now the one, now the other, but I lacked the courage and certainty to declare for literature. But I shall never forget that it was he who first really encouraged me.

### 4 January 1951

In London. Went to lunch with Harry Leon,* the County Court Judge, who asked me to explain to him the rudiments of pictorial art. He entertained me at the Lansdowne Club in Fitzmaurice Place, a place less like a club than a hotel. Thence we adjourned to the National Gallery. He had informed me that he had never been able to take an interest in paintings but ardently desired to do so. The question was how to start. We strolled in and I suggested that he should tell me when he saw a painting that might attract him. But that did not work. Nothing caught his eye. So we reached Leonardo's *Virgin of the Rocks*. I began to praise it, but felt that Leon did not share my enthusiasm and sure enough presently he observed that the vista of blue rocks in the distance might have been done by a pavement artist. Looking about in desperation I espied Mantegna's *Agony in the Garden*. I explained to him that its excellence depended largely on its magistral construction and pointed out how the tensions were achieved and the tightness of the balance. He followed with difficulty but became interested. The idea of tension, balance, construction intrigued him. I point out how different was Bellini's *Agony* which hung next to it, which had a looser construction laterally, but had colour depth. I then took him to Titian's *Noli me Tangere*, showing him how it had perfect and not over-emphasised construction and also wonderful colour depth, and how the colour depth was fused into the constructional design, both together exactly expressing the tremendous mood of the subject. I now had his attention and he began to be deeply interested. And I showed him Rembrandt's *Flora* as an example of impasto texture. Then I showed him Hals and Gainsborough and Rubens for brush work, and Chardin for design, without much colour or texture or brushwork or drawing. Cosimo Tura I showed him as an example of drawing and little else. I surprised myself for as he became enchanted, as he did, I began to see more than I had ever myself seen before in these paintings. The battle was won; he was converted.

* Novelist. Author of many books under the name of Henry Cecil.

*20 March 1951*

I had promised to take Marion Topolski to the National Gallery to enquire whether a painting they have is a Desiderio, as they suppose. I found her in trousers with her hair knotted on the top of her head, evidently quite unprepared to go out. However she quickly threw on one of her embroidered oriental gowns and we set off in two cars. We got separated in the traffic and when I reached the Gallery there was no sign of her. As I waited I saw John Rothenstein. His face was exceptionally mongolian. He gave me a nonchalant saluation. On my explaining that I was waiting for Marion and that we intended to go in to see Sir Philip Hendy, the Director, he said: 'Oh, but I am taking him out.' He went up the steps to the private door, rang and was admitted.

At last I saw Marion hastening towards me. 'For twenty minutes I was stuck in a traffic jam,' she cried. 'We may have just missed Hendy,' I said, and we hurried to the private entrance where we saw Hendy with Rothenstein standing by a car as if about to get into it. We increased our pace and caught them, explaining that we wanted an opinion on the Desiderio which Marion held in her hand. Hendy in his elegant, almost too elegant, manner glanced at it over his shoulder and declared: 'That is not a Desiderio.' This was too off-hand an opinion to accept and we asked whether we could show it to any of his assistants. He named Martin James and embarked with Rothenstein. Accordingly we rang at the private door and were admitted. In the flurry, neither of us could remember the name he had mentioned. By getting the porter to run through the names of the various assistants, we re-captured the right one and asked if he would see us. In a few moments Mr Martin James arrived. He immediately said that the painting was by Desiderio.

*10 April 1951*

At 7 p.m. I went to the Conway Hall in Red Lion Square where the art critic Herbert Read was to deliver a lecture on *Art and Evolution*. I had been asked to sit on the platform. Topolski was also there and sat beside me. The audience, about two hundred, were plain earnest people of moderate education. Herbert Read, looking as usual quiet, withdrawn, amiable, yet authoritative, read his lecture (his delivery is not very clear). It was totally unsuited to the audience, being a recondite survey of various metaphysical conceptions drawn largely from German sources and quite incomprehensible for his hearers, and, indeed, too vague and formless for anyone who liked a clear statement. Nevertheless, the sea of faces looked up at him without boredom or impatience, as if his very unintelligibility impressed and pleased them. When we left we found a man outside the door selling a newspaper. *The Anarchist*, he said, adding: 'I don't think I shall be able to sell Mr Herbert Read a copy.' At that, Topolski immediately bought one. What body it was the mouthpiece of I have no idea nor can I imagine why the seller took up his stance outside the Ethical Society's door. Certainly the audience did not look rash enough to fancy anarchical opinions.

*16 April 1951*

While I was talking in Topolski's studio about an art film, a river yacht moored in the canal outside his window. He looked out and the owner, a tall lank man, asked to be allowed to put a pipe into his tap to fill his water tank. Topolski agreed and the man came in, introducing himself as the labour peer, Lord St Davids. He invited us to visit his yacht, saying that it was his town residence, as he had given up his flat and kept on only his country house in Wales; he moved about the canals, keeping a convenient distance from the House of Lords, when it was in session. As we approached the yacht, a shower of stones fell, directed by a troop of boys behind a wall on the other side of the canal. The stones continued, many hitting the yacht. Feliks telephoned for the police. On board was a girl of about 24, who was travelling with Lord St Davids. He did not introduce us. We explored the interior, two rooms and a bathroom, and drank some home-brewed Welsh beer. The stones fell for a time and then ceased. A mild policeman arrived, but did nothing. A curious episode.

*17 May 1951*

Had lunch with Mervyn Peake at the Victoria & Albert Museum. The Royal Society of Literature has just awarded him the Heinemann prize, worth £100, for his book *Gormenghast*, which I reviewed for *World Review* and declared to be a work of original art. This award has pleased him, but he is in such straitened circumstances that his great need is money rather than honours. He had a strained wild look, as if life was very hard. He had started on the third volume of the story, of which *Gormenghast* is the second. It deals with the adventures of Titus Groan* in the world. I remember when I first met Peake in 1942 or thereabouts and asked him down to Maidenhead, how when I rowed him on the Thames he told me that he was contemplating these books and sketched the story. He had made a name for himself since, for, as I assured him, he is already a famous author, though not yet recognised in the way that he should be and will be. Our conversation lasted over two hours.

*29 May 1951*

Leave Maidenhead on a visit to Manchester to see L. S. Lowry and talk over with him the writing of the book commissioned by Reid and Lefevre.† Arrive Manchester at 1.45. Met by Lowry. Go to Salford Art Gallery to see Lowry's paintings there and the view from the terrace which he painted often in earlier days. Then down the Oldham Road, off which is the old quarter, where Lowry got much of his subjects and inspiration. As we sat in this part by a children's playground, a scene he had often painted, he spoke of his loneliness. All his friends dead. He said his painting was not so much a pleasure as an anodyne. He was just carrying on from day to day. Yet he could not have lived without it and was deeply grateful to Reid‡ for having enabled him to do it. In this way he unbosomed himself, forgetting his normal shyness. We dined together and he continued to talk, giving me gradually a full understanding of his character and art, which I shall recount in detail in the introduction to his book. It will be a moving and unusual story.

*30 May 1951*

Lowry called for me at 10 a.m. and we took the bus to Pendlebury, where he had lived from 1909 to 1940. He showed me the spot which had started him in 1915 on painting industrial subjects and which led to his evolving a special style. It was called Thomas St and Stump Park and was a view of two approaching lines of miners' or cotton

* The hero of *Gormenghast*.
† *The Discovery of L. S. Lowry*, published 1951.
‡ Director of the Reid & Lefevre Gallery, who gave Lowry his first exhibition in London.

spinners' dwellings against the high square front of a cotton mill, in front being an open space with stumps, called a croft.

Thence we visited Station Road, No 117 being his parents' house where he had lived so long. He was sad and tender as we walked about it. His mother was everything to him. He lived at home till her death, which was in his 52nd year. It was a very ordinary semi-detached house in a row, but to him it seemed lovely, a loveliness from which he was now cast out, for he had left it and taken a house in a village called Mottram-in-Longdendale. We went to this village in the afternoon to see his house and studio and work. I obtained all the information necessary for my 10,000 word introduction. I was moved and impressed. Lowry became quite at ease and natural.

### 12 June 1951

Visited Lefevre Gallery and had a look at some Lowry paintings which they had in store. The most significant one was a desolate landscape of crater-like lakes. This was a late painting of a purely imaginative sort, and pointed to a desolate state of mind bordering on madness. I was very glad to have seen it, as it throws much light on his state of mind in conjunction with what he told me in Manchester.

At 1 p.m. I went to the Savage Club where R. J. Minney* had asked me to lunch. I found that the other guest was Cecil Scott Forrester, the creator of Hornblower and a best-seller novelist. He makes £50,000 a year from his books and the films etc. founded on them. He suffers from some arterial disease and can only walk a very short distance. Though only fifty-two years of age he seemed old. His books have no literary value, but are widely read because they are exciting. His appearance was not that of a man of culture or character. On the whole, however, his immense success had not spoiled him entirely, though he was certainly not a pleasant character. His conversation was fairly interesting as he had been about so much. The lunch passed off pleasantly. Minney asked me to stay with him at his house near Harwich. He is well acquainted with the film people.

### 28 August 1951

Topolski had rung up to say that Gandhi's son, Devadas, was in London; was making a collection of pictures and drawings of his

* Author.

father for an Indian museum, and wanted to see my painting of Gandhi by Topolski. This was done in 1946, two years before Gandhi's assassination, and represents the Mahatma disappointed by troubles and tensions of the time, which his gospel had been unable to allay, leaning in dejection on two women, while a British soldier with a gun keeps order. The attitude and details in the painting seem to fore-shadow his murder. Devadas was said to wish to buy the painting. I told Topolski I would sell it, but would buy from him with the proceeds another picture or pictures. Accordingly I brought up the canvas and left it with Topolski, arranging to return when Devadas Gandhi would be there. Arrived back at Topolski's studio at 7 p.m. Devadas Gandhi appeared, accompanied by the Swiss editor of the London branch of his newspaper and a Hindu qualquoque. Devadas was a small man, more prepossessing in face than his sainted father, earnest, precise, rather winning in manner and quite self possessed. We adjourned into the other room where the painting was set on an easel. Devadas looked at it, liked it, and said that he would get it reproduced in colour for a book which he intended to get published of Topolski's many drawings and paintings of his father. He enquired the price, which I said was £150, though I would make a gift of £20 towards the Indian museum in honour of his father. He replied that when the book was published he expected that funds would become available. So it was left at that. During this conversation Devadas showed caution and there was a hint of suspicion, as if he was accus-tomed to have to do his negotiations with rather tricky persons and was so much in the habit of being on his guard that he could not recog-nise frankness. He is a lawyer by profession.

When he and his party were gone, we went to dine at Topolski's house in Hanover Terrace. It was an easy and delightful evening.

### 16 October 1951

Met Frank Dobson, the sculptor, who is head of the sculpture section at the Royal College of Art, and had lunch with him. He told me that he had been commissioned to carve a memorial for Shelley and Keats in the Poets' Corner of the Abbey. In preparation he was reading their works and had not yet hit on a suitable symbolism. He also spoke of Ezra Pound, whom he used to know and who is now in a Home for mental defectives in America, following on his capture by the Americans in Italy after he had been broadcasting for the Italians in the war. Pound was the most conceited man he had ever met, but a striking personality, who threw himself into every subject, like translating Chinese poetry, when, though he knew no Chinese he caught the spirit and was often very successful. And I remembered and told him that Arthur Waley had included in his life of Li Po a translation of the poem called *The Exiles' Letter* done by Pound, a paradox.

### 1 November 1951

I spent the day reading the letters I wrote from Oxford to my mother (1907–1912), preparatory to writing the chapter in my auto-biography covering that period. One of the questions that I have to answer is why I decided to go in for the Indian Civil Service. I think that ultimately it was the desire to be independent as soon as possible. I saw it as a career with prizes at the top; I thought it would give me a free hand; the out-of-door strange life attracted me in a romantic sense. Though I had inclinations towards writing, I had no subject, I was not a journalist, and I evidently did not believe I could succeed as a writer. Moreover, the decision to try for the I.C.S. was made in March 1908, too early for me to have a conception of my literary aptitudes. Having taken the decision, I went on with the implication of it and was not tempted to change in the direction of writing when my degree showed me where I stood. The fact was that my writing at that period showed little literary promise. In a long view the decision was fortunate, for it spared me the horror of the First World War, which I would probably not have survived, and eventually provided me with a subject.

### 5 November 1951

Went to a cocktail party at the Hanover Gallery. The first person I saw was Somerset Maugham, to whom I had never spoken. He is a man of seventy-seven, small, with a large mouth and a face like a frog. His appearance is therefore undistinguished. We had a short conversation. He said that Epstein had just finished his bust of him and that it made him look like a *condottiere*. He wondered who would buy it. I said surely some of his readers had a fine hall in which the bust of a *condottiere* would look just right. He replied that readers never did anything like that. I then told him that I had long been one of his regular readers and had read his stories many times. He did not speak of my books. He gave the impression of being tired and of making an effort to keep going. Life and success seemed vanity to him, though he still (perhaps by force of habit) thought it worthwhile to appear at a cocktail party. At the moment he is at the very height of his reputation, but how can he at seventy-seven take such plaudits seriously?

I then went to see Pearl Primus and her African dancers. This was a remarkable entertainment. The dancers were presented with real art and were above the heads of the average Londoner who goes to see native dancing. There was a splendid solo by a drummer, which could be compared to a river, now violently leaping over rocks, now sweeping along in a vast tide, now almost motionless on the flat. It was the most magnificent piece of drumming I have ever heard and I will never forget it. I had no idea that a drum played with two hands could by force of rhythm and the monochrome of its notes convey the effect of a symphony. Pearl Primus herself was very good in various roles, but she gave the effect less of Africa than of the West Indies.

### 28 November 1951

I met L. S. Lowry and took him to lunch in Soho. After a conversation when we discussed the book on him and his future plans, we attended the Egon private view to look at our respective portraits. There was a fair crowd, mostly to do with those whose portraits were on the walls. I spoke to a few, including Markova, the dancer. Mervyn Peake came in, had a look at his portrait, declared his dislike of it, decried many of the drawings and came along with me to tea at the Kardomah café in Piccadilly. There he told me that his play,* which Vivien Leigh wants to act in, is held up for want of a producer. He proceeded to sketch the plots of two more plays, one a sort of atom bomb plot,† suited, I thought, only for one of the club theatres, as there was insufficient action, and the other a farce about a school with no students,‡ an inspector who talks officialese patter and has to have an interpreter, and a tyrannical headmaster—Peake at his most natural. I urged him to write it.

* *The Wit to Woo.*
† Subsequently called *The Cave*. Never produced or published.
‡ Never written except for a few notes.

*15 January 1952*

The Burmese Ambassador, U Ka Si, late of the Indian Civil Service, asked me to call at 11.30 today and I presented myself at the embassy. U Ka Si was at his desk in English clothes. We sat down on a sofa. The two matters of interest that we talked of were: (1) that the British would not have lost Burma if they had handled the Burmese better and studied their interests, rather than those of the English merchants; had we devoted ourselves to the task of acting as trustees for the Burmese and always put their interests first, had we, instead of using the word 'pro-Burman' as a term of opprobrium, adopted it as our policy, the Burmese would never have asked us to go. (2) The Ambassador asked if the Burmese should return to the Commonwealth. My view was that they could not return, for no government could withstand the left-wing opposition there would be to such a return; and that the Commonwealth was already becoming old-fashioned and would be swallowed in a united nations organisation for world peace: it should be to that that the Burmese should make sure of belonging. The Ambassador was in close agreement with me. We both felt that the British had thrown away a great chance.

*26 February 1952*

At 8 p.m. I reached Hampstead, where Desmond Fitzgerald, the editor of *World Review*, lives. I had my autobiography* with me, as he hopes to find passages in it which will be suitable for the *Review*. I dined there and met Stevie Smith, the novelist and reviewer, an amusing odd woman of about forty-eight or so, very human and intelligent, with exceedingly bright eyes and a flow of pleasant conversation. She is the most entertaining reviewer of novels in England. Her reviews contain a humorous malice, but there is no malice in her conversation or apparently in her nature, which is sweet and indulgent, as seen at a dinner. The Fitzgerald interior was unusual, there being a wicker birdcage hanging from the ceiling with a pot of ivy inside, the life-size statue of a negress in one corner of the kind associated with Edwardian hotel lounges, and a wicker bull's mask on the wall—Mrs F's taste, I guess.

* *The Journey Outward*, 1952.

*4 March 1952*

I went to the Leicester Galleries to look at the Zadkine exhibition. Suddenly Mervyn Peake came in and we went to have a cup of tea. His play hangs fire, because the Oliviers are in America and he hears nothing from them. It is the usual story, The stage people are spoilt and heartless, they encourage a poor author to believe that they will do his play and then leave him in the lurch without even a message of explanation. Peake looked worn and dispirited, but was yet planning a new book that he hoped would bring him money. He related the plot and asked my opinion. It was to be called *The rise and fall of Icarus Pye*,* a fantasy where a man is terrified to find that he is growing an angel's wings, because of his good works, and to counteract them does ill and grows horns, an equally alarming phenomenon.

*8 April 1952*

By staring at these deliberately clumsy shapes† you can imagine anything. But you may be deceiving yourself. A great deal of modern art is like that; it is so removed from life and appearance, so disguised in archaic or abstract forms, so much an abstraction from natural forms, that you can get nothing from it unless you play the game of let's pretend and enter its world without prejudice. But when surrendered to its world you begin to imagine what may not be there. That is the problem of some modern art. It sets you off dreaming in a queer way and you like it, provided that your surrender is complete, but you have no assurance, no standard of judgment, to convince you, on awakening from your trance, that you have really been in the domain of art. As the great majority of people can see nothing at all, whether by themselves or when the thing is explained, you find that art becomes a private withdrawal, quite a different thing from the main current of painting and sculpture, which is essentially public and for general uses, as to please, excite, elevate or decorate.

*22 April 1952*

At 4 p.m. I went to Slatters in Bond Street where Harold Nicolson was opening an exhibition of Dutch pictures in aid of a charity.

* Published as *Mr Pye*, 1953.
† At an exhibition of sculpture.

Nicolson, who is two years older than me and has had a varied life in diplomacy and letters, is rather the man of affairs and club type of English gentleman in appearance than the scholar, artist or poet. He has no knowledge of, interest in, or need for, pictures or works of art, but is a commonsense critic. As literary reviewer in the *Observer* he has great influence. His features are somewhat puckered up and small, his manner not very assured or easy. The speech he made was pleasant, and in no way boring, a most exceptional thing. I spoke to him before and after it. He is, I imagine, a kind and human sort of man. His books are respectable, but perhaps none of them, except that about his experiences with Curzon, are of permanent interest. He had told me that he has long kept a daily journal, the contents of which could never be published in his life time as it reveals too many secrets, and which he is leaving to Balliol. That might prove his memorial, as his experiences in diplomacy, journalism, literature, the B.B.C., Parliament, have provided wonderful material.

*10 May 1952*

I have read quickly Augustus John's *Chiaoscuro*, his autobiography. Though very fragmentary and not more than a medley of impressions of places and people, arranged without reference to chronological order, it gives some idea of the man, but not an altogether attractive one. His judgments of the character of the many people he met as a portrait painter and wandering artist are, one feels, very sane. Many are unpleasant or, apparently, boring after a short acquaintance. He does not seem to have made real friends. The café table, the glass of pernod, a lively disputation, a sense of excited high spirits, a taste for low or exotic company —but never a sense of quiet content or reward. When I visited John a few years ago with Topolski I had the impression of a man who still could not sit still but must have the fictitious jollity of the bar and a crowd of admirers. One is left with the impression that he is more a character than a man of character, more a figure than a great man. He lacks seriousness, and his opinions are trite. Nevertheless, his character studies of people like Gogarty and Joyce are extremely true.

*9 June 1952*

At 7.30 I arrived at Topolski's house. He was giving a reception.

He told me as a secret that the leading newspaper in Japan had invited him to that country for a stay of three months, all expenses paid. The Japanese, he said, admired his painting. He bound me to secrecy because he feared that, if the cliques in London heard that the Japanese were choosing him as the most interesting contemporary painter in England, a spoke would be put in his wheel. The guests now began to arrive: the foreign editor of the Japanese paper in question accompanied by the paper's Paris correspondent, a half Japanese, half English woman, smart and pretty. There followed some members of Parliament, including the eminent K.C. who had been Maxwell Fyffe's assistant in the Nuremburg Nazi trials, and Vernon Bartlett, the celebrated journalist, an old rather commonplace man to look at, but pleasant, quick and modest to speak to. The K.C. told me that Goering dominated the trials; he was the big man. Mr Justice Lawrence was foolish enough to dispute with him on one occasion on a political issue and got the worst of it. Also, when sentence of death was pronounced, he scored. Lawrence delivered it in English and it was instantaneously communicated to him through the headphones in German. He pretended that the headphones were out of order and that he did not understand. A man was told to test the circuit, while the court waited. He declared it was not out of order. Goering smiled; he had succeeded in getting a rise out of the solemn judge.

Other guests included three Indian dancers, pretty and very self possessed, friends of Mulk Raj Anand, the novelist; finally the ex-Cabinet Minister Bevan arrived, red-faced, low-browed but making an effort to be pleasant. He thought the Japanese editor was the new Japanese ambassador and called him Your Excellency till Topolski explained.


*7 October 1952*

Went to see Feliks Topolski at Hanover Terrace. He remains low spirited. 'You cannot work', he said, 'when you feel the public is against you.' What his plans are he did not say. 'One does not require much to be happy,' he declared, and cited the case of a Polish friend who, obliged to become a gardener to support himself, filled his leisure happily with a hand press with which he printed de luxe editions of his friends' writings. Topolski continues to get publicity, for he showed me an article in *Architecture* describing with many reproductions his murals on the block of flats north of Holborn, and another in an Indian art publication about his big Festival painting. He said: 'Artists ought to get salaries like civil servants. What an irony it is when you see the Arts Council people drawing a regular monthly salary for distributing pictures and the artists who painted the pictures without enough money to pay for their food.' And he cited in particular the case of Lucien Freud, now starving though his pictures are so much admired. 'Why should the state pay James* for patronising Freud, but not Freud for being worthy of patronage?' I made the usual objection that if artists were paid by the state they would have to paint what the state wanted, and that they would not like that. 'Not at all,' said Topolski. 'They would paint what was required. Look at them now. You have a vogue, started who knows how, perhaps in Paris or by somebody like Herbert Read, and artists adjust themselves to it at once and begin painting according to the dictates of the moment. Artists never stand out against contemporary ideas. A state order would be no different.'

### 23 February 1953

L. S. Lowry, the artist, came down to lunch here today. I met him at Taplow station. He has become yet more eccentric. His manner is to talk in a very loud voice and to repeat several times the same assertions—such as 'I don't want to go anywhere now' or 'I am getting old' or ask abruptly questions, 'You really think my painting as good as it was?' All this is a reflection of his melancholy and unrest. However, he seemed to enjoy his visit. When I took him round the house he was indulgent to the work of other artists to a degree unusual among painters.

### 26 February 1953

The great Mexican exhibition opens on Tuesday and the Arts Council arranged for some art critics to have a look at the pieces today. On arrival at the Tate I found all in confusion. An army of workmen were putting up show cases. Half the objects were not in position. Members of the British Museum staff were helping. Philip James was rushing about. Even so, there was a great deal to see and I stayed there for three-and-a-half hours. To grasp the various cultures

* Philip James, Director of Art at the Arts Council.

that come under the general head of Mexican art cannot be done in one afternoon. By the end of the time, however, I had seen enough and understood enough to realise that America has as large and interesting a heritage of ancient art as has Europe. There is no need for any Americans to seek inspiration outside their continent. There is ample in the dozen cultures of old Mexico to provide them indefinitely. I met John Skeaping, the sculptor, potter and draughtsman, who had lived 18 months in a Mexican potters' village. He told me that in the deep country the Mexicans, though Catholics and having churches, retained some of their ancient religious beliefs. He had seen statues of the old gods in churches and seen animal sacrifices to them. He had even heard of human sacrifice in the foundation of new buildings. His impression was that an unbridgeable gulf divided the original Mexicans and the white inhabitants, chiefly Spanish. The original Mexicans did not want to leave their accustomed round of ideas and come up to date. Another point he made was that the scenery and weather of Mexico are highly dramatic—volcanoes, earthquakes, violent storms, great mountains—and that to understand their art one must allow the influence upon it of the dark and frightening forces of nature.

*3 March 1953*

Went to the private view of the Mexican exhibition. There were many people I knew. I spoke to Arthur Waley, who looked bloodless and was quite lacking in any cordiality. He had Beryl de Zoete with him. I was afraid to speak to her at first, having heard so much about her madness, but did so eventually and found her quite sane. She spoke of her recent book on Indian dancing, which I said I was reading. We had tea with Stanley Spencer and his old friend Daphne Charlton, whose portrait by him hangs in the Tate. He is at work on drawings for his great last judgment, commissioned for Coventry cathedral.*

*17 March 1953*

The newspapers have been full of the destruction of Reg Butler's representation in wire of the Unknown Political Prisoner. A Hungarian entered the Tate, seized it and crushed it in his hands and then stamped on it, saying: 'That is the end of that.' He was arrested and

* The commission fell through.

is to be tried. Reg Butler's thing was only a scale model and can easily be done again. But a great sensation was created, the greatest in my experience of the art world. The section headed by Herbert Read and the Institute of Contemporary Arts, of which he is president, has put forward this wire sculpture as real art. The rest of the art world is very sceptical. Perhaps the trial will turn out an amusing debate on the state of modern art. As I looked in at the various galleries, I enquired what was being said. The subject had been the talk of the town. But no one knew anything of the Hungarian iconoclast, who he was or why he did it.

*28 April 1953*

I went to Feliks Topolski's house in Hanover Terrace. He was wearing a morning coat, striped trousers, dove-grey waistcoat, white collar, a dress I had never seen him in and which suited him well. He and Marion had been to some society wedding. The excursion had set them wondering about those sort of people. They had seemed so gentle and yet sure of themselves, and all looked alike, very English and without culture, yet charming, It seemed that they had made much of Feliks and he was flattered. I was taken to the kitchen and given a snack. The telephone went and I heard Feliks inviting two people to come round. On his returning to his seat he said they were called Empson and asked if I knew them. I could not remember until he said the man had an untidy beard under his chin which straggled down in front, giving him the air of a monkey. That identified him. He was the man who on 9th Dec. 1952 had addressed the China Society at lunch. Shortly afterwards they arrived. Empson spoke to me in a manner which I found very eccentric, saying that a certain diplomat whom he knew in China had always referred to me as 'that cad Collis'; I assured him that I had never met or heard of him. It seemed that he made his observation because he disliked some passage in my *Foreign Mud*. I was rather put out. When he saw this, he was sorry and insisted on sitting down with me and conversing with studied amiability. I daresay he may be all right if you get used to his style of humour. He said he had been appointed Professor of English at Sheffield University. He is now enjoying a belated reputation for poems written in the thirties. He has become quite a vogue among a certain set. His poems are extremely difficult to understand and are written with an allusiveness and compression unusual even for modern poetry. In an anthology of verse selected by a man called Fraser, and just published, a set of contemporary poets are called Empsonians.

## 19 May 1953

I went to the Tate, where Graham Sutherland was having a private view of a big selection of his *oeuvre*. It was 5 p.m. when I arrived and not a great many people were there. I saw Sutherland and went up to speak to him. He looks remarkably young and has rather a dapper military appearance. Hailed by the pundits as the greatest living English artist, he has no more than the air of a beau type. When speaking to you, however, his eyes have unusual intensity. There is some sadness, also, in his air. He was very modest. I spoke of the rather unpleasant review of his exhibition which had appeared this morning in the *Times*. He said that Clutton Brock, *The Times* critic, had never liked his work. And added that he had received more blame than praise. This praise, however, was much in evidence in his catalogue, for he had three separate prefaces to it, written by Philip James of the Arts Council, Kenneth Clark and Herbert Read, each of whom wrote in very strong support. Indeed, in the ten years since his emergence, he has been more supported and pushed forward than any of his *confrères*. He said to me how hard he had to work to live. I asked why he did not do at least one portrait a year at the big figure he now commands after his successful portraits of Somerset Maugham and Beaverbrook. He replied that he did not do portraits easily. The Beaverbrook portrait took him six months. There was no gain there, particularly as he could not do his normal painting at the same time. Moreover, how to find subjects which would really stimulate his interest? Just to do a portrait to get money would not ensure its success. It was evident that he did not want to do portraits as a regular thing. In all this he spoke diffidently. Some critics, he said, declared his art had no more meaning or basis than his discovery that a novel and bizarre effect could be achieved by looking out for unusual natural objects, say of curious twisted shape, and fitting them into a design. Perhaps they are right, he said. Yet, creation is surely a more mysterious process than concocting shapes from bits of things noticed by hazard. When he turned to speak to someone else, I looked closely at some of his paintings—for instance *The Deposition* and *The Thorn Trees* both painted in 1946 and was quite astounded at the sensation I received of power and at the vigour of the brush and the quality of the paint. Nevertheless, I do not care for the subjects of the pictures, if you can call subjects the shapes represented. I have no desire to possess any of his works.

*28 May 1953*

At 7.30 I dined with Michael Rothenstein at his mother's house at 10 Devonshire Place. Old Lady Rothenstein is practically stone deaf, but will not use a hearing aid. She is very pleasant, smiles and says amusing trenchant things, but, as she cannot hear what you say, she is very fatiguing. She has the upper flat in the big house, though it preserves the appearance of being simply the first floor of a private house. You find yourself in a large sitting room with some objects of oriental art, the remains of Sir William Rothenstein's collection. She keeps a butler-cook factotum. We three sat talking and behind us was the dinner table. At a certain moment her man, having cooked the dinner, appeared in his rôle as butler, and as if it were old times and they were still living in the state kept by Sir William, announced, 'Dinner is served, your ladyship'. One looked round, saw the soup on the table, and moved back four feet into position. After dinner the old lady went off to bed and Michael Rothenstein showed me his new aquatint process.

*12 June 1953*

Drove to the Kingsway Hall, where a reception for Nehru, Prime Minister of India, had been arranged by the Indian community of London. A great crowd was present. I found myself in a large room where coffee and Indian sweetmeats were being served. A man touched my sleeve and turning I saw it was the Burmese Ambassador. He introduced me to the Indian High Commissioner, a Bengali of the most charming manner, so much nicer than his predecessor's, Krishna Menon. Nearby Nehru was standing in a circle of admirers. He was dressed in a white Gandhi cap, long black coat and white jodhpur-type tight trousers. His hair is white but despite his 63 years he looks young, his face being fresh, tanned like a bather's and unlined. His manner was grave, quiet and a little distant, yet sweet. Seeing my opportunity, I went and introduced myself by name, saying that I was Feliks

Topolski's friend. We spoke of his oil portrait by Topolski and I told him I thought it an admirable work. He said that rumour had reached India that Topolski's drawings had been damaged by water leaking through the roof. I assured him the damage had not been important and that anyhow his portrait was in good shape. He said he had never seen it. (It was made from drawings of Nehru done from the life in India.) I was going on to speak of Epstein's bust of him when he had to speak to another person. He has practically no accent. His manner is very perfect. As a personality he easily dominated all those who were present. He is, of course, more than Prime Minister of India. He has become a great international figure. I stayed a little longer and heard the beginning of an address that he made to the many hundreds who were present.

*28 June 1953*

I went up to Cliveden and lunched with Bill Astor, who has recently succeeded as third Viscount. I came on him outside the front door and said that I believed his victory in the Oaks betokened the beginning of a period of good fortune. His misfortunes were in the past. He replied that he hoped I had second sight. He has just emerged from a most disastrous marriage. His health, never very robust, was affected by the sufferings he endured over having to part with his wife Sally. On entering the hall I remarked that it seemed much as it was in his father's time. He pointed out that he had removed from its centre a particularly hideous statue. On entering the study he introduced me to the members of his house party, who included the celebrated writer Freya Stark. She is a woman of about fifty-six, stoutish, rather a bundle of a woman, who possesses a marvellously bright eye. Having corresponded with, but never met, her, I was delighted at seeing her, particularly as I felt a strong sympathy for her at once. The gong went and we passed into luncheon. I noticed that the late Lord Astor's old butler was still in service. His present Lordship kept more state than when I used to lunch at Cliveden in his father's time. There were two or three other men servants waiting at table. The lunch was excellent and I was able to carry on a pleasant conversation with Freya Stark and my host. After lunch we sat on the terrace. I found that Astor wanted to tell me about the breakdown of his marriage. Going aside with him we sat on chairs in the arbour above the steps by the great magnolia. He said: 'She suddenly told me one day that she had been in love for three years with an Oxford undergraduate. It was a complete and shattering surprise. She was not the sort of person who has lovers. It seems that her feeling for the young man was romantic only. She was not his mistress, but she wanted to marry him.'

## 5 July 1953

I have written about a third of the Cortés book.* I have never undertaken a bit of work which absorbed me more. As one continues to ponder the story, it becomes stranger and more difficult to understand. Madariaga does not probe deep enough in his biography. There are too many loose ends, too many *non sequiturs*. But he points the right way to treat the subject. As you study Prescott you find him superficial on the Mexican side. He covers up with such words as 'barbarism'. It is a subject that can become a muddle if you go into it too much or try to reconcile the varying statements of people who obviously did not understand the essence of the drama, which was, as I see it, that everything Montezuma foresaw came true. From first to last he was right. An overwhelming fate was marching upon him and his people. It seems to me that to understand the story correctly is the greatest task, not research into more detail, when in a book of 60,000 words there is not room for such detail. Moreover, the audience is not suited to such a work of research. What is required is an intelligible and original reading of the known facts, presented shortly and clearly, step by step.

## 20 July 1953

We left the reception† in time to reach Jack Yeats's‡ studio by 6 p.m. It had been arranged that Louise and I were to see him alone. Since I had met him last (about two years ago, I suppose) he had become rather more feeble and had some of the slow stiffness of a very old man. Yet his face was not old nor his eye. His features were little lined, his colour was good, his eye limpid. And his conversation was as amusing and downright as ever. In his usual way he went behind

* *Cortés and Montezuma*, published 1954.
† Given by the Provost of Trinity College, Dublin, to the International Association of Art Critics who were holding their annual congress in that city.
‡ Painter, brother of W. B. Yeats.

the screen and came out carrying a tray with whisky, sherry and biscuits. He poured me an immensely strong whisky and Louise a claret glass of sherry. In the course of his talk he showed us some of his latest paintings, each of them an autonomous creation, an original comment of a man watching with intense emotion the pageant of life. I told him that James Sweeney, the American art critic and head of the U.S.A. section in the Congress, had said something to me about wanting to see him. He replied firmly that he did not wish to see Sweeney. He was too old and detached to have any motive for assuming a pleasant welcoming manner with a man who had, it seems, been a little facetious about him in the American press. Yet I think that had he seen Sweeney, he would have found him a charming man. But Yeats was too grand and proud to make any effort to win over a man he supposed was unsympathetic. As I knew that at 7 p.m. his housekeeper brought his supper and moreover that an hour's conversation was enough for him, we took leave at that hour. I wonder if I shall ever see him again.

### 23 July 1953

Turning left* downhill through Killiney village we had the view of the Big Sugarloaf† and Bray Head which used to refresh me as a child returning on Sunday mornings with my father and mother on foot from the depressing service at Killiney church and the sermon of the dry old creature, Canon Stoney. The route we were taking would bring us past the upper gate of Kilmore and I strained out of the bus hoping to see the roof of the house which from 1893 till 1912 was my home and from 1912 to 1950 I constantly visited, always with deep feeling. But I forgot that the hill is far too steep at that point. The house lay below the line of sight. We raced past the gate on which I saw the, for me, magical word 'Kilmore'. I could never have imagined that one day I would pass my father's old house without halting and going in to peep from the top of the steps further down the drive, pass without a glimpse of the rhododendrons, the lawn where my mother's flower beds were, the steps on which she used to sit for long hours in the sun, the rockery plants she so much loved (descendants of which still grow in my garden at Maidenhead), pass

* Travelling in a bus full of art critics attending the Congress.
† A mountain.

in company with a crowd of cold, foreign, sophisticated, clever, narrow and rather inhuman art critics. The picture that rests most clearly of all in my mind, Kilmore garden, the tennis court, the palms my father planted and the eucalyptus trees he was so proud of, the daffodil bank, the walled vegetable garden, and the steep path to the lower garden with its iron gate whose screech (it was never oiled in fifty years) used to welcome me home from journeyings to Burma. All this flashed through my mind as I sat by Louise and flitted by the top gate, and I was surprised to find that it gave me a pang. I might have still been living in that house, for my father left me the residue of his lease, some thirty-five years I think. But I did not choose to go there and leave London. Indeed, to have done so would have been the death of the mind, a surrender to sentiment, a wallowing in old memories, a refusal to continue growing, a premature plunge into old age. I was right not to go, yet to pass the house without a salute and in such company seemed in some sort a desecration.

### 11 August 1953

I went to the British Museum to see Burland (the Mexican expert) and ask him questions about Montezuma. I found him in his room among the vast Maya reliefs (in plaster). He was very friendly and informative. In general I checked against his specislist knowledge some of the conclusions I had come to, and was relieved to find them correct. After an hour's conversation he took me out to tea with a young friend of his, a clever woman of striking appearance. He told me of his early struggles and how he had gradually won his way to the head of his department and his position as the leading expert on Mexico. While I was talking to him in his room, the anthropologist Fagg came in with an iron spearhead in his hand. He said that it had been forwarded to him with a letter stating that it had been found in some diggings for Roman antiquities and asking him to date it. He told us it was African and perhaps thirty years old. It must have been dropped in the excavations. He said he had heard of a man who, having inherited a quantity of African spears, used them as bean sticks, and remarked that in time no doubt his garden would be declared by the local archaeologists to have been the scene of a Roman battle.

*9 September 1953*

At a party at the Hanover Gallery I saw Baron, the photographer, tall, burly, with his maimed arm and smiling strong profile. He was accompanied by a young French actress or dancer, carefully made up and quite stupid, though fashionably pretty. I went to speak to him and he threw his arms round my neck in an heroic gesture. He has recently been much to the fore with his photographs of royalty. His only rival is Douglas Glass. They share the glamour at the top of the profession.

Then suddenly I saw Augustus John coming in. I do not know his exact age, but it must be about seventy-six. He wore a beret and the loose coat and trousers of the working artist. Years ago I had visited him with Topolski and we had spent some time in his studio, though he was impatient to get to the Antelope in Sloane Square where his friends were awaiting him. Seeing him again now I was struck by the mellow humanity of his appearance. It is certainly something to be very remarkable looking. He went upstairs to look at his bust, one of the exhibits, and talk to Fiore de Henriquez, (the artist exhibiting), who is a great friend. Presently, I followed upstairs, as I wanted to have a quiet view of him talking to others. Sitting on a chair, with Louise on the arm, I studied him. He was quite close, in conversation with various people. His face was very expressive, like an actor's. He had very great charm. Affection, intimacy, indignation, sadness, flitted across his features. There was emotion of some kind showing all the time. He has one of the most remarkable old faces I have ever seen, not intellectual, not kind, not even very intuitive or sympathetic for others, but human and greatly experienced in life. One sees very few Englishmen with such faces in the upper classes, but tramps, beggars and poets (old style) sometimes have that look. Augustus John in his old age is the perfect bohemian type of the Paris of the twenties.

*30 September 1953*

I made my way to a party given by the Lefevre Gallery for L. S. Lowry. On entering I saw him there, tall, awkward, saying in his jerky way 'I did not write, I knew you would hear of the exhibition', and repeating the phrases several times. All the rooms filled up and I noticed that, though he was no party man, he was not unable in spite of his shyness to greet the guests, going from one to the other in quite a professional way. From scraps of conversation I had with him I gathered that he was less of a recluse, went about more, did not sit at home listening to music in quite the distraught manner he used to and as I have described in the introduction I wrote to his paintings. I studied his pictures and came to the conclusion that few of them were as good as his best. They had been done quicker as the demand now obliged him to produce more. His habit had been to linger for years over each painting and with loving care improve its quality. He cannot give so much time now. Nevertheless I think there was little fall.

## 22 October 1953

I dropped into the Lefevre Gallery to enquire how Lowry's exhibition had gone. While I was talking he chanced to come in, having arrived that day from the North. I was interested to see that his rather sudden promotion into a premier place in British art had in no way changed him. I said, 'You have now become a great man.' In his startled manner he replied: 'Do you think so?' One detected in him a shade more self-assurance, and something of the toughness and power which had enabled him to get where he is peeped out from behind his distracted old face.

## 26 October 1953

When walking to my car in Berkeley Square, I ran into Henry Moore, whom I had not seen for some time. He looked well though a little haggard. We stayed talking awhile. He said that, though a man who had not been laid up in bed for thirty years, he had recently had to have an operation for stone. It happened out of the blue and made him realise how uncertain was the strongest man's health. I looked at him closely to see if his international fame had in any way changed the charming simplicity of his character. It did not seem to me that it had. He spoke with candour and modesty of his art. We were standing only a stone's throw from the four strange abstractions of his which are on the Bond Street façade of the *Time & Life* building. 'It was lucky,' he said, 'that they were put in position during the coronation and what with the decorations and very different ideas that were running in people's heads, they were not noticed. In that way I escaped the press attacks and notoriety which would have been

10 Nov. 1968 As Louise and I were walking along the towpath of the Thames we met Geoffrey Baker, one our milkmen, who became an artist, exhibited at the academy, taught at an arts school in High Wycombe, came under the influence of the Beatles meeting the Maharishi Mahesh Yogi and joined him in the foot-hills of Himalaya, while meditating in retreat. Baker has just returned to England. He has a luxuriant beard, so bushy that I did not recognise him at first. He told me how he had become 'one of the Maharishi's missionary preachers' and was shortly going to South America to spread his master's tenets. He begged us to go forthwith to India city at the Maharishi's Himalayan institute. 'You will have a lovely room with a vast view towards the eternal snows.' And he gave us samples of the Maharishi's sayings and interviews over the river, some of his catchwords, such as 'Wait on, wait on.'

It was very interesting to see the milkman might come, and come quickly.

1 A manuscript page of the Diaries

Maurice Collis in
his studio

3 Maurice Collis' mother aged 85, drawn by Feliks Topolski

4 Maurice Collis' Burmese horoscope

so disagreeable. There is a female figure of mine inside, done more naturalistically than even the Northampton Church Madonna. Do go in and see it. The *Time & Life* people like visitors to enquire for it.' And he went on to speak of his present activities. 'An artist is only happy working. Or at least,' he corrected, 'an artist is much at a loss when he is not working.' Then he told me that the Brazilians were having an exhibition of his sculpture and that he had been invited there, expenses paid. His expenses were also being paid for a visit to Mexico, 'a thing which has always been one of my dreams'. With Cortés and Montezuma fresh in my mind I envied him that chance. But, indeed, if I were offered such a tour, I would hesitate to go, on account of the strange malaise that overtakes me if I am far from London. Still, with Louise to accompany me, I would go.

## 7 November 1953

Yesterday I was phoned by Lord Astor's secretary who said that King Gustav of Sweden was staying the weekend at Cliveden and conveyed a message that I was expected to dinner today. On getting there at eight I found the front of the house in darkness except for the inner hall. In the darkness I could not find the bell and knocked. There was no reply. I wondered if the secretary could have given me the wrong message. By searching about, however, I found the bell and pulled it hard. Almost at once lights were switched on and the butler appeared. 'Lord Reith is coming,' he said. 'I had better leave the lights on in case he too cannot find the bell.' I was shown into the study. In a moment or so Bill Astor appeared. He looked well after his stay in Scotland. He had also been to America. I find myself having a genuine affection for him. Suddenly there came in Lord Hailey, the Indian Civilian who made the greatest career of all Civilians in my time, being Governor of the Punjab and then of the United Provinces and afterwards on retirement Chairman of a quantity of important public commissions. He is eighty-two. He has not a very agreeable expression; with his long nose his appearance is rather Jewish, though as far as I know he has no Jewish blood. He looks the old autocrat, and has a cold smile. Though a classical double first, he does not look cultivated. We spoke a moment of Corpus Christi, his and my college. He was very civil. He was followed shortly by Lord Reith, late director of the B.B.C., a public man if ever there was one, who has been a Minister of State, and has been chairman of numerous corporations. He is immensely tall, has a sword cut across his face, rather a hump, a wild eye and a dominant manner. I had never met either him or Hailey before. Hardly had he shaken hands before a very elderly lady appeared, whom I did not recognise as the dowager Lady Astor until she spoke with one of her unmistakeable gestures. I had not seen her for, I suppose, four or five years. She had aged much in appearance. There was now a short pause and I saw Bill Astor go to the door. The King of Sweden came in looking very much as I had seen him ten years ago when as Crown Prince he used to come sometimes to meetings of the Oriental Ceramic Society. He is now said to be seventy, but does not look more than fifty-five. He has not much of a head or a presence, but is immediately likeable. His face is very lined, his English quite perfect. He is in England on a private holiday and arrived without even a valet. His personal interests are in the arts, but he has very wide inclinations for administration in general. He is probably the most quietly cultured reigning monarch in the world.

We went into dinner, Hailey delivering himself of a long Latin quotation as we politely urged each other to go first through the door. At dinner the atmosphere was pleasant. The King did not speak much but seemed happy. I talked to Bill on whose right I sat. His nerves have much improved. He said that he had much enjoyed reading my *Into Hidden Burma*. Old Lady Astor sat at the far end, with the King on her right and Lord Hailey on her left. We had soup, lobster, grouse, an iced sweet, a savoury, fruit, coffee. Sherry, sauterne, port and kummel were offered. Lady Astor, as was her wont, tended to monopolise conversation. She found it hard, apparently, to forget that she had for so many years been Cliveden's famous hostess. Though she intended to treat Bill as the Viscount-in-being, she could not forego altogether the old habit of bullying him. But he seemed much more able to hold his own. She treated me with more indulgence than I expected. Her manner to the King was a mixture of licence and respect. In her time Cliveden was teetotal. To show her disapproval of the drink, moderate in quantity though it was, she said to Lord Hailey, 'You are having too much. Being so long in India has demoralised you.' Lord Hailey seemed to like her badinage. He said: 'I see you suspect me of lining my pocket in India,' and he told the company of how an upright judge there was the man, who, having taken bribes from both sides, gave back to the man who lost his case. Many interesting things were said by Hailey: that Kashmir wanted to solve the problem of which state it was to go to by demanding the status of an independent state; that Neguib, who looked exactly like an English colonel had offered to put up the capital sum to compensate the British civil servants in the Sudan if they would leave at once; and that Stalin had looked exactly like a Scotsman.

I had brought with me one of my two red, silver and gold Ch'ien Lung bowls, in case it would interest the King to see so unusual a piece, and I asked Bill if it would be correct for me to suggest showing it after dinner. He agreed, and when we were in the drawing room I told the King. He became at once very interested. On my fetching it from the hall he examined it with great care. Not being able to satisfy himself he went off to his bedroom to get his magnifying glass. On his return Lady Astor said to Bill in her loud deep voice: 'Fancy letting His Serene Majesty go and get his glass!' By using 'Serene' she made fun on purpose of her protest. The King took it quietly. He was evidently very glad to dispense with ceremony. 'Not at all,' said he. 'It was good to have to go.' He examined the cup, made a number of true observations—e.g. that the bouquets on the exterior were founded on the T'ang style (a point I had never thought of, though I had wondered at their Greek appearance) and agreed the cup was Ch'ien Lung. He had never seen anything like it. This led to our having an half hour's conversation in which the others made no attempt to join, as it was concerned with the arts, a subject in which Hailey, Reith and Lady Astor had no interest, though they respected his interest. He spoke of his collection of Chinese antiquities. He said he was very fond of the Ming and of early classical bronzes. I asked him if he had a collection of modern art. He described his collection of Swedish drawings and Danish ceramics. He also mentioned Staite Murray and said he had some of his pots. It interested him when I told him of S. Murray's strange abandonment of his potting and his remaining in Africa as his studio disintegrated. He said: 'I have been over to England fifteen times. I manage to stay as much as a month. I have not a great deal of work in Sweden. Since coming this time I have had a look round the antique shops. There are about six big collectors of Chinese antiquities in Sweden. Our museum is very rich in the earliest Chinese art, particularly neolithic pots. I am still adding to my collection.' He realised suddenly that he had been neglecting Lady Astor and moved over to speak to her.

I now joined Reith and Astor. Reith was saying that he had been up all night writing a report, had had a bath at 6.30 a.m. and been hard at it all day. He thought he ought to get home to bed. But what about having to wait till the King gave the sign? Astor said he could mention it to his mother. 'Don't tell her I am tired,' begged Reith. He was afraid of her raillery. He has the reputation of being tireless. On second thoughts he decided to wait. He did not look tired. He spoke of how interesting it was that perhaps England was the only country in the world where a King could put off all ceremony and stay as a private gentleman. Meanwhile Lady Astor, having the King and Hailey by her, exerted herself to amuse. She told of her famous visit to Moscow with Bernard Shaw during the war. The things she said straight out to Stalin were staggering. 'Your régime is no different from the Czars'.' 'Why?' 'Because you dispose of your opponents without trial.' Stalin laughed: 'Of course.' She also spoke of Bernard Shaw's last illness. 'I went to see him the day before he died. I sat by him stroking his head. He was quite clear. Suddenly he said, "That reminds me," and told me this story. "Lord X gave a great party to all the local gentry. As they were about to eat, the butler came in and said to him: 'Excuse me, your lordship, but Mr So & So is in bed with your wife.' At this Lord X, rising in his place, said to the company: 'Go home, go home. There is a man in bed with my wife. The party is cancelled. Off you go.' The guests, much disappointed, for there were quantities of drink, began to disperse. The butler came in again and spoke to his lordship. He got up. 'Don't go, don't go. The man has apologised.' " Those were G.B.S.'s last words.' This story was well received. If it was not Shaw's last words, it might well have been. 'And now, your Majesty,' said she to King Gustav, 'it is time for you to get to bed.' The King rose, pleasantly, easily, and the party broke up. He shook hands with each of us before leaving the room. Said Bill Astor: 'What time would you like breakfast, sir?' 'Whatever time you have it.' 'Would you like it in your room?' 'No, I would prefer to come down.' 'About 9.15 then?' 'Yes, I will telephone.' After thanking me for showing him the cup he went off. Lady Astor was ecstatic. 'A wonderful man! A wonderful man!'

*8 January 1954*

The Princess Fahrunissa, my old friend, rang up to say that she was back from Paris for a while and would like me to take her to the Tate to see the Dufy memorial exhibition. So I drove up and called at the Iraqi embassy at 3.0. The butler was on the steps, as he had apparently noticed me arriving. He (not the older drunken butler but the one who generally had to carry in and unroll her immense paintings) seemed more bloated than before and had taken to painting his face, which was pink in places and brick red in others. I imagine he was a little drunk. Long service in that fabulously rich household had evidently debauched him. 'Yes,' he said, 'Her Royal Highness is awaiting you in the drawing room.' I went in and found the Princess, as always, seated on a small divan with a table handy on which were bonbons and an assortment of drinks. She got up to receive me and made me sit by her on the divan. I was soon drinking brandy and eating a bonbon. After this we set out for the Tate in her Cadillac. *En route* she said that she wanted to buy a monthly French publication which gave astrological predictions and lucky days and asked me where it could be procured. I gave her chauffeur the address of a shop at the bottom of Museum Street. I told her of the Cingalese exhibition and asked her whether she would like a ticket for the party at Mrs Lessore's gallery, the Beaux Arts. She said she would and enquired whether it would be in order to bring Madame Lessore a bottle of brandy. I replied that a bottle of brandy was never out of order.

*12 January 1954*

Went up to London and called first to see Burland at the British Museum. I had the photos for the illustrations in my *Cortés and Montezuma* and asked Burland to interpret them for me. This he very kindly did in detail. With the explanations and considering that they have never been published before, they ought to add greatly to the interest of the book. Burland told me that he had spent New Year's Eve table-turning with a circle of friends. The evening had begun by his talking of the Mexican magic books, which are full of the supernatural. Then the party set to work with the table. By chance they were suited psychologically for the experiment. A most uncanny atmosphere was generated. The table rose from the floor, icy blasts of wind blew, there was tapping everywhere, and ectoplasm rose from the people, in the case of the women from the inner side of their thighs, in the case of the men from their abdomens. Its presence was manifest by a dampness at the place it sprang from and by the way it threw the table about, but it was not visible. Messages of all sorts were tapped out. Burland related all this in the same manner that he relates the curious explanations of the Mexican magic pictures.

### 10 February 1954

Went to a party given by the Mrs Dangerfield I had met at Princess Zeid's. I found the Princess there already. The company did not look interesting, but contained people with names and reputations. Sir Ronald Storrs was there, but I did not speak to him. He might not have been friendly on account of my reference to his boots, when he was Governor of Jerusalem in 1918, the reference in my *The Journey Outward*.* Anyhow he is a self-important and not really distinguished man. The present Lord Birdwood was there, the son of the Field Marshal and C.-in-C. of India in 1926. This Birdwood was not interesting. He had spent all his life in Indian cavalry and had not risen beyond the rank of Lt. Colonel. I saw also a small old person, very plainly dressed and was surprised to see the attention which the Princess paid her and the length of time they conversed. Later, when this old lady was seated alone, Mrs Dangerfield said 'Let me introduce you to the Duchess of Atholl'. The introduction was broken off, but I sat down beside her and introduced myself. The Duchess has had a learned and political career. She speaks with clarity and calm. We talked for a while about affairs connected with Egypt and the East. I was on the point of leaving when Mrs Dangerfield asked me whether I would give the Duchess a lift home. This meant going a bit out of my way so I suggested that perhaps the Duchess would be more comfortable in a taxi. She replied: 'She is too Scotch for a taxi. Unless you take her, she will go by bus and that means that I shall have to go out and get her on to a bus.' That being so, I begged the Duchess to let me drive her. We set out, conversing quietly and apparently with ease and mutual understanding. I conceived a regard for her as a wonderful old person who had survived from an age so different from the present as to seem another life and who, though a *grande*

* The reference is admiring.

*dame*, had been an M.P. and so had mixed much with men of all sorts. Out of politeness she invited me in to have something to eat, but I declined.

*3 April 1954*

Cambridge. At tea time Gwen Raverat arrived. She was a Miss Darwin before her marriage. Now seventy, she has had a stroke and was wheeled into the room in a bath chair. She has a round young face with big eyes, and an air of downright sense. Till recently her reputation has been as an artist, being well known for her woodcuts and illustrations. Then in 1952 she published *Period Piece*, an account of her childhood in Cambridge, a remarkable book that went into five impressions. Now it has become a book of the month in America and is earning big money. It is surely very unusual for a woman of her age to publish for the first time and to write something comparable to Mrs Gaskell's life of Charlotte Bronte. Though stricken with a paralysis of the greater part of her body, she is calm, clear, quick and strong in mind, with merry eyes and giving out a sense of robust warmth.

*6 April 1954*

At 6 p.m. I went to the Burmese Embassy where I saw Lady Cripps and went up to speak to her. The conversation turned on her daughter who married the West African. The two are renting the outbuildings of Topolski's house. Lady Cripps seemed resigned to the astonishing marriage. She said her only condition beforehand had been that her daughter should go out to Africa and stay there for four months. If after that she persisted, it would be on her head. She went out, said Lady Cripps, and made friends with the African women. That, I said, was more important than anything else and presaged success. Lady Cripps gave me to understand that her daughter had a sense of mission. She would work to bring Africa and England closer together. A baby is due in May. After that they go out to West Africa. Lady Cripps seemed sad. She had not got over the long illness and death of Sir Stafford in the height of his fame as Chancellor of the Exchequer.

I was introduced to Sir Reginald Dorman-Smith, late Governor of Burma. I had never met him before, though I had heard much of him, some to his discredit. But I found him engaging to talk to. He was very modest about himself. Apparently he has been wanting to write an account of what happened during his rather disastrous tenure of the governorship. 'But I cannot write,' he said. He hinted that he wanted my help and asked me to dine with him at White's.

*9 April 1954*

I journeyed to the Whitechapel Gallery where a large exhibition of Barbara Hepworth's sculpture, from 1927 to 1953, is well displayed. She herself was there, a slight figure on a sofa with a ravaged face and uneasy eyes. I talked to her awhile, recalling my visit to her studio at St Ives two years ago. The colossal nature of her *oeuvre* and her smallness physically immediately strikes you. In the centre was a monolith some ten feet high, a dream figure or presence suggested by the abstract form. Round the big hall were all sorts of shapes belonging to rock and shell, and suggesting the passage over them or through them of wind and sea and long time. It was all forlorn and wave beaten, the storm humming and the ages passing, prehistoric Cornwall, Cornwall before man, a lonely cape of ultima thule inhabited by supernatural presences.

*17 April 1954*

After meeting Sir Reginald Dorman-Smith at the Burmese Embassy I wrote to him, and he invited me to come and see him at Liss where he lives. I arrived at 11.30 a.m. and found him having a gin with an Australian. All day up till 7 p.m. he talked of his experiences as Governor of Burma and made it clear that I only could get on paper what was certainly a series of dramatic events, all of historical importance. It became clear to me as he talked that there was a good book to be written, provided I could find the proper form for it. Should it be a fully documented 'Last Days of British Burma' sort of volume or should it be Dorman-Smith speaking of his personal experiences during those days?* That question will have to be settled later. He gave me some papers which will help me to get an idea of the main outlines. But it seemed that it will be his personal recollections that would make a book live. It seemed a practical proposition to me. He appeared the sort of man who could express himself

* The book was eventually called *Last and First in Burma* and published in 1956.

64

sufficiently well by word of mouth to give me the added material, much of it, judging from what he told, unique. For instance, his last evening in Government House, Rangoon, with the Japanese marching on the city. I think that what I want is to get the framework clear and then take him methodically over the ground to hear his personal reactions and doings, which my secretary can take down in shorthand. He seems to have been a very unusual Governor and to have been treated badly. Among other confidential matters he told me that a Burman had set out recently from here for Burma to force Thakin Nu to enter a monastery and to take his place as Premier. I shall get into touch with him again and see what can be done. I saw what seems a Gainsborough in his house. He wants to sell it. I said I would put him in touch with a dealer.

*17 August 1954*

I have been working so hard on my book about Dorman-Smith that I have not been out much. The weather too has been atrocious for the time of year. The book advances. There is a good tension. All one can say is that it absorbs me. Dorman-Smith himself is pleased, though of course the presentation is very different from anything he imagined. It is a big drama, with a lot of characters. He however has the leading part because he is on the stage from first to last. The book is very exciting to write. I do not think I have ever been so completely wrapped up in any composition.

*10 October 1954*

I went up to dine with Lord Astor at Cliveden. It was on the occasion of the publication of *Cortés and Montezuma*, which is dedicated to him. Kilmartin, the literary editor of the *Observer*, was present with his wife. They were most agreeable. Bill Astor enquired about my book on Dorman-Smith. He said that he could introduce me to Mountbatten when he returned from the Mediterranean. He is godfather to the baby Astor. It would be useful to meet him when I am writing the last part of the book.

*7 November 1954*

Stanley Spencer came to tea after his visit to China. He looked a little thinner and more weatherbeaten. As before, he talked endlessly.

The excursion, through Prague, Moscow to Peking, alarmed him because of the feeling of powerlessness in those sinister countries. 'I longed to be back in my little cottage in Cookham', he said. 'The Chinese, however, treated me like royalty. I was given a studio. They made me presents. But underneath they seemed sad and suppressed.' He made a few drawings of people and an oil painting of the Ming tombs. He found it all a great strain and became ill and could not eat. I drove him back to his 'little cottage' afterwards. Since his return he had continued work on his long saturnalian picture,* as if nothing had happened. I do not think the experience can have any effect on his art, which is too personal and English to be deflected from its set course. But I did notice more authority and aplomb in his manner than before.

*8 January 1955*

I went to a dinner given by the Burma Association at the Le On restaurant in Soho. On being shown upstairs I was invited into a side room where I found Mr and Mrs Attlee. I had never met him before. They introduced me and I had a short conversation with him. He gave the impression of toughness, a small man of great determination, without charm, very clear and collected. We spoke of his being on the Simon Commission† and how I must have met him on the Rangoon wharf in 1929/30. I told him of my book on affairs in Burma from 1941 to 1948 and he was interested. The proprietor of Le On's, a sort of Chinaman, was serving drinks to us from a cabinet. He gave me a stiff whisky. About 220 people were in the dining room. I was seated next to the First Secretary of the Embassy. Opposite to my right was a good-natured-looking man who turned out to be the Rt Hon Arthur Bottomley, M.P. The dinner was good Chinese, most palatable. It was followed by speeches. Attlee paid a tribute to General Aung San, the dead Burmese national hero, and to U Nu the Premier. He also said, and was applauded, that he regarded Burma as an honorary member of the Commonwealth.

*17 January 1955*

Went to London. I was having lunch at a little place near the

---

* *Love on the Moor.*

† A parliamentary commission headed by Sir John Simon, sent to Burma to examine the question of certain proposed changes in the constitution.

London Library* when Tony Keswick† came in and joined me. He is a curiously distinguished personality, full of good heart but affecting a bluff manner. He was leaving for Africa on business in a day or so. He said that a conversation with me cheered and braced him. He suffered from fits of impatience and fears, he said. He is too much in a hurry and finds it hard to enjoy small things.

*8 February 1955*

At the Lefevre Alexander Calder was exhibiting a quantity of his mobiles. The interior of the gallery had the air of some kind of Christmas fair. A Calder mobile of moderate size in a verandah where a wind blows softly, or in a bow window, has an idle charm and can be watched a while for its graceful movements and the outlines that it makes. One may dream of waterweeds and strange water creatures. It provides a distraction for an aesthetic set. But the many mobiles in the Lefevre, some of them as heavy as bits of machinery, others as small as waving insects, were on the whole ludicrous. These things are no more than empty toys.

I went on to dine with Veronica Wedgwood in St John's Wood. Among the guests was a wonderful old lady called Miss Lynda Grier,‡ who used to the Principal of some college. I had met her once at a China Society gathering and had been much struck by the depth of her voice, the purity of her accent and the clarity of her mind. She exhibited all these qualities again. Her age must be seventy-five. She stated that she was reading Gibbon for the first time and with great enjoyment, though she found his view of Christianity distasteful. I spent a good deal of time talking to Veronica about the first volume of her Stuart history, *The Great Rebellion*, the volume in question being called *The King's Peace*. I am reading it slowly and find it very well done, written in a masculine prose and full of excellent sense. It has been very well received by the press and is an exceptionally level book for today. She inscribed my copy with too great kindness—'Inscribed for Maurice Collis with gratitude for example and encouragement'. She is a woman of much charm. Having a great interest in the executive

* Cheap Italian café in Jermyn Street.
† Sir William Keswick, Director of the Hudson Bay Co., Jardine & Matheson, etc, etc.
‡ Dr Lynda Grier, Principal of Lady Margaret Hall, Oxford, 1921–1945.

side of the author's trade and being much liked, she is continually on committees or in the chair at lectures, or giving them herself or contributing to journals—all making it harder to find time for history, yet perhaps giving her the balance, tolerance and understanding of character which comes out in her writing and gives it weight.

I much enjoyed the evening.

*31 March 1955*

I have finished my book *Last and First in Burma* (if it is to be called that) after ten months' work. It has taken me longer than any other book and has given me more trouble. I received a few days ago a letter from Captain Brockman inviting me to call at the Admiralty today, when Admiral Lord Mountbatten would be pleased to have a talk with me about the book. Accordingly at 4 p.m. I presented myself at the N.W. door of the Admiralty, by Captain Cook's statue in the Mall, adjacent to the Arch. From there I was conducted by a young naval staff officer to an ante-chamber, where I found Captain Brockman. He announced that the Admiral was ready to receive me and ushered me in. Mountbatten, who is still Designate First Sea Lord, as he does not take over for three weeks, got up from his desk and welcomed me warmly. After lighting a cigarette, he listened while I shortly gave him the structure of the book, saying that it was in connection with his dealings with Aung San that I particularly desired to hear him speak. Then followed an animated conversation lasting three-quarters of an hour. I thought Mountbatten wonderfully young looking for his fifty-five years. He was full of spirit, throwing himself about in his chair, sometimes tilting his head right back, sometimes leaning towards me till his face was only a few inches from mine. He said that he could have saved Burma for the Commonwealth. 'In 1945 I was young and inexperienced. As Supreme Commander, South East Asia, I had the power to name, if I wanted to, the Civil Governor who would take over from me in Burma. I should have said that Dorman-Smith was unlikely to reach a settlement with the left wing, Aung San and the League,* and suggested another man. But I did not. I thought Dorman-Smith was so sympathetic to the Burmese that he would manage it.' I objected that Dorman-Smith was bound by the White Paper and could not offer more than it allowed. He replied that he

* Aung San's party.

had latitude. I further objected that Aung San and the League had from the first determined to have a republic. He denied this or argued in alternative that if they had been handled properly they would have foregone their resolution; Aung San had told him as much. (My impression is that though Aung San may very well have said this, he was only expressing a polite possibility, but so vaguely possible as to be out of the question.) This being Mountbatten's view, what he was saying was to accuse Dorman-Smith of mishandling the situation with the result that Burma left the Commonwealth. The papers I have seen, however, preclude so simple or dramatic a view. Thus, though what Mountbatten said was most interesting and explained precisely the grave differences which developed between him and Dorman-Smith, to the ultimate detriment of the latter, it did not require me to alter what I have written. If I add a passage here and there summarising Mountbatten's point of view I shall be doing all that is required. The interview was very pleasant and warm; we parted on agreeable terms. I found him a person of exciting personality. He gave me the impression of immense resolution and courage.

### 9 April 1955

Lord Astor, having just returned from the States, asked me up to dine tonight. I found Bill in the study, sitting by a wood fire. He seemed well, but said he was not, that he had trouble with blood pressure, an ominous symptom at his age. He was taking some Indian drug, which he said had been used for centuries by old style Indian physicians. He complained of tiredness and said his doctors advised him to take things easily. He is evidently not at all strong. The collapse of his marriage was a shock from which he is not completely recovered. But he appears less nervous with guests than he was a year ago. His old mother is so tough. She still, he said, plays eighteen holes of golf and does gymnastic exercises night and morning, as well as taking a cold bath. She is about eighty. But I suppose she was in her day the best-known woman in England. Bill Astor in the course of the evening said he would like to make the acquaintance of Stanley Spencer and John Piper. He would give them commissions to paint things for him. I said that could easily be arranged. If he would act as Spencer's patron it would be splendid, as perhaps he would build the hall in Cookham which Spencer so much wants to decorate with his paintings. I dropped the hint and Astor listened.

*13 April 1955*

Met Lord Astor to take him to Stanley Spencer's. He was in his new Bentley and was accompanied by one of those well-born but colourless chits of girls who are often to be met with at Cliveden. I led the way in my car to Spencer's house, that queer little wretched residence where he lives alone and paints in his bedroom. He came to open the door, his usual debonair talkative self and we went up the squalid stairs to the bedroom. The bed was covered with cardboard, drawings and photographs of paintings. There was not really much for Astor to see, as all Spencer's completed works were at Tooth's in London. However there were drawings and some unfinished paintings, and there was Spencer himself, chatting at large about his visit to China last year, amusing, original and not tedious as the visit was short and this was Astor's first experience of him. He spoke of his grandfather, the grocer, of his father, the organist, of his many brothers, of his patrons in the past. Astor was impressed with him and asked him to come to Cliveden and choose a subject in the park for a picture. 'I will send my car for you,' he said. 'Only for the first time,' said Spencer. 'I would rather be free and come by bus after that.' So it has been arranged. It remains for me to arrange a similar meeting with John Piper. 'I suppose if I have two artists working for me at Cliveden at the same time they will not quarrel?' Astor asked.

*21 May 1955*

On getting to Cliveden at 8.0 I found that I was first on the scene because the dinner hour had been changed to 8.30. However, the Dowager Duchess of Rutland soon came in. The other guests, all staying in the house, followed. There was Lord Hailey, once in the Indian Civil Service, Lady Worsley (a lady-in-waiting to the Queen Mother), and the King of Sweden. The old Lady Astor was also there. This was the rather formidable party of elderly people which the young Lady Astor, Philippa,★ just back from her honeymoon, had to manage. Bill whispered to me, 'It is her first important party.' We went in to dinner. I was placed next to the bride, on her left, the King being on her right. Old Lady Astor was on the King's right. I talked

★ Astor's second wife. They were married on 26 April 1955.

for a while to Philippa Astor. It appeared that when I first saw her, as Miss Hunloke, when Bill Astor, she and I visited Stanley Spencer, the engagement had not taken place. Astor proposed the next day. The King now joined in the conversation. He spoke of the constitution in Sweden and that the Upper House there was elected, not hereditary, like our Lords. Our system he declared was much better. Of his tours abroad he said that he had more freedom in this respect than our Royalty because when he left Sweden a Regent took over automatically and had full powers and responsibility during the King's absence. In speaking of these matters the King, who is seventy years of age though he does not look more than sixty, used the manner of an Englishman in, say, the Athenaeum. He had *not* the vivacity of the people one meets at White's, the somewhat exaggerated society manner, apparently very friendly and easy-going, though sometimes masking a malicious tongue. He was more like a savant or professor, with much dignity, some authority, yet perfectly natural, kind and collected. One of his expressions was: 'For a man in my position . . .' I told him that I had brought a Sung dish to show him (the one mentioned in my *Into Hidden Burma* that was brought up by a Japanese diver at Mergui after being in the sea for 800 years) and said I would take an opportunity after dinner. Philippa Astor meanwhile was doing her best. She was keeping an eye on the butlers and aiding in the conversation. When the ladies left Astor came round and sat by me. I reminded him of Stanley Spencer and John Piper and he said that he would be getting in touch with them. Meanwhile another of the guests, Isiah Berlin, a Fellow of All Souls, was amusing the King and Lord Hailey. Berlin, a philosopher, is a decided personality and reminded me of Guedalla.* He is a little dark laughing imp of a man, a wit and a raconteur. When we rejoined the ladies, old Lady Astor took the floor, taking the lead away from her daughter-in-law in a ruthless manner. Indeed, she completely ignored the girl, and might have been mistress of Cliveden, as in former days. She sat on a backless divan and gathered a party about her. Lord Hailey, who had drifted to a side table where there were newspapers, was hailed by her in a loud voice: 'Come on, old Hailey' and when he pretended not to hear, she shouted again in her deep contralto and he had to join her group. He evidently did not like it much, but his knowledge of her

* Philip Guedalla, author.

ways and of the world enabled him to capitulate with grace. Having secured the King also, she initiated with Berlin a rough and tumble political discussion.

I made no move and presently Lady Cadogan came across the room to speak to me. The time passed quickly and Bill and Philippa flitted about, feeling a little out of things, as old Lady Astor was conducting the evening, rather overdoing her part as outrageous female, her one and only part and which had made her famous. Since she is nearly eighty one felt she might fittingly have been a bit quieter and given her new daughter-in-law a chance. Suddenly she jumped up, exclaiming at the late hour (it was 11.30) and led the women off to bed. I now took the opportunity to ask the King whether it was too late for me to show him the plate. 'It is never too late to look at antique Chinese porcelain,' he replied. 'It is in the hall,' I said and we went out. He was much pleased with it, and it is certainly a curiosity, worn so smooth by the sea and sand. 'A good piece,' he pronounced, 'Sung or Yuan.' I had also brought my book, *Cortés and Montezuma*, and asked whether I might present it to him on the ground that it was dedicated to Astor and was to appear as a Book Society choice in a Swedish translation. 'Of course,' he said, 'I would like to have it.' I fetched it from a table and he looked at it, enquiring whether it was history or fiction, and evidently pleased when I assured him it was the former. I then asked if he would like me to write in it. He said yes and when I looked doubtfully at Astor's pens on the table where we stood in the main hall he took out his own, a splendid gold mounted affair, and handed it to me. I quickly wrote: 'Presented by his kind permission to His Majesty the King of Sweden by the author Maurice Collis'. He looked and it seemed to me that the thought passed through his mind that he would have preferred me to write 'King Gustav of Sweden'. But he only thanked me and put the book under his arm, going off to bed. Astor took me to have a drink. I said: 'It went off all right.' We both hoped the plate and the book would please him, and it seemed that they had. The King however had not gone to bed, for a few minutes later he approached us and asked Astor what was on for the next morning. On being told that nothing special had been arranged, he said: 'Well then, I can wear my country clothes.' And he went off again at a good pace.

*14 June 1955*

I have been continuing my deliberate holiday from writing, doing a good deal of work in the garden, which seems to agree with me. The long hours writing my last book over nine months caused me to put on weight and look older. Air and exercise have rejuvenated me to a noticeable degree. I have also read with avidity. For long I wondered why Thomas Mann had so great a reputation and as a first taste of his work have read *Transposed Heads*, probably one of his minor works. In translation it certainly does not amount to much. The Hindu legend he takes, he strives to make real in spite of its incredibility and, I think, fails. Then *To the Lighthouse* by Virginia Woolf, which though certainly an original book and composed in a style and technique both beautiful and very skilful, cannot really be given unqualified praise. The second half is too vague and the conclusion is not brought sufficiently home.

At the moment I am making my first acquaintance with Kafka by reading *The Castle*. Its dreamlike quality is immediately evident, a curious combination of detailed clear facts which, instead of creating a clear narrative, create an increasing mystery, which is seen to be the mystery of life itself. Not only have I never read a word of Kafka, but I have never read anything on him. So I come to the matter with a plain mind.

*6 July 1955*

At 4.0 I met Louise and we went to a party in Hampstead. We were agreeably surprised to find that among the guests were people interested in letters. Julian Huxley and his wife arrived. In the talk we had he spoke only of mathematics, saying how at school and college he had not got as far as the Differential Calculus and, indeed, found the subject beyond him. Yet in later life, with the constant desire he had to broaden his knowledge, so that one thing should throw light on another, and he be able to draw wide conclusions, he had sought to discover in general what mathematics were about. His conclusion was that though what he did gather certainly gave him a better all-over view, he felt that mathematics was a world of its own, into which non-mathematicians could not enter. 'The tendency is for science, theoretical and applied, to rest more and more on a mathematical basis, and also the interpretation of phenomena, the cosmos, reality and unreality. But as only mathematicians, and only a small inner ring of them, can grasp the subtleties of the strange, almost musical, metamorphoses of the subject, in future the ultimate explanations will be possessed by an elect, like the Egyptian priests.' My contention (as a writer) was that mathematicians should, if they had creative genius, be able to express in intelligible words what secrets they possessed.

*6 November 1955*

Lunched at Cliveden. Lord Astor had some anonymous lords and ladies (their personalities and their names did not impinge on one) but he also had that interesting person Freya Stark, just in from Asolo. I sat next to her and had an animated conversation, the best I have had this long time, as the butler plied us with the very choice eatables which Bill Astor always provides and the series of drinks. She told me that she was done with travel books and was now going to devote herself to history or historical disquisitions on Asia Minor. Her next book will have to do with Alexander the Great's march up to the battle of Issur. She mentioned, what I did not know, that Alexander's march was conditioned by his main object, which was the destruction of the ports, etc. of the Persian fleet. For my forthcoming book she expressed interest, repeating however the general belief that Dorman-Smith was an unsatisfactory Governor. I assured her that the documents I quote would show him in a very different light.

In the course of lunch Bill Astor made it clear that he had no intention of building a hall in Cookham for Stanley Spencer to decorate. I was surprised that he knew that Spencer hoped he would do this. I had never said anything about it, because I felt it would be better for Spencer to get friendly with Astor, painting this and that at Cliveden, and then the major project could be mentioned at a chosen moment. But evidently Spencer must have said something. And it has not convinced Astor or attracted him as an interesting project. Perhaps someone else may come forward.

Freya Stark is stouter than before and was, I remarked, careful to eat very little. But that may have been because she was sick in the night, through having eaten too much at dinner or something that disagreed with her. She is small and has a very pleasing manner.

Though she must be fifty-five, her hair is not grey and she looks in full health and strength. She is very quick to take a point and is exceedingly well-informed. She has an admirable conception of how talk should go and, I imagine, would never be dull. She evidently is a very hard worker and a person immensely interested in acquiring new knowledge. She is a very considerable celebrity, though this is partly due to the fact of her former intrepid travels, and does not rest altogether on her books.

*10 January 1956*

My sixty-seventh birthday. My state of health remains good, though I suffer periodically from rheumatism. My nerves are much stronger than when I was younger. My mind is capable of greater concentration. I take more trouble over my work. My interest in things has, I think, increased rather than diminished. I have the impression that my education is continuing. I could hardly have expected that at my age I should feel inclined to take up the study of a period in English history, working from the original Latin and early French texts. Yet I have found the exploration of the fourteenth century, of which I knew nothing whatever a year ago, an absorbing occupation. My new book, called *The Hurling Time*, whose theme is the 1381 rebellion, seems to be developing quite satisfactorily.

*3 February 1956*

I drove down to see Reggie Dorman-Smith and arrived in time for lunch. As we walked in the garden after lunch Reggie told me something I knew nothing of. He said that about two years ago, when attending a local meeting, he suddenly realised that he could hardly see. He went out to his car and sat down quietly. Slowly the sight of one eye returned. But the other completely darkened. He drove home as best he could. A Harley Street specialist said that he had a thrombosis of the eye and asked him whether he had had much worry. He said yes. The way he had been blamed for his conduct of affairs in Burma had of course gravely upset him. Perhaps the departure of his two daughters for Australia had added to his worries. 'For two years,' he went on, 'I have been going about blind in one eye. I could see nothing from it, only a faint blur of grey light. But the other day my sight came back. I can see you now out of that eye,' and he closed the good one and looked at me with the other. The explanation of his returning sight, he thought, was the news that my book was considered by those who had read it as a vindication of his conduct. This moved me greatly. One must hope that the publication of the book (fixed for 24 February) will be a public vindication, and that he will seem a different man afterwards.

*6 March 1956*

Went to a party given by Julian Huxley and his wife and found people I knew: Henry Moore, Sir Philip Hendy and his wife, the artist Julian Trevelyan and his wife, and the cousin Michael Huxley and his wife, besides some half dozen more. We had a fork supper and then went to Julian's study where he projected on a screen some of the coloured photographs which he had taken during his recent tour of Siam, Cambodia, Java, Ceylon and India. They were excellent and he accompanied them with a short commentary. One saw Angkor, the palace at Bangkok, Ayuthya, Fatepur Sikri, Jaipur and the ancient sites in Ceylon, Polonaruwa and Sigiriya, all taken from new aspects. Afterwards a woman who was there—I don't know her name, though she was not English—asked me whether it was true, as she supposed was the case, that Mr Huxley had himself discovered the existence of all the remarkable things he had photographed and was the first to describe them. I replied that it was not true. She seemed dashed. When I told Huxley that one of his guests had believed him to be the discoverer of Angkor, Borobodur, the Taj Mahal, etc, he was evidently pleased to think that he was so great a figure that such glories were automatically attributed to him.

I had a good talk with Henry Moore. He is quite unaffected by his world fame, but seems a little worn. He wants me to pay him a visit in the spring and I intend to do so. He spoke amusingly of the effects of publicity: 'I have never had anything wrong with me in my life, except a few years ago a minute stone in the kidney which kept me in hospital a fortnight. This got into the papers and even still people ask anxiously about my health. The public thinks I do no work because when occasionally I have to open an exhibition of my sculpture in Yugoslavia, say, or Brazil, this is represented as my continual practice and the impression is given that I am always rushing over the globe in luxurious aeroplanes.'

I also had a talk with Lady Hendy about Veronica Wedgwood, whom she had known well for a long time. I wanted to know why it was that Veronica did not concentrate more on writing her history but wasted her time in writing a quantity of journalistic articles and presiding over conferences and taking the chair at all sorts of wretched functions. Lady Hendy said: 'She knows all this well enough. It is a kind of restlessness she cannot control. Also she does not want to fall into the complete academic life. She was offered the headship of one of the women's colleges at Oxford but refused for that reason. Her father was very academic in outlook and there is a reaction there. She wants to be in touch with contemporary life. She is also extremely kind-hearted and finds it very difficult in any case to refuse an invitation to lecture or preside. However, she is now again in her American university and is writing hard and regularly. Her second volume is getting on.'

*17 April 1956*

Walking towards Bond Street came on Arthur Waley and Beryl de Zoete sheltering in the doorway of a restaurant, as a shower was in progress. He hailed me. 'Here comes Maurice Collis.' I stopped and standing under my umbrella talked to them. Waley was wearing a battered beret and looked wonderfully well and vigorous. His eye was very keen. Beryl de Zoete nowadays is a shrunken little figure, bent and huddled, with a nervous tic in her face, which causes her to make grimaces. After a little chat on the step Waley suggested we should go into the restaurant and have an ice. When we were seated at a table the conversation grew interesting. I asked him why he did not occasionally take a European subject, literary or historical, for I assured him that his comments, backed not only by a vast Oriental scholarship but also by a wide general reading, would certainly be fresh and interesting. He replied that he did not think they would be, and that in any case he could not undertake such an excursion into a new field without an exhaustive exploration of the background. Here he spoke more as a scholar than as a literary personality. Meeting him again after some years' interval, I was greatly impressed by his incisive brilliance, his teasing humour, the vitality of his mind. I have, of course, for twenty years considered him to be one of the very few eminent writers of today. All his books read as fresh now as when they came out. There is a good deal of malice in his composition and I confess that a shrinking from it has prevented me from seeking his friendship. Nevertheless, I have a great admiration for his style and the poetic feeling which informs his writing, and astonishment and awe in contemplating the enormous industry and perseverance which has enabled him to master the Chinese and Japanese languages. He left with his old companion to look at the Japanese porcelain at the Arts Council. On bidding him goodbye and telling him what a great pleasure I felt at seeing him again, I noticed with surprise, for I had forgotten it, the abrupt cold manner in which he made his adieu, an unfortunate trick of his, which must have offended or abashed many people, until they understood that it was no more than a mannerism and meant nothing personal to them.

From there I went into the Hanover Gallery. The lady assistant there, whose name I do not know, told me she had recently returned from Bahrein, and that she had met in that desert an engineer who stated that he never read any books except mine. He had, she said, copies of most of them in his house.

### 18 April 1956

Louise and I set off today to pay Henry Moore a visit at his studio in Perry Green. It was a longstanding invitation. At 3.30 p.m. we arrived at the very small village, where on a green to the left one sees Henry Moore's house and studio. He was visible standing outside his studio on the grass where a large stone sculpture of his, a man and woman seated, with a child on the woman's knee, a variant of the bronze group at the Tate, was being admired by two visitors. We got out of the car as Henry came forward and were introduced to the visitors, a father and son, the father with some idea that it was necessary to talk in an artificial, confused and difficult way since he was with Henry Moore and had just been introduced to a writer, the son an uncouth gauche youth who seemed to protest against every-thing, even before it was said. As the visit went on they both became intolerable. As Henry said, they had happened to drop in to see his sculptures. He gets every sort of visitor. How normal it was for him to find himself conducting visitors was evident when we entered the studio. He fell into a sort of peripatetic lecture style. There was not much to see in the studio except odds and ends, plaster casts, bits, a few early works, notes, etc. Henry Moore is now so celebrated, not only in England but all over the world, that he is unable to keep up with the demand for his work and he has little or no stock. The large stone group outside the studio had been commissioned for the new town of Harlow, where on May 17th it is to be unveiled by Sir Kenneth Clark, who is now Chairman of the Arts Council.

After seeing what there was to see in the studio, we went into the house for tea. It is a charming place, rambling, rooms opening off each other, two storeys, many of his drawings on the walls, a selection of his smaller bronzes arranged on shelves or tables, and a few antiquities from Peru and Oceania. Tea was served in a glazed verandah. The sun was full out and it was pleasantly warm under the glass, though a bitter wind, with occasional flecks of snow or hail, blew outside. More visitors arrived, including a mathematician from one of the universities. I asked how it was that Herbert Read had suddenly been attacked so violently in the correspondence columns of *The Times*. He replied that Read had brought it on himself by injudiciously stating in a letter published earlier that works of art exported for exhibition and sale in Europe had to conform to the same rules which governed the export by manufacturers: they had to be what the inhabitants of the continent wanted to see or buy. This called down on him the wrath of those who held that it was the duty of bodies organising such exhibitions to show a true selection of the best English art in the widest sense, irrespective of whether it conformed with European taste at the moment. I agree with Sir Herbert that it is not practical to ship abroad what foreigners are not interested in.

After tea the programme was a stroll in the grounds to Henry Moore's new studio some hundred yards from the house. This was a large, airy and modern structure designed by himself. In it were some larger pieces, one a new bronze, Greek warrior with shield, a powerful mutilated shape, which had been bought by Florence and was to be set up there in a public place. In the loggia of the studio were three tall pole-like sculptures, in plaster, with a distant resemblance to totem poles. These, in bronze, were to be put up outside a public building of a modern sort—where, I forget.

Beyond the studio were vegetable garden and fields with bushy trees. Here were dotted about plaster casts of more sculptures. On walking back to the house, I asked Henry Moore about his attitude to commissions. He said that if he accepted all the offers he had, he would be busy for the rest of his life, though he now has two assistants. But he would not accept so many that he had not time for personal work, done without reference to any place, position of site, or subject or public. He must have freedom to work *in vacuo*, if he were not to dry up. I agreed very strongly, and said that from the first he had imposed his vision of the world of art, and had never conformed to the usual restrictions which a commission involved. It must be a great satisfaction for him to feel that after many years of struggle and small means, he had now brought so large a section of the art public to accept his creations.

He looks his age, something under sixty. His face is resolute and authoritative in a pleasant way. His manner is kind and indeed charming, though blunt and hearty like a countryman's. He has no pose, no conceit, no absorption in himself. The extraordinary shapes of his creations, apparitions which have fascinated people of today, though they could not explain why, look like the projections of a haunted personality, an introverted tortured creature, yet they are not, for he is an extroverted character, and has produced these original creations as if from some deep source in his personality which does not touch his normal pleasant self. For he is a plain man of excellent commonsense and practical ability, very natural and genuine, and, what is unusual for an international celebrity, full of simple wonder and interest in everything, common things, other people's thoughts and talk, and an ingenuous admiration for his own sculptures. In this connection he told me that my friend Tony Keswick had become a purchaser of his sculptures and was placing them on a large moor he owns in Scotland at points in the landscape which harmonised with their wildness. Moore had been up there and seen his *King and Queen* seated on rising ground by the shore of a lake, from which, as he said, they seemed to be surveying their dominion. Also the very strange emaciated bronze of a man, which I had first seen when it was exhibited some six years ago in Battersea Park, is there on top of a boulder by the roadside. When he was driving with Keswick over the moor after dark, the headlights suddenly showed up the figure in its solitude and he saw it, he said, as he had seen it in his imagination before he had created it, a wilder, lonelier, stranger being than it looked in his studio or on the lawns in Battersea Park. 'He speaks of buying more of my figures,' he told me, 'and peopling his moor with them.' 'It will become a place of pilgrimage,' I said. 'Well, tourists have begun to come,' he admitted. 'Keswick told me of two busloads lately and wondered what he should do.' I said: 'Perhaps it will be your sculptures on his moor which will preserve you best in the mind of posterity.' He did not dislike the notion; he is really a romantic.

*4 June 1956*

Went to a party at the Gimpels given for Barbara Hepworth who was showing a new series of sculptures. She looked tired, worn and aged. Her sculptures represented an immense effort. She told me that she sought to reproduce in wood, stone or bronze shapes which were suggested to her by the contemplation of the Cornish coast. It is true that many of her sculptures looked like rock smoothed or eaten into by the waves. It is individual for that reason, for no other sculptor seems to get his inspiration from landscape.

Spoke to Herbert Read. He was quiet and affable and less inclined than usual to want to go aside with someone else in confidential conclave.

*11 July 1956*

When at the Savile Club this afternoon I met Compton Mackenzie, whom I had not spoken to before. He is an amusing raconteur. He did a very pretty piece taking off W. B. Yeats talking rot about astrology to some eminent scientist. He left hurriedly to see the Queen Mother, altogether the successful writer in the swim. L. A. G. Strong was also there. I found him looking a good deal older. He was going over to Ireland to conduct a film on peat and had written on commission a book on peat manufacture for a firm. 'The new patrons of literature,' he said.

*31 August 1956*

On the 23rd I received the following letter from Sir Francis Rose, Bart:* 'St Ann's Heath, Virginia Water, Surrey. Dear Maurice Collis. I have been very ill and just avoided a nervous breakdown but now I am really feeling well and working madly. I have already

* Artist and past friend of Gertrude Stein.

finished ten pictures and am working on more. This is a fantastic red and white Gothic madhouse. The dining-room had a wood lace work, false 15th century vault, from which gilded angels trumpet judgment, doom and most of all, dust, on our heads and food. Around the walls are shiny oil paint frescoes, copies of Watteaus in the Louvre framed in painted Gothic traceries; not at all "fête champetre" but rather rather more "Blackpool gloom". The patients are mostly Harley Street doctors, a number of clergy, very old Guards colonels, and a sprinkling of Q.C., and of course some actors. If you would like to see this "Crystal Palace" glory, I would be delighted to see you. I can also show you a Japanese garden with Gothic decorations. Bridge, cricket and the television are rather over-coming. Luckily I have a large and modern studio to myself, except on Wednesdays and Thursdays. Do let me know if you can come. With all best wishes to your family, yours very sincerely, Francis Rose.'

On receipt of this letter I fixed today for going to see him. When his wife Frederica came over with him from Paris to put him in this queer institution, I met her and she related that he went off his head in Paris and imagined that in various awkward ways he was mixed up with the man called Crabbe, who dived under the Soviet cruiser during the visit here of Bulganin, and was never seen again.

I set off by car for Virginia Water, a half hour's drive. On getting there I was directed to a portal in a high brick wall. By the entrance was written 'Holloway Institution'. I enquired from a man standing near in an attitude which suggested that he might be an inmate whether the Holloway Institution was the same as St Ann's Heath, the name on Francis's letter. He replied that he had never heard of the latter. Afraid to ask him whether the Institution before me was a lunatic asylum in case he was a patient, I drove in and immediately perceived that I must be right, for rising up, high, outrageously faked and hallucinatory, was the facade of the pseudo-Gothic monstrosity. I parked at the base of an immense flight of steps. Various people were strolling about aimlessly, or, rather, slouching past in a melancholy way, coming and going in the large garden. I entered and enquired from the lodge porter for Sir Francis Rose. 'He is in the art studio (I thought he said archery studio) and is expecting you.' He led the way (I wondering whether Francis had taken up archery) until after following long corridors of the most depressing kind I was shown into the studio, where Francis was awaiting me. In appearance he seemed as I had always known him. He was dressed in a pullover and a pair of disreputable trousers, his studio dress as he explained apologetically, for generally he is carefully turned out. It was clear at once that he was as collected as he normally is, in some ways more collected. He showed me his recent paintings. We then went to see the building. It is immensely large, and had been put up in the second half of the Victorian era by a person called Holloway, who made a fortune in pills before he was thrown out of business by the more famous Beecham. Influenced by the Gothic revival and the pre-Raphaelites he had concocted with his architect and internal decorators something so hideous that one would have to be John Betjeman to take it for what it was intended, a work of art. I was shown the dining room, with the Watteau frescoes in oil and a great hall whose walls were frescoed with oil portraits of various national heroes. Across the end wall, in the place of honour, were portraits of the Holloway family and their women. After all, they had paid for the place and it must have cost hundreds of thousands, because it was about twice the size of the Victoria & Albert Museum (and twice as hideous). Francis had many amusing stories to tell of the inmates. He was in a ward reserved for the upper classes, where the types listed in his letter were lodged. There were several noble lords. In one ward was a woman who kept a Rolls and chauffeur. In another was the lady secretary of some company whose reputation for sanity was only harmed when it was discovered that she had laid in a hundredweight of mothballs. 'For throwing at the moths,' she explained. Francis told me he liked the place and would be happy to settle down there. 'But as I am well, I have to go,' he declared sadly. He seemed, however, to be suffering still from some delusions, for he spoke in a confused way of his supposed association with Crabbe and also of his son, or alleged son, Louis, whom he said the French threw into prison in order, apparently, to abstract from Francis a confession of his complicity in a spy ring.

*28 December 1956*

Went to London with Louise. Called on Mr Howgrave Graham, Assistant Keeper of the Muniments, Westminster Abbey. One enters the Muniments office from the cloisters. I rang the bell at an ancient door. Presently a youth opened and led us into the library (the monks' old dormitory). Mr Howgrave Graham was presently seen coming down the high winding stair from the office above. He seemed very old, frail and rather taken aback. Perhaps he thought that I would remonstrate with him for having done nothing about the photos of Edward III and Richard II. We sat down and were soon in pleasant conversation. He has extraordinary charm. He appeared as before overwhelmed with work, behindhand with his duties and in confusion over his papers. But he promised everything readily. He told me that he possessed what he believed to be two or three hairs of Edward III. He also said, as a curious fact, that lap dogs' hair was used for the eyebrows in funeral effigies in the fourteenth century. I felt sorry to leave him, as he seemed on the point of making other historical revelations, but the cold in the monks' dormitory was too intense.

*30 December 1956*
During these last days I have been bitten by an odd desire to paint. I bought some gouache and powder paints. I found to begin with that I could do calligraphic flourishes which assumed what seemed to me interesting shapes. From single colour flourishes I passed to flourishes in two or more colours. The abstract pictures which resulted surprised and excited me. I found that I had no facility whatever in representing natural objects. I have also begun to do multicoloured designs which look like folk art, as in textiles of a rustic sort. I became so intensely absorbed in this that I had difficulty in giving my attention to the final revision of my book.★

*1 January 1957*
I delivered *The Hurling Time* at Fabers. On my way out, when in the hall, I saw T. S. Eliot descending the stairs. He was dressed in dark clothes, an overcoat, a soft hat. His face was exceedingly lined and weary. He seemed very melancholy, old and shambling. He passed by and out through the hall door, drooping with gloom, as it were dazzled by despair.

*8 January 1957*
At 6 p.m. I went to see Henry Channon (Chips) who was made a knight in the New Year's honours. His grand house in Belgrave

★ *The Hurling Time*, finished December 1956, published 1957.

Square is as it was. I was ushered into the front salon on the ground floor by the butler. I had not seen Chips for two or three years. He shows little sign of advancing age, except a tightening of the skin of his jaw. We sat down on the sofa under his old masters. He asked me whether I had seen Bill Astor recently. I said about three months ago. He then surprised me very much by saying that his wife Philippa had left him. This was a very startling piece of news. He had only been married to her just over a year. It is true that the last time I was at Cliveden I noticed that there was little cordiality between him and her, a marked contrast to the tender relationship one had noticed soon after the marriage. Chips had no information as to what had occurred. She had gone home to her mother just before Christmas, a day before Astor returned from a visit to America.

Chips also said that Bill Astor's speech in the Lords on the Suez crisis had offended many people and that he had been cut in London. Altogether it seemed that poor Bill was having a trying time and I decided to write to him.

The conversation now changed to Wavell, whom I had met in Chips's house just before he set out for the Indian Viceroyalty, and had written of in *Last and First in Burma*. Who was going to undertake his biography? Lady Wavell had all the papers, which had been carefully arranged. There had been an idea the son would write it but he died before undertaking to do so. Chips then suddenly suggested that I should. 'I will approach Lady Wavell,' he said. 'You will both come to lunch.' It would be a big undertaking, but Faber would much like it and one might expect good terms. It remains to be seen what her reaction is. She may, of course, have made arrangements.*

I did not stay after this, as Chips by some hardly perceptible movement suggested that he was going out to dinner and must change.

*29 January 1957*
London. Lunch with Sir John Smyth V.C. at the House of Commons. One enters by St Stephen's door and goes to the main lobby. Smyth was waiting. He is a small dapper man with rather a ravaged face. During lunch he said that he was writing a book which would compare the Dunkirk evacuation with the evacuation of Burma. He arranged for me to see question time in the House. I had

* She had.

a good seat just above the bar. The House, now repaired after the war damage, is an ugly dreary chamber. When I arrived the Minister for Labour was answering questions. Presently the new Premier, Macmillan, took his seat. I had not seen him before. He wears his hair rather long and has an anxious peering expression. When it was his turn to answer questions he moved down the front bench till opposite the despatch box and clutching a large book containing questions and answers hurriedly turned the pages to find the right place, giving the impression of an old woman scrattling in her bag. He lacked dignity and presence and did not in any way dominate the House. Smyth said at lunch that he appeared to be afraid of the Commons. He also gave that impression to me. The Commons are not an impressive sight. They look on the Labour side like shabby intellectuals, and on the Conservative like club men. On the way out I had a glimpse of the palace in general. It is a hideous interior, hardly superior to that of the Victoria & Albert, with which it is contemporary.

## 14 March 1957

Louise and I went to see Mervyn Peake's play *The Wit to Woo* at the Arts Theatre. He had shown me the play years ago, but had in more recent times assured me that it was much changed. Now when one saw it acted it was inclined to drag. Not enough happened and the plot was too slender. It was less a play than an interesting commentary on Peake and his semi-serious Gothic fantasy. He appeared after the first act and we had a talk. It seems that the audience's reception on the first night was so enthusiastic that he felt certain of glowing reviews and a West End contract. The next morning he bought several papers and in happy anticipation took them into Sloane Square, where he sat on a bench, still thrilling with the plaudits of the previous evening. He was horrified to find that the press notices were nearly all, not only unfavourable, but almost savage in their ridicule. All his hopes crashed, hopes built up during years of waiting and disappointment. Had he been older he would have realised that his talents were unsuited to the popular stage. The failure of this play has no other significance.

## 20 April 1957

Dined at Cliveden with Astor. There were present, besides his trainer and secretary, an American (with his wife) called Findlater, who was secretary of state for defence in the Truman presidency, and Mrs Churchill, ex-wife of Randolph Churchill. It was an animated party. We stayed talking till 12.15 a.m. Mrs Churchill said that Winston had rather suddenly become senile. He had lucid intervals but more often than not had lost touch with reality, could not remember anything, repeated questions and remarks, and seemed plunged in melancholy, as if brooding over past mistakes. He could not write any more or paint. His health, however, was good and he might live some years.

Astor himself was in good spirits because he had been given a senior Order of St John of Jerusalem for his services in rescuing and raising funds for Hungarian refugees.

*4 May 1957*

Dinner at Cliveden. The chauffeur arrived with a note this morning and I went up as usual at 8 p.m. Astor had a few people staying the weekend, including his mother, the famous Nancy Astor, and the Dowager Duchess of Rutland. At dinner I found myself seated between these two. Lady Astor was clearly pleased to find herself in her old place at the foot of the table. I reminded her that I had been sitting at that same table with her on the day when the atom bomb was dropped on Hiroshima. I had heard the epochal news at 6 p.m. on the B.B.C. and told her. She did not believe it, but it was, of course, confirmed on the 9.0 news. We spoke of the disaster of Bill's second marriage and she said she hoped very much that no reconciliation with Philippa would take place. 'But perhaps he had better not seek a divorce, as he will only marry a third damn fool. I wanted to come to Cliveden and stay, to support him. But he would not have it. And there is the cottage on the estate, which my husband left me, where I could stay, but Bill does not want it.' So she rambled on, making me confidence after confidence; though the same wonderful Lady Astor of legend, she seemed sweeter and gentler than I had known her, and more exceedingly feminine. After we had had jellied soup, prawns in white sauce, beefsteak with quantities of early vegetables, and a cream pudding of particular excellence, she called down the table to Bill, saying she supposed there would be a cheese course. This remark sent him nearly into hysterics. He had evidently taken trouble to provide a particularly good dinner, and waving his arms about he almost shouted that it was the last straw to be asked for cheese when he had chosen in profusion the best dishes and her favourites. 'There isn't any cheese!' he cried. This ebullition did not appear to her out of the ordinary and she continued her conversation with me. After she had recalled her youth in Virginia and some of the guests she had entertained at Cliveden, making such observations as 'I had to forbid the Churchills the house; they were too rude,' and 'The most important thing I have done has been to foment Anglo-American friendship. I was inviting Americans when the ordinary run of hostesses were inviting Germans,' and, 'The people invited to Cliveden were invited for political reasons, not social. All my entertaining had that object,' I said to her that she ought to write her memoirs of the many celebrated people she has known. She replied: 'Anyone who writes an autobiography ought to be taken out and shot.' Presently she called out to Bill to give the signal for the ladies to withdraw. I took the opportunity to say across to him that I had been urging his mother to write her memoirs. He replied at once: 'You must write her biography.' At that the ladies departed to the drawing room. When the men reseated themselves Bill repeated that if it could be arranged he would so much like me to write a book round her and her numerous acquaintances, who included everyone of note over fifty years. He said: 'There is no one else in the world I would trust to do this.' I replied that I was ready to do it, because I desired more than anything to please him. The reply pleased him very much. All would depend, of course, on whether his mother would consent to give the information. I said it would have to be a sort of collaboration *à trois*, though the book itself would have to be mine. He said that was exactly as he looked at it. After dinner in the drawing-room nothing was said to Lady Astor, but as I bade her goodnight she said that she hoped that I would lunch with her in London. I promised to do this.

*3 June 1957*

The Princess Zeid held a press view of her pictures at 6 p.m. today in the newly opened Lords Gallery by the cricket ground. A party was given. Louise and I attended. The art world was poorly represented. Before the end the Princess invited the two of us to supper at

5 L. S. Lowry

6 U Nu, Maurice Collis and Sir Reginald Dorman-Smith

7 Maurice Collis with Burmese officials and editors (*far left* U Thant)

8 Stanley Spencer in 1956

the embassy. She also invited Lynn Chadwick, the sculptor. At 8.30 we drove there. The Princess's butler had been helping at the party. On the way to the embassy we saw him emerging from a public house. Apparently, he and the Prince, who was at the exhibition, had dropped in there for another drink, though they both had quantities at the party. On arrival at the embassy, the butler was in the hall and the Prince in the garden, though how they had got there ahead of us was hard to say. The butler, who was three-quarters drunk, whispered to us that he had been into a public house with the Prince. The supper began on this note. Chadwick had taken so much that he was stupefied. Before sitting down more drinks were handed round. The supper was a big dinner. The Princess was very gay, picking carnations from a big vase on the table and distributing them. (The flowers had been flown from Baghdad that morning.) The butler and the assistant footman were now so drunk that they staggered with the dishes. Chadwick sat bolt upright, speechless.

## 22 June 1957

Julian Huxley invited me to his birthday party today, when he attained the age of seventy. I arrived at 9 p.m. and went in with Julian Trevelyan and his wife. The guests were members of his family, old friends and colleagues, and a few prominent people. I met Henry Moore, J. B. Priestley, Rose Macaulay, and Craxton, the artist. There was champagne, vin rosé, whisky, iced coffee, with smoked salmon and cake. Henry Moore invited me to visit him and see his new studio. Rose Macaulay spoke of the surprising success of her last curious novel* in America, Trevelyan of his forthcoming book of memoirs, *Indigo Days*. So far all was amusing, normal and pleasant. Then it was announced that there would be speeches. I found a seat on a radiator, knowing by experience how tiring it is to listen to speeches standing up, but all the rest stood round in a circle, some fifty men and women. The first speaker, some kind of a junior colleague of Huxley's, made a long, incoherent and dull speech in which he praised Huxley in the manner of a sycophant. Huxley, who was in the front row of the circle, received the adulations with a calculated expression of modesty which did not conceal his pleasure. This speaker was followed by another, who after a laudatory pre-

* *The Towers of Trebizond.*

amble announced that there were present six persons from countries overseas, India, Africa, America, Mexico, etc, who had come to declare their admiration for Huxley. He proceeded then to mimic the speech and mannerisms of six such fans. His mimicry was excellent and very amusing, so amusing indeed that the compliments these persons poured out became farcical and tended to make the company laugh at rather than admire Huxley. However, this part was an excellent joke, though hardly in keeping with what was intended to be the solemn congratulation of Huxley on a life's work. When this speaker had done, he led out Huxley and clothed him in a red doctor's gown and placed a laurel wreath on his head. Got up in this way, Huxley began a long rambling speech in which he recalled the principal events of his career. He is a bad speaker anyway, and made ridiculous by the wreath, the effect he created was not happy. I saw Rose Macaulay's face in the first row; she was haggard and tired. Her expression told nothing, but no doubt she was making her own ironic reflections. The autobiographic speech dragged on. When Huxley concluded, Tom Harrisson*, who was immediately behind me at this point, for I had left the radiator to get myself some iced coffee and cake, nudged me, as if demanding support, and suddenly broke out into the terrible school ditty 'For he's a jolly good fellow'. The guests followed obediently. Huxley listened, as if surprised, bewildered, moved and delighted. He had presumably agreed (or planned, since it was his party) to have speeches and had prepared his own, as he used notes and he must have known about the wreath. All this may have been suitable for a group of fans but it was a risky thing to do before the well-known people he had also invited. I noticed that J. B. Priestley looked very queer. In sum, it struck me as definitely not the way to celebrate one's seventieth birthday.

*1 July 1957*

Went to London to attend Steven Runciman's annual garden party. We reached Elm Tree Road by 6.30 and were shown the steep staircase down into the garden, at the bottom of which the Honourable Steven was receiving his guests. He had written to say how much he appreciated my desire to dedicate *The Hurling Time* to him; he

---

* Curator of the Sarawak Museum, Borneo.

now received us with much affability. On these occasions he asks members of the embassies and a few well-known people. I saw Mrs Julian Huxley in conversation with Rose Macaulay and went up to them. Rose Macaulay, looking like a corpse except for her eyes and humorous expression, began speaking of fruits, prompted by the fruit trees in view. She declared she was certain that our first parents were not tempted by a mere apple and that the fruit of good and evil was, in fact a mango, the most paradisal of all fruits. Her uncle, she said, used in the old days to send boxes of mangoes from India, which arrived in their prime of ripeness and convinced her they were the premier fruits in the world. The famous tree in Eden could only have been a mango tree. Even the Serpent could not have contrived the fall of man if he had only had an apple to work with. This took her on to the subject of figs, which she praised highly and, always erudite, quoted a line from Webster's *Duchess of Malfi* to prove that in Elizabethan England they were greatly appreciated. She was about to discourse in the same manner on bananas when somebody else caught her attention.

I then took the opportunity of enquiring from Mrs Huxley how her husband was after the birthday party of the previous week. She replied that he was in bed with painful knees and that she had sent for a favourite doctor. Before leaving I also spoke to Lady Whyte, chairman of the Council of the China Society, a woman despite her age of very great charm. She spoke of having known Runciman since he was a small boy. He had recently, she said, been invited to Hollywood to advise some film company on the Crusades. The film companies get over at great expense scholars and literary people from time to time, but one has never heard that they take their advice on the production. It may be that they only parade them as part of the advertisement.

### 2 July 1957

I was rung up by the Maidenhead house agents to say that Staite Murray, the celebrated potter, had arrived from Rhodesia after an absence of nineteen years and would like to speak to me. He wanted to see me and I went to the agents to fetch him to the house. I found him, as was natural, very much aged. He is now seventy-six. He said that his immediate plans were to stay with his tenants in his original cottage at Bray* and sort out the pots and other things in his studio, which have been lying there for years. I have looked into his studio and seen the hundreds of pots lying there in the utmost confusion, covered with dirt and in some cases with trees or plants growing in them. I found him as I had known him, though perhaps more mellow. His sensitivity to beautiful objects is great and strikes one as remarkable and spontaneous. In my house I showed him his own pots, carefully preserved. I did not gather from him why he had deserted England when at the top of his fame and given up potting and painting, and cut himself off from the London art world. But he said something to the effect that he did it because his wife (since dead) wanted to live in Africa. When I see him again perhaps he will explain more fully.

*13 July 1957*

Presented myself at Cliveden at 8.15 p.m. Lady Astor sat at the other end of the table. Before dinner Bill Astor told me that he had brought up the subject of a book by me about her and that she had discouraged him. Immediately after he said this I spoke to her. She was in her usual state of animation and talked at once about biographies and their vanity. Addressing me earnestly she said: 'There is nothing to tell about my life. No secrets. No sensations.' I said: 'It is what you can tell about other people. The book need not be about yourself.' Then she made a mot: 'I don't care if people accuse me of adultery because it is not true, but I do care if they accuse me of talking too much because it is true.' She also related an amusing story of some important dinner party where Lord X says to the Duke of Z: 'The Prime Minister has his hand on my wife's knee. What should I do?' The Duke replies: 'How long has he had his hand on her knee?' 'Since the soup,' says Lord X. 'In that case,' says the Duke, 'let it rest.'

After dinner I went up to her at once in the salon, as I wished to find out whether she would like to do the book. She began talking away. 'The salon doesn't look as it did in my time. It doesn't look lived in. Do you see these chairs? Waldorf's father bought them. Paid £1,000 each. They are Louis Seize from the palace, with the original tapestry. No one was let sit on them, but now Bill sits on them. It

* Two miles from Maidenhead.

will destroy them. I bought that French bust, paid £200, wonderful profile. And I had all these books bought, the classics. Come into the other room.' To enter the boudoir or small salon one opens a door of dummy books which match the books lining the walls of the large salon, more like a library than a salon (perhaps it is called the library). She led the way and continued to talk: 'The Astors have no taste. I bought that painting over the fireplace. The ceiling is wrong. It should have been white. Look at this drawing of me by Sargent. He also did my portrait in oils. That's in the hall.' We set out to see it and she continued: 'He swore that he would make it the prettiest portrait he had ever painted.' We continued round the hall and she pointed out the tapestries, the portraits of previous owners of the house (there have been three Clivedens) and finally came to Sargent's portrait of her late husband, Waldorf. 'It's like him in a way,' she said, 'but I don't care for it. He had a stronger face.' Wanting to turn her thoughts to the book, I drew her attention to the pile of guest books on the hall table, which go back to 1906. She went to them and began turning over the earliest, commenting shortly on the names, many of royalty and many of famous people like Churchill who seems to have stayed often. Jameson of the Jameson Raid, Rudyard Kipling and his wife ('When they stayed they would only talk to each other'), Curzon, etc. 'You remember them well when you see their signatures?' I asked. 'I can see their faces perfectly,' she replied, with the intense flickering look she has. And running her finger down the Christian names signed by royalty, she said: 'You will think me a snob. But I have always looked up to my betters.'

We rejoined the guests in the salon. Bill was playing canasta with an actress; the rest were talking. We sat down by a group. She continued in reminiscences. 'When Waldorf and I set off on our honeymoon he received a letter every day from the Queen of Rumania. I didn't mind. It was all on her side. But when we got near Rumania I said "Waldorf, this must stop or I am going home."' It was getting late and she began saying it was time for bed. When I said goodnight to her, she pressed my hand warmly. I said: 'We must meet soon and talk more.' She replied: 'Ring me up and come.' So it was left.

*7 September 1957*

I visited Staite Murray to ask whether I might bring to see him the

Siamese whom I met on Tuesday and who has since written to say he is coming with wife and nephews. S.M. agrees. He will be delighted to see Buddhists. Before I left he invited me to say whether some pots of his should be broken or not. We went into the house and he showed me three pots. As they were not good enough to exhibit nor to sell nor give away as signed work, I advised destruction. He immediately took a hammer and, holding the pots over a wheelbarrow outside the door, butchered them.

*16 September 1957*

At 9 p.m. there was a party at the Institute of Contemporary Arts to open an exhibition of paintings by two chimpanzees, one belonging to the London, and the other to the New York, Zoo. The London chimpanzee painted with a brush. The method was to set about five different colours ready before him and hand him in sequence brushes charged with the colours. The chimpanzee then made marks on the paper. The result was not unlike certain kinds of action painting. It was not a mess. A design emerged. As several dealers who were present said to me: 'If a young painter had brought these pictures in and asked me to show them, I would have done so.' The American chimpanzee used a different method. He dipped his paws in a colour mixture prepared for him and wiped them up and down the paper. The colour was a brownish red. The result was quite different from the London monkey's. A sort of queer landscape effect was produced. It was quite attractive.

The animals were reported to enjoy painting. The result can, however, only be attributed to chance. The pictures shown were no doubt selected from a large number, the majority of which had no merit. The fact that action painting is produced by haphazard or accidental movements of paint over a surface gives it an appearance like the monkeys'. A hen whose feet were smeared with paint and which was set to walk on a large sheet of paper on which grains were scattered would produce a sort of action painting, which in a few cases might well be pleasing. This rational view was not that taken by the introducer (Julian Huxley) in his speech. He and the I.C.A. as sponsors claimed that there was a psychological creation of sorts by the chimpanzees. There was quite a big gathering, an amusing occasion.

*2 October 1957*

Called to see Staite Murray in his caravan at Bray. He took me into New Court Cottage, where were some pots of his and asked me if they were good enough for his exhibition. In four cases they were. Talking to him in his caravan, he told me of his lonely life in Africa. His house is on the hills 15 miles from Umtali and 5 from the nearest European. But he goes often into Umtali, where he is President of the Buddhist Society. At home he writes poetry, reads and meditates. He did not want to make this visit to England, but felt he had to come in order to sort out his belongings for the benefit of his heirs. Nevertheless, he speaks of the possibility of another visit at the time of his exhibition. 'Not that I care now for such things. It matters little whether the pots sell or not, and what the critics say.' He remains, however, practical and businesslike.

Murray looks remarkably well considering his age, the way he is roughing it, and the indigestible food he consumes, cooked by himself in the caravan, though it is mostly out of tins. He said that after his supper last night he went to sleep sitting upright where he was till midnight, when he crossed over to the studio and spent the rest of the night on the abominable old settee he likes. He had supped, he says, on a beef and suet pie and Guinness. He might, I think, live to be a hundred. We may see him back in Bray several times, though he is clearing up like a man who settles his affairs for good. His physical condition is rather better than his mental, but he was never at any time at all an intellectual.

*26 December 1957*

Invited to Cliveden. At dinner Lady Astor was very amusing. She recounted story after story, sipping a glass of Dubonnet, though an extravagant teetotaller. Of her stories the one I thought the most droll was, she said, told her by one of the FitzHerberts. As Livingstone was going along in Africa, he passed a naked black girl. He stopped his people and opened a trunk, taking out three yards of calico. This he gave the naked girl, remarking: 'After all she is one of God's creatures.' Such a story illuminates in a flash the minds of Liberal Victorians. The blacks really were God's creatures and as such deserved to be clothed with propriety. Lady Astor also told a Vanderbilt story: Mrs Vanderbilt opens a room door saying to her guest:

'This is my Louis Quinze boudoir!' 'What makes you think so?' asks the friend.

Bullitt\* then began to talk at large about life behind the scenes at the White House. His description of Wilson and Roosevelt was that they were kept going by drugs and by being painted for public appearance. They became through ill health and the drugs like puppets, controlled by the White House gang whose aim was to keep their places and make their money. The same he said was now happening with Eisenhower. After dinner Bullitt asked me to dine tomorrow at Claridge's with him and his daughter. I accepted. He is an interesting man, of great experience, who has known pretty well everybody of importance in the last thirty years. He talks too much and perhaps all he says need not be believed, but he has a wonderful memory for names, events and dates, and has certainly heard all the secrets of the Wilson and Roosevelt régimes. We joined Lady Astor in the study. Bullitt became rather rough with her, but she answered back. Her repartee is one of the amusing traits in her character. Thus —Bullitt was saying Mr So & So was always drunk. 'No, no,' says Lady A, 'I disagree with you. He was *generally* drunk.' Before I left I asked for an appointment to see her on Saturday about the book. She asked me to phone that morning. She gave the impression that she was against the book.

Bullitt's subjects also included General Marshall and Chiang Kai-shek. He said Chiang lived like a saint, up very early for prayer, then exercises, then calligraphy, then breakfast. The explanation of his downfall was over-devotion to Mme.

*28 December 1957*

I went up to Cliveden at 11.0 a.m. hoping that the matter of the book could be settled one way or the other. The old lady took me into her boudoir and we sat down on the sofa. I came to the point at once, saying that I wanted to write a book which would be in no sense a biography but which would consist of the stories she could tell of the famous people she had met and any other amusing stories. I said that such stories, when told of prominent people, were part of history, in fact the part of history which people often remembered to

\* William C. Bullitt, American diplomat and friend and adviser of Presidents Wilson and Roosevelt.

the exclusion of the rest. Considering the pessimistic view which her son had taken, I was surprised when she immediately agreed to my proposal. She said she had no objection to a book containing her stories of other people, and that it would amuse her to recall them. I then asked her when she could begin. She said it would be during the summer that she would like me to come, so that we could get to work. She suggested a dictaphone. She also suggested that I should familiarise myself with her background—Virginia and the House of Commons—during the interval, so that I should know what questions to ask her. The Cliveden visitors' books would serve, she said, to remind her of a host of tales.

If all goes as planned I now feel sure an amusing and interesting book could be written.

*28 January 1958*

The Princess Zeid asked me to see her at the Iraqi embassy. I brought my new book, *The Hurling Time*, which will be published on the 31st. I found her seated on the sofa in the salon. She was very pleased with the present of the book, and after turning over the pages, looking at the illustrations and enquiring about the contents in her simple manner, she said she wanted to buy four copies, one for the King of Iraq, one for the Princess he is going to marry, one for Prince Zeid and one for somebody else. How could they be got and got quick enough for me to write dedications before I left the house? With her permission I asked her secretary to ring Fabers and myself talked to one of the directors. In result the four copies were put in a taxi and delivered before I left. I then wrote three dedications, to the King, the Prince and the fiancée. The whole was an example of the Princess Zeid's large and generous kindness.

In the course of conversation over a tray of smoked salmon and a glass of Irish whiskey, the subject came up of the Princess's life. What about a book on her, describing her adventures from the harem in Istanbul to her present unique position as Her Excellency and a noted painter? She would have to provide the documents, an account in French, preferably, of her life, the people she met, her art, etc. She enquired whether she would have to pay anything. I said not. Fabers would pay me. She seemed much attracted by the idea and said that her friends in Paris had urged her to put her experiences on paper, but she never had, as she did not think a publisher would take them if she wrote them.

*23 February 1958*

Went to dine at Cliveden alone with Bill Astor. He described some of the private stresses and troubles which existed in the background of the brilliant Cliveden period of the twenties and thirties. Nancy, though sexually frigid, had a great need for men friends. Her affection for Philip Kerr, Lord Lothian, was very deep, and Waldorf was jealous of the friendship. She had also a very deep fondness for Bernard Shaw, who stayed frequently at Cliveden and wrote *The Apple Cart* there and would read the scenes to the assembled guests in the evenings as he completed them.

*25 March 1958*

The Princess Zeid, handling a sheaf of papers written in her large sprawling writing, began talking of her early days. It seems that on the death of her father's brother (about 1900) who was Grand Vizier to the Sultan Abdul Hamid II, her father, General Shakir Pasha, broken-hearted at his brother's death, sold up his residence in Istanbul and bought a property on the island of Principo, the largest of the group of islands in the Sea of Marmora about two hours' steam by boat from the city. Here in 1903 the Princess was born, her father's third daughter. The notes she had written contained these details, she said, and she now began to speak of her governesses, of one in particular. The Princess is an amusing mimic and she made her face to look like the Fraulein's, with enormous arched black eyebrows and cavernous eyes. The woman was lame. Her talents were remarkable. Not only was she an accomplished linguist, but an artist, a poet, an embroiderer and full of fancy and contrivance. Her knowledge of European languages was invaluable. Shakir Pasha, who was engaged in writing an immense work on the Ottoman empire, employed her to translate documents for him. She was so useful that he overlooked her shortcomings, which were startling. She had Sunday off, when she visited Istanbul. 'When she returned,' said the Princess, 'I would see her come up the avenue and, instead of entering by the hall door, slink up the back stairs. She wore a long voluminous skirt and in the folds of this, as we children found out, she concealed a bottle of absinthe. That night she would get very drunk and next morning be unable to give us our lessons. We would loiter outside her door and hear her moaning inside, "Mein Gott, mein Gott!" But my father ordered that nothing was to be said. Sometimes her door was open and she was to be seen lying naked on her bed. We children were fascinated by her. I was her favourite and adored her stories. I liked seeing her come in with the bottle of absinthe. It did not revolt me that she got drunk. The only thing my sisters and I did not care for was when, as she often did, she took us to the parents' house of a certain François, a Levantine, of whom she was enamoured and contrived to see in this way. This was very boring for us.'

The Princess then went on to relate how she knew by sight and reputation everyone on the island. 'I remember with surprise a cruel thing I did. There was a Rabbi who had six or seven daughters. They lived in the village not far off. Sometimes the daughters would pass our door. When I saw them coming, I would go to the front of the house and throw stones at them. I was just a child, of course, but I think they invited stones, because they cringed so much.' As she said this, the Princess mimicked how they cringed so that I was enabled to see the Rabbi's daughters.

She continued to recall her childhood in this way. Her aunt, the Vizier's sister, also lived on the island, a very formidable woman. On her pilgrimage to Mecca, or visits to the Hedjaz, she would purchase Nubian slaves and on her return to Istanbul, give them as presents. The Princess and her sisters each had a Nubian slave to attend on them. The Pasha's headman in the house was a eunuch. He still lives in Istanbul.

At lunch time the Prince came in from his office. 'A plain lunch,' said the Princess, 'as I know you prefer that.' And directing the butler, she said, 'Give Mr Maurice Collis a very full plate of soup,' indicating with a sweep of her hand the high level the soup was to be at. The soup was followed by poussin. 'We always here eat this sort of thing with the fingers,' she said, 'but you can wash them afterwards.' So I ate with the fingers, a very agreeable picniclike relaxation, and washed them in a finger bowl.

In conversation with the Prince, I said that I was reading the new translation of Juvaini's immense *The History of the World Conqueror.*\* We spoke of the Abbaside Caliphs and I asked about their strange titles. 'They are the names of God,' he said. 'God has ninety-eight names.'

## 3 April 1958

Heard from Staite Murray in Africa. His letter mentions his efforts to convert the inhabitants of Rhodesia to Buddhism. He does this, he says, not from learning, for his reading of the subject is not wide, but by talking of his pots, which, he declares, he made according to the principles of Zen Buddhism, without being aware of the fact when he did so. I am very happy that I have not got to listen to such confused rubbish, propounded at most tedious length by a very conceited and self-deluded septuagenarian. When I was afflicted by it in the caravan he inhabited here, I always excused myself after a few minutes. How terrible it would be to have to listen to him in lonely Africa with no escape! He has left open the question of his return for his exhibition. He may come, he may not. It would be better for him to come, because I shall get no thanks for managing it for him.

## 17 April 1958

The visit to Nancy, Lady Astor at Eaton Square. I arrived at 11 a.m. and was shown into the drawing-room by the butler. I had the room to myself for a few moments. It was beautifully arranged, old masters on the walls, very valuable period French furniture, cabinets of continental porcelain, an immense carved Chinese lacquer screen, curtains, carpets. While I was inspecting it, Lady Astor came in. 'Come along with me,' she said and led the way to her boudoir at the opposite side of the drawing room. This was furnished with the same high level of luxury and taste. I remarked on it and she said: 'When Bill was here the other day, he declared that everything in the house was his.' Then changing her tone, she asked: 'What can I do for you?' I replied, 'It is in your power to do something wonderful, if you will.' And I spoke of the project of the book. She immediately expressed willingness to do what I desired. 'I have some American books here about Virginia, which you should read,' she said, and in a moment was on her knees searching about among a quantity of new books piled

\* 'Ala-ad-Din' Ata-Malik Juvaini, born about 1226 in Persia. The history is of Genghis Khan and his three successors.

underneath a side table. She selected six large volumes—all books about the south, the civil war, the Union and its results on the south, long books of from four to six hundred pages.

At this point, the butler announced that Lady Somebody or other had called. 'Tell her to wait ten minutes or so,' says Lady Astor. We now sat down by the fire and she began talking at large. Her conversation is a mixture of anecdote and comment. The anecdotes are invariably amusing, the comments human and revealing. 'We must instal a dictaphone,' she said, and repeated that if she had the Cliveden visitors' book, she could reel off stories and descriptions about the many notable persons who had stayed there. 'Dr Jameson (of Jameson's raid) stayed,' she said. 'I remember at a dinner I gave at my St James's Square house that I asked him to pretend to be my husband, Waldorf. I said a lot of rough things to him, so as to make one of the guests, Balfour I think, believe I treated my husband badly. He was very shocked. We had a good laugh.' She went on to tell of the old Duchess of Connaught as one of the most able and intelligent women she had ever met. And quoted a remark to her by Henry James, that 'the English were the most dauntlessly decent people in the world.' She repeated her mot: 'The welfare state may be the farewell state,' saying that people so coddled could not survive in this hard world. 'For the first time I find myself pessimistic of the future. How can we hope to continue selling in foreign markets once other states get their export trade going?' I suggested we should have to produce what other states could not. 'Yes,' she said, 'machinery and biscuits. Our biscuits are unique. The soil gives the flour a particular taste. It can't be copied.'

She now remembered Lady Somebody and hurried into the hall, calling the butler; he announced that the lady had left, as she could not wait. Our conversation was resumed, after she had examined a list of engagements which her secretary, Miss Jones, had placed on her desk. She appeared to have engagements hour by hour, and I wondered how she would ever have time to devote herself to providing material for the book. 'I don't care for London,' she said, 'and yet it might be the place to do the work, because when I am in the country I like to be out of doors.' The name of Lady Patricia Ramsay came into her head and she said: 'One should never be rude to servants or familiar with royalty. Lady Patricia was always saying to me "call me Patsy," but I never would. Royalty's existence depends on us. If we start calling royal persons by their Christian names, they will go out of existence as royal persons.' She changed the subject to her first speech in the Commons. A member said afterwards: 'Your voice is your fortune.' I said I had remarked how well her voice carried and what a relief that was, as I particularly wanted to hear all she said. 'My voice,' she declared, 'is not attractive but everybody in the place can hear it. And if you hear distinctly what is being said, you are held by it better than by the best arguments which are inaudible.'

She went on, 'I feel I have accomplished nothing in life.' I don't know what she was thinking of; she has done a lot—British-American friendship owes much to her, for instance. Perhaps she was thinking that she had failed to bring in prohibition. There was as much drunk as ever. She speaks vehemently and gaily always, and sometimes as it were dreaming and not remembering exactly, but letting the words flow, for there is no hesitation.

I spoke of how I must read her speeches in Hansard, and asked the years. She said, from 1918 to 1945. It will be a job to find them, as there are so many volumes of Hansard a year. The subject turned to Catholicism, because I said that I came from Ireland. This made her tell a story of a Belfast man. He met with an accident of some sort in southern Ireland and while unconscious and evidently dying was given extreme unction by a Catholic priest. He recovered consciousness just before he died and his last words were: 'To Hell with the Pope.'

After an hour the time came to go and I made an effort to fix a definite date to begin work on her reminiscences. But she evaded this, saying, 'I promise to do it, but leave it to me to suggest the time. I believe Cliveden would be good. You could come up there.' So it was left.

### 29 May 1958

Lunched with the Princess Zeid and her elder sister, a blonde woman with blue eyes and hair which once was golden, one of those fair Turks. She had a quiet collected manner and much charm, due partly to the attention with which she listened to what you said. When in Istanbul, she related, we children each had two Circassian slaves. They were village girls but had a natural flair and after being instructed in polite usages were wonderfully dignified, tactful and accomplished, as well as having striking good looks. They were married off later to

Turks in government employ of various ranks. I was also told of the children's attendance at the Friday prayers at the mosque when the Sultan arrived with his Janissaries. All stood as he came in, the women careful to adjust their yashmaks. Even as a small girl she had to wear one on that occasion and her mother held her tight so that she did not move. When visiting the palace they were given toys and presents. Her uncle once asked what she would like for her birthday, expecting she would want jewellery. Her fancy had been taken, however, by a workbox owned by her English or French nurse and she asked for one for herself, a mistake, she said, for had she been smarter she would have got an emerald ring or a rope of pearls.

### 1 June 1958

I went up to Cliveden at 8.0. When I was ushered by the butler into the library I found old Lady Astor there with a few guests. She came forward and with a rather delicate appealing smile said she was very glad to see me again. She then introduced two persons who were standing by the fireplace as the Duke and Duchess of Brunswick. As there is no such title, I knew that this was one of her little tricks and I waited to know who they might be. Almost at once Lord Palmer (the Huntley & Palmer man) came in with his wife, and the girl who rides for Astor, and Lord Gowrie's mother. Astor himself did not appear for a moment. It now transpired that the so-called Duke of Brunswick was Prince Giri, whose wife was an American. The Prince was a White Russian of Tartar descent. When I spoke to him he claimed descent from Genghis Khan through the son who was made Khan of the Golden Horde.

Then Bill Astor opened the door from the big salon and, although it was really he who was late, pretended that he had been in the salon waiting where all the drinks were, and asked us why we were sitting in the library. His mother, protesting that drink was the ruin of the world, reluctantly let us go into the salon where he rapidly made a very strong Martini. He had hardly done this, however, before the butler rang the gong and everyone gulped the drink down and we went into the dining room. It was so exceptionally strong, however, that what with gulping it so quickly, everybody was already a little drunk, much to the disapproval of the old lady.

She sat at the bottom of the table. There was a glass of Dubonnet at her place. 'I don't mind Dubonnet,' she said, 'it isn't any stronger than cider and I don't count that.' As dinner went on she tended to bait her son, who was sitting at the other end of the table. She said loudly so that he could hear, 'If I were to raise my finger I could take his cook.' I said, 'But surely you have an excellent cook?' She said, 'Yes, I have, my chef is first class, but the Cliveden one is better and if I was to give a hint he would come running. Isn't that so?' she said raising her voice. But her son was not to be drawn. And she went on to me, 'It is a funny feeling living in a flat; I have never lived in a flat before. What is the butler to do without a hall door? He has got nothing on earth to do. But they never leave me, my servants, I let them go to bed early.' And she shouted across the table: 'Bill, why do you keep your servants up late?' He said: 'I'm away half the year, in America or Scotland, and when I'm here I keep them up or they would only drink in the kitchen.' 'Ah,' she said, 'that drink.' And she said to me, 'Look at the way that girl is drinking there, she has had more than enough. Once when very young in Virginia I had been riding all the morning and I came in very hot and they gave me a drink. I wasn't experienced and I gulped it down and was practically insensible for two hours afterwards, and have never touched another drop since.' I replied, 'Perhaps it was because you were not accustomed to it that it had that disastrous effect.' 'No, they made it especially strong. After the birth of my son, when I discovered that my husband drank, I resolved never to live with him again. I don't know how I ever had the strength to do such a thing. I was only eighteen but I just couldn't, I had such a horror.'

Then suddenly changing, she shouted down the table to her son: 'What I want now is more money.' Somehow or other this remark somewhat discomposed Bill and he refused to be drawn or to answer. Which when she saw she gave up. She said to me under her breath, 'What I want is to settle in here.'

After coffee had been handed round, the old lady said: 'Well, we can't sit here all night; get up you girls,' addressing the Princess Giri, Lady Palmer, Lord Gowrie's mother, and the girl who rides the horses. They said: 'But we haven't finished our coffee.' 'Well, drink it down, I can't sit here.' She got up and strode off. In all these things however, it would be a mistake to think of Lady Astor as in any way offensive or rude; she has some kind of extraordinary indefinable charm which enables her to do all these things without giving the smallest offence.

When the ladies were gone, Astor made me come and sit close to him because he wanted me to tell him again how much I liked his speech of the day before on Stanley Spencer, which I did. Astor said that he had invited Spencer to dinner not very long before and at the end of the meal Stanley said: 'This is the first time in my life that I have ever been asked to dinner; I have only been asked to functions before.' Astor said that it was rather amusing because at the table there was also the famous cartoonist Osbert Lancaster. Stanley and he seemed a little jealous of each other, or at least they both wanted to hold the floor and both being inveterate talkers there was rather a struggle between them to do so.

Then we joined the ladies in the library. I spoke to Prince Giri about the Crimea and the background of his youth. He said that the Soviet were anxious to entertain him as a sort of museum piece and he thought it would be quite safe for him to go, but, though tempted to do so, and see the old family house, he had decided on the whole not to risk it, particularly as his uncle had been hanged by the Soviet only about ten years back.

After a time I found myself again talking to the old lady. She made it very clear that Stanley Spencer's painting was disagreeable to her. I said to her 'Can we settle now about meeting and making a start on the book?' She said, 'Yes, we must,' but yet would not come to the point. I said, 'You said that you would like to have the visitors' books to remind you.' We went over to where the books were piled up and she took the first one, 1906, and we turned over the leaves with all the names of famous people there, including the Archduke who was killed at Sarajevo, Lord Kitchener, Dr Jameson, various royalties, literary people like Henry James. 'What good company I used to keep in those days!' she said. 'When I first entered the House of Commons somebody said of me—is it that she is intelligent or just that she kept good company? Yes, yes, everybody was here. You know I have been in my time called the friend of the poor but as you can see from this book I was really the friend of the rich.'

The Giris and the Palmers having gone and I being the only guest left, she said, 'Are you staying the night?' I said no, and she said, 'Then why haven't you gone?' I said, 'It is not so late.' 'The Astors all have to be in bed by 11,' she replied. This statement seemed to satisfy her, because she then again entered into further conversation. Astor was standing by the table of drinks and offered me a parting whisky which I refused. She said loudly, 'I have heard it said that Mr Collis has taken to drink.' I said, 'Do you mean in general, Lady Astor, or just that you think on this particular occasion I am a little drunk?' She was very satisfied with this reply. Finally wishing me goodnight she made her way towards the stairs and said: 'I promise, I promise.'

As Astor saw me to my car he said, 'It may be that you will never be able to get more out of my mother than what you remember from these sort of evenings. And your book will have to be a kind of Ebury Street Conversations.' I said I didn't think it could be constructed on those lines; there would not be enough, we would have to have more material; and he said, 'I hope it can be managed.'

### 26 June 1958

I drove up to my appointment with Lady Astor, bringing two volumes of the Cliveden visitors' books (1914–1925), enormously heavy and large and quite a job to carry up to the first floor. Lady A had her usual rather distracted air, as if she was in a hurry and had a lot to do; she welcomed me with her half shy, half hardy glance, saying as before: 'What can I do for you?' a formula of hers, evidently, for opening a conversation. 'The book,' I murmured. 'Come on,' she said, leading the way to the sofa on which she sat. I drew up a chair. She began skipping over the pages of the first volume. 'Look at all these names,' she said with a trace of distaste, as if the job before her of having to talk about the people there was not exactly what she wanted to do and as if she did not intend to spend much time over it. However, as she looked her interest was aroused and memories began to crowd into her mind.

One of the first names she noticed was Kipling's, who stayed at Cliveden first on 4 July 1914 and came again twice more, the last occasion being 24 Nov 1917. Said she: 'There was something comical about him.' And then she checked herself. 'I mustn't say that. But you couldn't get him away and talk with him without his wife, on whom he leaned and to whom he would refer. His manner was dour. He was very poor company; he didn't seem able to take things lightly. His wife was American. He was one of the Round Table men with Curtis,

Lothian and Geoffrey Dawson.' My impression was that she found Kipling very heavy on hand, and without sparkle or wit, and unable to throw himself into her gay moods. James Barrie, who stayed in 1920, she did not find congenial either. 'He was spoiled,' she said. 'He lost all his homely Scotch ways after being taken up by high society; his cottage charm went and he became a ridiculous snob.' And she went on: 'I was never a snob, because the Virginians already thought so much of themselves that it never occurred to them to cultivate titles. We used to say in America: "Don't say you're from Virginia because it will embarrass people."'

Another important literary person who stayed at this period was Lytton Strachey. Him she liked. He was a congenial spirit. 'I was very fond of him; he was nervous but excellent company, so droll, and lively.' I spoke of *Eminent Victorians* having established itself as a classic despite the efforts of some critics to belittle it; on hearing the book mentioned, her manner changed and her expression became respectful. She has a genuine awe of brains. Her constant remark: 'I know my betters' or 'I have always looked up to my betters' is true in the sense that when she felt herself in the presence of intellect she felt humble. People like Bernard Shaw must have found this trait attractive. It was flattering that a woman so well known for the trenchancy of her tongue should feel humble in their presence; perhaps this was the secret of how she made such fast friends among really clever men.

I was anxious to bring the conversation round to parliament, as she was elected for Plymouth in 1919, and asked her whether the people she asked to Cliveden at that time helped to turn her mind to a public career. Her reply was that it was Waldorf's translation to the Lords in 1918 on the death of the 1st Viscount which persuaded her to stand instead of him at Plymouth and keep the seat, as it were, in the family. I asked how the MPs received the first woman MP. 'They did not want me in the House,' she said. 'I knew it was an intrusion into an entirely male world and outside the Chamber I kept as much as possible to myself. I had my own sitting room in the House where my secretaries worked. After debates I went back there. I never went into the dining or smoking rooms; nor mixed with the members, like the Socialist women MPs later. I did not meddle in anything outside my particular interests, improving the legal position of women and children and in legislation to control the drink trade.' 'If it was a shock,' I said, 'for MPs to see a woman in what had been their preserve for centuries, how was it that the Plymouth electors, as unused to the idea of a woman representative, voted you into Parliament?' 'I think that they admired my courage, for Plymouth people have always admired courage and have themselves had the courage which saved England more than once. Before the election I made a speech against the drink trade; I was never a prohibitionist but I thought seven pubs on one side of the street too much. That speech was thought to have killed my chance of getting in, for the trade opposed me all it could and it had great influence in Plymouth. But I called all the sailors to a meeting. "If you want more drink, don't vote for me," I said. But I told them the trade was too powerful and showed that it should be controlled in their true interests. This seemed to the sailors and the general population very courageous; they admired it and voted for me.'

This said, Lady A began flicking over the thick pages of the visitors' book and letting fall observations on personalities, life and manners as she did so. There was a page on which was inscribed the childish signature of George V and the more formed signature of Queen Mary, dated in 1915. 'What was the procedure followed?' I asked. 'How did you manage with them for a weekend?' 'They did not stay the weekend, it was just a visit; and very exhausting it was. George V was a terrible ass. He was so rude to notabilities from abroad that it was enough to precipitate a war. I remember once, when the Duke of Kent came to see me at Plymouth, that I said to him: "Why doesn't your father consult your mother and take her advice?" I forget his answer, but the fact was that Queen Mary was never accepted at her right value. It had something to do with her having been engaged before to the Duke of Clarence; it seems that King George never quite got over the fact that he had to marry the woman who would have been, had he lived, the elder brother's queen. The day King George and Queen Mary came was more tiring than it might normally have been because after they left Henry Ford turned up and that night I had to go to London to attend a dinner at the American embassy.' She went on to say that George V was essentially a stupid man, but by some happy intuition he acted during the First World War in such a way as to win popular affection, a thing which in fact surprised him very much. This was partly because he acted strictly as a constitutional monarch and, though he hated the sight of Lloyd George, was guided quietly by his advice.

At the mention of Lloyd George, whose name appeared several times as having stayed at Cliveden, Lady A remarked that he had once said to her about public speaking: 'It's not what you say that matters, but whether you hold your audience.' This observation was much to the point, for this was precisely Lady A's strong suit. In the House and in the country people listened to what she said. 'But they did not listen to Lady Atholl,' she observed. She was the third woman to be elected to parliament. 'When Kitty Atholl came in they said that they had got a real Tory. But when she stood up to speak she emptied the House.' The fourth woman MP, Ellen Wilkinson, was a great friend of hers, though not in the Tory interest. 'She was such a friend that she refused to speak against me when I was standing for Plymouth.'

Lady A had some further remarks to make about royalty. Of Queen Alexandra she said. 'She was a most beautiful woman but had no brains.' And of the Duchess of Connaught she said: 'She was the most intelligent of all the royal women; and she was also the most modest. When I said to her, "You must get tired of opening bazaars", she replied "That's all I'm fit for." '

Noticing the name Sylvia Pankhurst, I asked what her attitude to the suffragette movement had been before the First World War. 'I was never an active suffragette, but I was all in favour and much admired Christabel Pankhurst. Once when Christabel was addressing a meeting, she was heckled by a wretched little fellow who shouted: "Don't you wish you were a man?" She replied "Yes, don't you?" '

Returning to the subject of Lloyd George, Lady A said that on his first visit to Cliveden in May 1921, about 28 months after her election to parliament, he remarked, after he had a look round: 'If I owned a place like this, I wouldn't give it up for politics.' She also recorded his mot on Curzon: 'One moment he is as engaging and easy as can be, the next he is receiving a foreign ambassador as if he was a Basuto chief.'

Lady A continued to talk in this way about one person or another; nothing she said was dull or trite. She often spoke with earnest intensity, always with humanity, never with malice, always too with good sense. She never made a silly remark. Often she spoke lightly, with gaiety and enjoyment, with relish for the comic situation, and hit out half in fun to puncture make-believe, insincerity and bunkum. She showed a love of contrasts.

By this time she had been talking for a full hour; it was time for me to go. She got up from the sofa and we moved towards the door. She had become very animated and seemed to break off with great reluctance. 'I have been so deep in old times that I feel lost now back in the present.' We reached the hall. 'Why are you writing this book?' she asked and went on: 'What's the good; nobody reads biographies. I don't believe in them.' I said I wanted to write something which she and her son, Bill, would like. She accepted this. And somehow there came into her head the retort she had made long ago to an Irish heckler in America: 'You came to this country because you were hungry and you have been a nuisance ever since.' With that she scurried down the hall.

*8 July 1958*

Miss Jones, the secretary, announced me, but Lady A paid no attention and continued looking down at her letters. Miss Jones announced me a second time. Lady A let a further ten seconds or so pass without turning towards me; she then did so with either a real or simulated air of impatience and after shaking hands demanded to know my business. As this opening has now become routine, I was not surprised and mildly replied that I hoped she could spare a little time to comment on matters pertaining to her friends. Almost with what in someone else might have been annoyance, she said: 'I would rather do anything but this.' However, she sat down on the sofa, snatched open one of the visitors' books and began turning the pages rapidly and with, as it were, distaste. Her disinclination now seemed to disappear and she began talking in her lively fashion as her eye caught famous names.

'When Ribbentrop came to lunch some time in the middle thirties he raised his arm and cried "Heil Hitler". I said "Don't give us any of that nonsense here." I thought it was a joke; but in fact he was serious.'

Of the Speaker of the House of Commons, Fitzroy, she said: 'Once on a very hot day I offered him a peach in the House. I came up behind his chair when he was presiding. He said, "If you don't stop tempting me, I'll have you put down." ' Of Montgomery: 'Monty once said to me, "I don't like women MPs." ' I replied, ' "I don't like Generals, with one exception, General Evangeline Booth." That settled him.'

Of Lawrence of Arabia, she said, 'When he called himself Shaw and was a private in the air force, he was stationed near Plymouth and used to come in often and see us after dinner. When interested his conversation was brilliant. I used to ride pillion on his motor cycle, disguised of course; I could balance without holding on to him. My last ride with him was only a fortnight before his fatal accident; the story that he deliberately killed himself is rubbish. He left his mother to me to look after.'

The Communist minister, Maisky, appears several times in the book, accompanied by his wife. Of him she said: 'When he was coming downstairs one day at Cliveden he was overheard abusing his wife; it was alleged afterwards that the woman was not his wife at all, but a person sent by Stalin to watch him. He disappeared not long afterwards and was not heard of again.'

Bernard Shaw's name first appears in the visitors' book under the date of Christmas 1927. Anxious to hear from Lady A something of the visit to Moscow in the summer of 1931 when Shaw invited her, Waldorf and Lothian to accompany him, I asked what she could tell me. She said: 'Molotov met us at the station. Shaw was received like a film star; the Russians, regarding him as the great writer of the age, had been most delighted at the warm way he had written about Lenin. But he understood about as much about politics as I about the writing of plays. At the hotel G.B.S. had the best room; I was some-where up in the attic. The reception delighted him; he was very vain. One of the things he wanted to do was to call on Lenin's widow. For some reason the Russians kept putting this off. Eventually we were taken to a cottage outside Moscow. Here Lenin's widow and her sisters showed great joy in welcoming G.B.S.' On other occasions, however, G.B.S. behaved with his more usual puckishness. When asked to record in the visitors' book of some institution what was expected to be a solemn and weighty saying, he wrote, 'When you finish your Five Year Plan, I advise your taking a rest.' (According to a note by Waldorf recording this event, G.B.S. prefaced the above sentence with, 'My father drank too much; I have worked too much.')

Lady A had a few words to say about her interview with Stalin accompanied by G.B.S. and Waldorf. 'Going to visit Stalin in the Kremlin was like going into Singsing. The place was more like a prison than a palace. Stalin never received visitors from abroad normally. One of the questions he asked G.B.S. was: "How do you account for England getting possession of so much of the earth?" To which G.B.S. replied: "I'm an Irishman and know nothing about England." When G.B.S. did not want to answer a question he always said he was an Irishman. I answered for him, "I believe the translations of the Bible we distributed did it. That along with the justice and mercy we brought." Stalin replied: "If we don't do that we fail." '

Other impressions remaining with Lady A were of the churches turned into museums, with pictures on the walls depicting the atrocities perpetrated by the Church. 'I saw too the road from Moscow to Siberia. In one church was a terrified old priest. We saw too some of the crown jewels, but so poor a lot that I told them I had better jewels myself.'

Of Shaw generally she said that she believed she figured in his last play *The Millionairess* but had not read it. When I recalled that he wrote a good part of *The Apple Cart* at Cliveden, she replied indifferently that she did not know this. 'He was up in his room writing something all day.'

It was now about 12.30. Lady A said in a slightly testy voice that I should leave. 'There is a lot here for you to digest. I think I've told you all I know. But if you can later think of anything else to ask, I'm ready to help.'

*25 July 1958*

At Lady Astor's. When I asked her about Virginia she began talking with animation. 'I inherited my vitality from my father. He had a large estate and many slaves. My father and mother were married during the Civil War; at the end of it he was ruined. But he took up various jobs without complaint. He was a nightwatchman for a time at a hotel. He lost that job because one night as a joke he lit a bonfire which smothered the hotel with smoke. When the guests, thinking the place was on fire, ran out in their nightclothes, he hosed them. Later he was employed on a railroad. When asked for his qualifications he said: "I can boss up niggers." ' (Here the old lady interjected that

I must be careful not to use the word niggers if I quoted her). By 1861 he had made enough money to settle £3,000 a year on each of his children. Having made his fortune he refused to do any more work. 'Only Yanks and niggers work' he declared, and set up again as a Virginian country gentleman with a big house, Mirador, on the Blue Ridge Mountains, and black labour, now free. He farmed and shot and visited England to hunt. He had great natural charm and was exceedingly witty. But he had a violent temper. Other things she said about him made me feel that she had taken after him. 'Never hand me port again,' he said one night to the butler. Next night when the butler did not hand him port, he abused him. He engaged a valet in England and bossed him like a nigger. But the valet adored him. 'To me he'd say: "Here's a dollar if you sing." Then he'd say: "Here's two dollars if you stop singing." He bossed his sons too much. They came to nothing.' All that makes you think of the old lady.

In the book I will have to try to disclose what sort of a person she really was, what were her real motives, why she, so rich and well provided with pleasant occupations, preferred the turmoil and heavy work of politics, and social duties such as founding institutions to help women and children. To succeed she had to do battle against indifference, stupidity and selfishness and the weapon she used was her wit. This must have given her much pleasure; but it was not only a weapon, it was her natural way of expressing her opinion on all subjects. So much is it part of her that she never opens her mouth without using some sort of raillery. Yet there is the exception to this rule that when speaking of suffering, merit, honesty and good heart in others, she discards humour altogether and is serious. Only in such moments does she reveal her true self. In some sort humour is a kind of shield. She can conceal herself behind it. There is also something enigmatic about her expression, as if she feared intrusion on her inmost self and also sought in constant activity an opiate for some kind of secret unrest, an unrest arising perhaps from a fundamental distaste for a close communion with anybody, male or female. Afflicted with this shrinking one wonders whether she has ever had among her hundreds of acquaintances a real intimate friend, whether she could have borne to lower her guard and speak openly to anybody. Perhaps when I know more of her I shall be able to answer these questions.

Today I went to London. Fred Warner had asked me to lunch. I had met him at Cliveden, a very engaging personality, who recently had been first secretary at the British embassy in Rangoon and now is about to go to Athens. His account of Burma, as it now is, is extremely droll. He managed to establish a most happy relationship with the Burmese, was infinitely amused by their happy-go-lucky ways and was never bored in their society, whether in the capital or country districts. He was insatiable for company. Thus, when he arrived at some out-of-the-way place in the districts and put up at the rest-house, he would send a message round to the local notabilities to invite them over. A bottle of whisky would be put on the table. Presently his visitors would arrive and conversation would follow into the night. There was always somebody, he said, who spoke English, as of course he knew no Burmese. That sort of familiarity with the native inhabitants in any countryside can only be achieved by certain natures; most people would not find it interesting and would also be too fatigued. Of the Shan States he said that the Sawbwas* had retained all their power and were richer than before. Opium was the source of their wealth; they supplied Burma and Siam. Gambling was another source. The great annual festival at Kengtung, conducted by Chinese croupiers under licence, sucked into the Sawbwas' coffers the peasants' cash. I attended a similar celebration at Mong Mit in 1938 on the occasion of the Sawbwa's funeral. But the jollification at Kengtung, as described by Warner, was infinitely more picturesque, with its rows of opium saloons, the girls you could dance with and with whom you could retire into chambers behind. Having got rid of the English, the inhabitants had returned to a Rabelaisian abandon on such festive occasions, which was in keeping with their natural high spirits.

Another interesting thing which Warner said was that he accompanied Peter Townsend, the Princess Margaret's rejected suitor, on the section of his world tour from Assam to the east part of Siam. The road over the mountains was so bad that they only averaged 3 miles a day. Landslides had to be dug away and unbridged torrents negotiated by laying down a causeway of boulders. Townsend was moody. He thought of himself as pursued by the Furies. He slept fitfully and

* Princes.

would pace up and down the bamboo huts, where they stayed the night, for hours on end. He was eager to get on to the next place always, as if there he would find content. He was tremendously self-centred. At Myitkyina he refused to dine at the mess of the local army headquarters. 'I do not know these people,' he said. His best point was that he was an excellent mechanic. When the Land Rover broke down, which it often did, he could always mend it. It sounded to me like a nightmare trip. 'But we were never in any danger,' said Warner, 'except once when the opium of our Naga porters gave out. They got very angry, and blamed us for letting them start with an insufficient supply. They became almost demented and it looked as if they would go for us with their knives. By good luck a mule caravan with Chinese had passed us a little time before. I sent a man after them with money to buy opium. He returned with a good supply within three hours and the Nagas quieted down.'

*2 October 1958*

At Cliveden. A young man related a story about Nancy Astor, an occasion when she was worsted by no less a person than Winston Churchill, with whom she was never on very good terms. She said: 'If I'd been your wife, Winston, I'd have put poison in your coffee.' His retort was: 'If I'd been your husband, Nancy, I'd have taken poison.' When dinner was over I climbed upstairs again to Bill's bedroom.* First I told him what I had done about the book, asking him whether he was satisfied. He seemed perfectly so. He said in passing: 'When I was up in Scotland I got a wire from Mama as follows: "Please tell Mr Collins to stop writing my wife".' 'My wife?' 'My life.' 'Ah. And what did you do?' 'I tore it up and didn't reply.' 'I received a letter yesterday saying that your mother would see me next Thursday to continue with the book. What of that?' 'I don't know.' 'Supposing your mother really forbade the publication of my book. It would be very awkward having made an agreement with the publishers.' 'I could bring her round. One of the best ways with mother is to turn a thing into a joke. I remember once she wanted to change houses with me in London. She was almost hysterical about it. But when I said: "If you pack all your possessions and have them carted the 300 yards from Hill Street to Upper Grosvenor Street, and

* He was in bed with a sore throat and had not been present at dinner.

I pack all my possessions and have them carted from Upper Grosvenor Street to Hill Street, all London will laugh at us," she laughed and it was all right. Try and make her laugh and it will help.'

I then asked how the estrangement between Waldorf and Nancy, his parents, came about. He said that it was due to political differences of opinion, not to a private dislike of each other. It began at the time of the Second World War. Lady A supported Chamberlain; Waldorf, Churchill. Lady A was essentially a Conservative, though of the most liberal kind; Waldorf had become gradually much more left. They now could not agree on any political question. Their close collaboration before had been founded on mutually shared convictions. They found that they could collaborate no longer. The bottom fell out of their lives. They were continually bickering—Waldorf wanted Nancy to give up parliament and not stand again for Plymouth. This greatly angered her. But as she could not manage without Waldorf's help and guidance to stand, she felt obliged to resign her seat. This further exasperated her with him. 'When I returned from the war,' said Bill, 'I found the atmosphere here appalling.' The marriage, despite the remarkable comradeship of the two between 1906 and 1939, was broken up.

*8 October 1958*

I had an appointment to see Lady Astor this morning. I felt a little nervous how she would receive me after hearing from her son about her telegram demanding that I stop writing. On being let in by the butler I was shown into the drawing room and told Lady A was on the phone but would come in shortly. After waiting about ten minutes I heard a voice calling my name in the hall, and answering, got up. At that moment Lady A came in. She had a bustling determined air. 'Come here,' she said, drawing me aside, 'I cannot give permission for you to go on with my life; you'll have to drop it. Unless you go to Virginia. If Bill wants the book, he will have to send you there. And that will make him think twice. You can't possibly write a book on me without thoroughly understanding my Virginian background. Everything important to me happened in Virginia.' She did not seem to expect a reply to this and took her seat on the sofa. I drew up a chair beside her. Seated thus, very upright, and with an earnest manner, she continued to explain what Virginia had always meant to her.

Later her father's name came up. 'I inherited his courage but not his temper. I have never lost my temper in my life. It may be because I grew up with such a horror of lost temper.' One of the things about Lady A is that these sort of remarks are perfectly true; she is not a woman of hot temper, her wit seems to relieve her of all her irritations.

The mention of courage enabled me to ask her about the famous occasion when a half-demented man came to her house in Plymouth and threatened to murder her. It was about thirty-seven years ago now. She leant forward and wagging her finger and flashing her eyes acted how she had dealt with him. 'How dare you come here and threaten to kill me! Get out, or I'll kill you.' The man was so taken aback that he made off. 'He fled and I immediately pursued him. There was no time to summon help if I was to catch him, as I now wanted to do, so as to hand him over to the police. Indeed, it did not occur to me to call for help. I just ran after him without thinking. It was all over quickly. He rushed into a public house and was caught.' She then told me there was a curious sequel to the story. The man was sent to prison, not apparently for his attempt on her, but for some other charge. Time passed and one day in the House of Commons he sent his name in saying he wished to see her. 'At this I was rather startled because I thought he might have come to make another attempt. However, I went out to speak to him. He said: "I just had to come to say how much I admire your courage."'

She had been talking an hour and now got up. As I had observed before, her spirits were highest at the end and it was then that she was the most amusing. As we walked towards the drawing-room door, she remarked: 'The Sergeant-at-Arms once said to me, "I want to tell you I've always been in love with you." To which I replied: "If I had known that I'd have taken more liberties with you—in the House."' And capping this, she added: 'Another person in the Commons, I forget who it was, said: "I always hated you, but could not resist your feet and ankles."' I asked what reply she gave to that. 'It stumped me,' she said; she was now quite merry.

At the Hanover Gallery later in the day was Feliks Topolski, my old friend, an artist who has a power of drawing and characterisation far greater, in my opinion, than any other artist in England. He said that he was going on to a party given by the West African Produce Company at Claridges for the Black Kings of Darkest Africa, and asked me to accompany him, which I gladly did, being both pleased with his company and eager to see the Black Kings. On arrival at Claridge's and after being ushered in, I saw a large crowd of business-men (they all look alike, as the universal and paramount need to sell has obliterated all other interests for them), but scattered among them were African men and women, mostly in national costume. Seated by himself on a sofa was one such, a burly Negro with a curious headgear. Topolski, who had come prepared to make drawings, asked permission to draw him and got to work. I sat down on the sofa and asked the Negro to write down his name. It was The Fon of Bum. I said to him: 'Your hat is remarkable.' He said: 'Only kings or the sons of kings may wear such a hat.' I said: 'Are you a king or the son of a king?' He said: 'I am a king, I am the King of Bum.' I said, 'I suppose that in Bum it would not be done for a man to seat himself with you on a sofa as I have done.' He said, 'The fine for that is fixed at £35.' He was an agreeable king and was enjoying himself.

### 30 December 1958

Ewan Phillips and his co-director of the Kaplan Gallery arrived at 11 a.m. On seeing my gouache paintings they immediately said they liked them very much and offered to give me an exhibition this spring. Phillips said he liked both the earlier and later styles. This has been a great reassurance. It seemed hardly likely that I, who had taken up painting so short a time ago, could interest a West End Gallery. When one thinks of the keen competition by so many artists de carrière to get shown in the West End, one knows how fortunate one is.

At 8 p.m. I went to dine at Cliveden, knowing that Nancy Astor was there. At the door the butler told me that there would be just herself and Lord Astor at dinner. When I was ushered into the small salon I found Bill alone, reading. Presently his mother came in. She looked very frail after her illness, and as if she had lost some weight. She came in, for her, rather slowly and wanderingly, though speaking as if giving orders, as is her custom. I hastened forward to shake hands with her; she greeted me gently, without rallying me. We went into dinner. As she sat down, she said: 'My father before taking his seat at table used to say: "Thank God for what we are about to receive," and when in his chair would shout at the servants, "God damn you, shut the door!" ' The butler now came in with a bottle of Dubonnet and poured her about a third of a tumbler, this so-called soft drink to which age and more indulgence now inclines her.

A certain amount of baiting on her part took place and she declared Bill owed her £100,000 in some way connected with the racing stable. But he was not to be drawn and received her thrusts with unabated good humour. My impression was that at times her mind wandered. Always inclined to make rather wild statements, this tendency was more marked now that increasing age and illness had weakened and confused her.

We spoke of T. E. Lawrence. Bill asked her, 'Where are the letters he wrote to you?' 'Oh, I gave them away to so-and-so.' This caused her son to say that if this was so, he would strangle her. At this, she withdrew the statement, saying they must be somewhere in the house.

After drinking coffee, the old lady made it clear that she wished to leave the table. We got up and went out with her. Before climbing the stairs, which are long and steep, she chattered in the hall, speaking of the portraits hanging on the stairs, which she had bought at Christies, of the sedan chair, which contains a collection of old silver objects, including a coach and horses. 'When Queen Mary saw the coach, she wanted to take it from me.' The sedan is a very beautiful eighteenth century creation, painted with scenes and with a chinoiserie roof. I was surprised at this point to hear Bill say, 'You mustn't spit on the carpet, mother.' I had not observed this. When she at length decided to go, she said goodbye to me in a very charming manner, saying how pleased she was to have seen me and that she hoped to see me again. Nothing whatever was said about the book; no reference made to the occasions when I had gone to Eaton Square; no enquiry as to how I was getting on. One could not say whether she had forgotten about it, or did not want to hear about it. But inasmuch as she was more than usually friendly to me, I got the impression that she did not associate me with anything disagreeable and that in a vague way she was content at what I was doing. (I have now read some 45 volumes of press-cuttings relating to her and have salvaged a mass of stories and interesting anecdotes and occurrences. There remain a few more volumes and then I shall begin writing.)

Bill told me that Stanley Spencer had been taken suddenly ill and was to be operated on. It was said to be cancer of the stomach. Bill thought his chances small. He had seen him in the Canadian Hospital before dinner and had given him the present of a book of Osbert Lancaster cartoons. He told me that he had instructed the hospital to put down all expenses to him—a private room* and everything else. He also said that if Stanley recovered he had resolved to finance him so that he could finish the large picture of *Christ preaching at Cookham Regatta*, giving him £1,000 a year till it was done. 'Though where I can find room for so huge a picture in this house, I do not know.'

The conversation returned to T. E. Lawrence. Bill said that when Lawrence got to know his mother and himself, he had largely overcome the neurasthenia which overtook him in 1922. He came to Plymouth in the R.A.F. about 1929 and it was soon afterwards that the friendship began. 'He used to come to the house every night after dinner,' Lady A had told me at the dinner table. I told Bill that Villars, T.E.'s latest biographer, discussed the question of his homosexuality; what was his view on that? He said that T.E. was not a homosexual in any objective or practical sense, though he had ideal friendships with men of a highly emotional kind. 'He was a very austere man. There was something of the monk about him. One could think of him as a saint. When we knew him he was much calmer than before, and laughed and was very good and patient with myself and my brother, answering our questions with good humour.'

I left at 10.30. Bill went to the hospital to enquire further about Stanley Spencer.


*16 January 1959*

I had invited Mervyn Peake to lunch, and met him outside the London Library. We spent the afternoon together till 4.0, visiting various exhibitions. Since I saw him last Mervyn had had a mental breakdown. He told me that, exhausted by his work on the third volume of the Titus Groan trilogy, to be called *Titus Afar*,† he had lost consciousness of the past and was apparently largely oblivious of the present. He was lodged in a mental home and only after two months came back into consciousness. He was not discharged, however, for another six months. He had now taken up again his two days lecturing at the Central School of Art, and was striving to finish the book, of

* Spencer refused the private room.
† Published as *Titus Alone*, 1959.

9 Bill and Bronwen Astor

10 Cliveden

12 Barbara Hepworth at work on *The Spirit of Discovery*

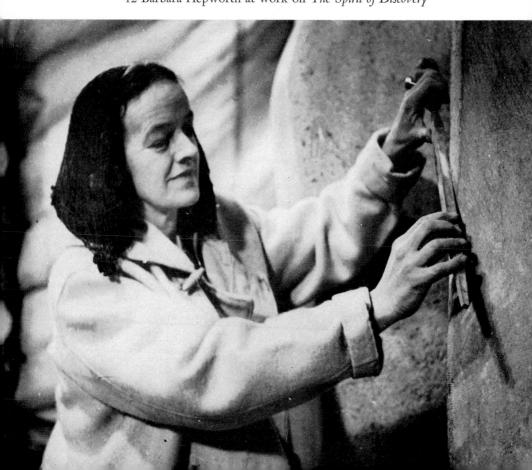

which only fifteen pages remained to be written. In appearance he was much aged and had the short hesitant step of a very old man, though he cannot be as much as fifty. He complained also that his memory was very uncertain and seemed unexpectedly to black out when in ordinary conversation.\* I had the impression that he was very fragile. In my view the two published volumes of *Titus Groan* are unique works of art. I ardently hope he will be able to finish the third.

*7 July 1959*

I went to Fabers to arrange about the photographs for the Nancy Astor book. As I was entering I saw Arthur Waley crossing the road to the far side. He caught sight of me and returned. It was a very hot day and he was dressed in a curious dark linen suit without a tie. Though bent, he looked extremely well, his face very keen, and his eye very piercing. He was exceptionally brown and though his cheeks were hollow he gave the impression of strength. He seemed immensely distinguished. He spoke of his book on the opium war and Commissioner Lin† in a mild way, saying he hoped that it was a contribution to the subject, and that anyhow he thought that Lin's diary was interesting from a literary point of view. He then said that for many years he had been contemplating the translation of *The Secret History of the Mongols*,‡ a contemporary account of Genghis Khan. It was a sort of saga, he said, part of which was in a kind of alliterative phrasing difficult to translate. He was not quite sure how it could be done as the use of alliteration might give it too much of a Nordic manner. I said I was quite sure he would solve that literary problem. He was exceptionally genial, very rare with him.

*13 August 1959*

Dropped in at Stanley Spencer's house at Cookham on account of what Astor had written. Ffrançon Davies§ came to the door looking very upset. He said, 'Stanley had a terrible relapse two nights ago. He suffered great pain. He is now asleep though he did not sleep at all in the night in spite of the drugs which were supplied.' I gathered from

\* His memory was affected by the electrical treatment he had been given.
† *The Opium War Through Chinese Eyes*, 1958.
‡ Published 1963.
§ Pianist. Close friend of Stanley Spencer.

the conversation that this appeared to be some kind of recurrence of the cancer and that the terrible operation he had undergone had not effected a cure as was hoped. This may not be so but it seemed to be what Davies feared. There was no possibility of seeing Stanley of course. I was informed he would go the next day to Cliveden hospital. The impression I carried away was that he was very seriously ill.

*3 September 1959*

Went to see Stanley Spencer, who has returned from hospital to his house in Cookham, to speak to him about the suggested book.* He said that proposals for such a book had been made to him by various publishers, but for one reason or another they had fallen through. He went on to say that in any book he would have to do a great deal of the writing. His *ipsissima verba* would be of interest and would give validity to the record of his life. In fact, he envisaged a book where the critic would only write an introduction; the rest would be culled largely from writings or notes of his own, which he had composed over the years. This did not seem to me promising, because his mind is too confused to expect from it a clear statement and his education and experience of books insufficient for him to avoid all sorts of naive statements, whose naivety might do him harm and be dull into the bargain. His writings could only be presented with very severe cutting. It seemed doubtful whether he would submit to this. I came away feeling the proposal was impracticable. Anyhow, it is for Fabers to declare definitely whether they want such a book and what form it should take. Let them make the next move. If he was more celebrated, more universally accepted, anything he said or wrote would have its audience and importance. But he has not quite that position.

*1 December 1959*

The party at the Kaplan Gallery, given to inaugurate my exhibition, began at 6 p.m. Neville Wallace, the *Observer* critic, had been in earlier when I was not there. He was reported to have said that he found the paintings 'gay and fey', by which I understand he meant to allude to their humour and something haunting about them.

Lord Astor and his mother, the famous Nancy, arrived early. He

* Astor had suggested it.

said that as he had to preside at 6.30 over a refugee committee he would have to leave before her speech, timed for 6.30. The old lady was in full character from the moment she entered. 'What's all this?' she exclaimed, pointing with indignation to the pictures. 'You ought to be ashamed of yourself,' she said to me. 'Who could live with things like that?' she demanded, her minatory finger directed towards the picture called *The Wandering Ecstatic*, the big face with the lowered eyelids and bitter mouth. We walked round. I drew her attention to some paintings which I thought would not seem strange to her. But she refused to accept any of them. They did not look to her like anything she had ever seen. Nevertheless, when we got to the *Potato Seller* in the inner room, one of the strangest faces I had on view, she exclaimed: 'I have seen people like that!' Her talk flowed out all the time. 'I know with artists one should not say these sort of things. I can't understand modern art.' And she wound up, 'You ought to be baptised,' meaning, it would seem, that I was some sort of pagan savage, who could be reformed by a knowledge of God. Having known her so long and studied her for her biography, I was not surprised or upset by what she said. It may be that she knew that, and so felt no necessity to pretend she thought otherwise. Moreover, there was something in her face which was very attractive.

If I had not known beforehand what sort of speech she would make, the dislike of my paintings which she had already expressed would have sufficed to inform me what I might expect. But I knew that all along. When I had asked Astor to make the speech and he had said that it would be far more advantageous for me if his mother did it. I had begged *him* to make it, apprehensive of her tongue. But he had insisted, 'It will be the best possible publicity.' So I was obliged to write and ask her. Last Sunday, when I dined at Cliveden, he had come up when I was writing Sir Edward Ford's invitation, and said: 'Mama is going to open Maurice's exhibition. She will say that his pictures are disgraceful, that he is a fraud and ought to be put down.' Even so, I felt no particular trepidation when I now went to Lady Astor and invited her to speak.

She opened with a couple of jokes which caused loud laughter and had no close reference to the matter in hand. She then declared her opinion of the paintings, monstrosities beyond toleration. But the diatribe was equally directed against all contemporary art except the kind she was accustomed to, the direct attempt to reproduce the appearance of things. This made some of the audience restive, some indignant, some astonished. When, pointing again to *The Wandering Ecstatic* she demanded to know who would care to have such a thing, some people waved their catalogues and said they would. Then switching, as her practice is, to irrelevant fancies as they crossed her mind, she gave an amusing imitation of a foreign notability opening a bazaar. Again her mind flickering, she spoke of how women always kept men under. She ended with a final denunciation of the pictures.

This entirely unorthodox and original way of commending the work of a man, whom she had begun by describing as a neighbour and a good neighbour, did not please her hearers. Derogatory remarks about her were heard. There was a kind of scene. Everyone was looking at me to see how I took it. I certainly felt rather embarrassed. The moment she stopped, the reporters crowded round me. 'What is your reaction to what Lady Astor has just said?' I said, 'I take it as a joke. When Lady Astor speaks in that way it is her style of humour.' The fact was that she was doing her act. As she said to me afterwards, 'I know nothing about modern art. For me to attempt an appreciation of pictures would be silly and very dull.' But her act is not dull. For years it has been news all over the world.

She left soon afterwards. I saw her to the door, and thanking her again said that I was greatly indebted to her. (And indeed for a Viscountess, a very rich woman, aged eighty and only just recovered from flu, to leave her palatial residence in Eaton Square on a foggy December night to open the exhibition of a man who had never exhibited before, was an extraordinary act of kindness, apart altogether from what she actually might say.) When I thanked her the expression on her face was humble and grateful. It was almost with emotion that she said goodbye to me. In her own undefinable way she is fond of me.

*18 December 1959*
The funeral of Stanley Spencer took place today at Cookham. His body was cremated yesterday and the little box containing his ashes was brought to Cookham. Louise and I arrived about 11.45 and found the church already full. On the way in I had a word with Astor,

who was standing outside the church door in a top hat and morning coat. I said that I hoped Stanley had not suffered much at the end; perhaps he had lost consciousness. Astor replied that he was conscious and in full command of his faculties to the last. A few minutes before he died, he had written a note (for he could not speak) to a friend (which friend I am not sure★) and having done so turned over and suddenly passed away. He had been in much discomfort but not in acute pain.

The congregation consisted chiefly of the inhabitants of Cookham. The service began by the procession to the chancel of the choir, a man carrying the box of ashes, and the vicar, Mr Westropp, reading out the opening words of the burial service. The organ played selections from Bach, favourite pieces, I believe, of Stanley's. After the lesson from Revelation XXII and the hymn 'Wake O wake the night is flying', Astor gave an address, standing on the steps of the choir. It was pitched in a personal and touching way. He described Spencer as a genius, spoke of the interest of his conversation, the freshness of his observations on life. He spoke of his own friendship with him (which dates back some five years to the day when I took him to Spencer's house on Cookham Rise). He made a correct appreciation of his art and lamented that he had not lived to finish his great picture, *Christ preaching at Cookham*.

The service in the church concluding, we went out to the church-yard for the burial of the ashes. A little hole in the grass, a foot deep or so, was ready to receive the box. Mr Westropp then read the final passages of the service and, after the words 'earth to earth' and slightly stressing the words 'ashes to ashes', he placed the box in the hole. This part was much less heartrending than the usual lowering of the coffin into a deep grave, when the fact of there being a body in the coffin, the form of the living person, and of that simulacrum being exposed to a slow and ugly corruption, is a chilling thought. But the little box of ashes seemed no more than a memento of a person who had gone. The body had vanished into the air. Its gases were already part of the living vegetable world. Nevertheless, the occasion had its poignancy. There was too the beauty of the language. When I heard the sentence: 'I heard a voice from heaven, saying unto me, write,' I was much affected.

★ It was the Rev. Michael Westropp, vicar of Cookham.

At 7 p.m. Mr Lee, the butler at Cliveden, rang up saying: 'His lordship finds himself a little short and wonders whether you can come to dinner.' I said that I thought I could just do it, and hastily changing presented myself at 8 p.m.

After dinner Bill insisted on charades, to amuse his mother, I think, as charades had always been the thing in her day. In the hall, where we had retired to, were two large wooden boxes containing clothes, wraps, hats, etc. I snatched from the women's box an extraordinary red cap which came well down over my head and seemed to have an amusing effect. On re-entering the room, Lord Grantley took my arm and we did some sort of a cabaret dance. The old lady looked on with indulgence. She has always liked this sort of thing.

After the charades it was close on midnight. The old lady now spoke of going to bed. She was in a very good mood. In the course of the evening she had been asked to do a few of her impersonations. 'Maurice wants you to do the Empress Dowager,' Bill first called out to her. 'I won't,' said the old lady, but immediately assumed the appearance of that personage. The women of the Peking *corps diplomatique* are being entertained to tea at the palace. The Empress Dowager, stiff in her chair, asks them personal questions through an interpreter—How old are you? How many children? Who is your husband? Is he rich?—the usual way Oriental grandees talk to inferiors. But only the voice of the interpreter is heard. The wives of the diplomatists see the Empress's face wrinkled in contemptuous grimaces, as she instructs soundlessly the interpreter what to ask; after each series of grimaces she composes her face and sits impassively, totally uninterested in the replies. I found the impersonation wonderfully amusing and a true revelation of Tzu Hsi. Lady Astor followed this up with mimicking an old woman. Though herself eighty, she made herself look as if she was ninety-five, nearly blind and half daft. The last piece was the impersonation of an old Jew, a tradesman or barrow man. For this she borrowed an overcoat, which was sent for from the hall, a blue overcoat far too large which hung on her in a ridiculous manner. She also had some man's hat. It was very funny; she became an old Jew.

With these histrionic triumphs cheering her up, she came to speak to me when there was the movement to go to bed. No reference whatever was made to her speech at the Kaplan Gallery. One could not guess what had passed in her mind about that affair. But, of course, it had never happened in her long life that when she spoke severely to people that she disliked them. Now, her manner to me was gentle and charming. We went into the hall. As we said good-night, she expressed great pleasure at meeting me, enquired whether my car was at the door, and told some parting anecdote, as is her way. When she went up the staircase, I looked for my coat and could not find it. Bill saw me and said: 'Oh, it's in the drawing room; Mama borrowed it for her old Jew turn.'

*30 December 1959*

Received a letter from Wingfield Digby, Keeper of Textiles in the Victoria & Albert Museum, saying that he had been much impressed by my paintings at the Kaplan and asking whether I had received my inspiration from 'a technique of meditation or by the use of drugs'.

*19 January 1960*

At 5 p.m. I went to meet Irene Stirling, of the Harvill Press, a part, it seems, of the publishers Collins. The Harvill Press want to publish a biography of Stanley Spencer and they want me to write it. That was what Miss Stirling said. I replied by explaining to her what had already occurred about such a book on Spencer, how Lord Astor was most keen on it, how Faber & Faber turned it down, and how during his last days Spencer was too difficult anyhow to have made such a book feasible. Now that he was dead, it was a question of getting hold of the papers which he had left. The first thing was to get into touch with his daughters, who presumably had inherited them. I also pointed out that a life of Spencer involved problems of a delicate nature. There was an erotic element in his art, and several women had an important part in his life. What attitude would his daughters take up in that regard? Irene Stirling seemed to think that the daughters would be sufficiently modern to wish to see their celebrated father truthfully depicted. The matter was left that I would write the book if the difficulties could be overcome and if the Harvill Press made the terms attractive.

Dined at Cliveden. I was introduced to the American Admiral Robert Dennison, who commands the Atlantic Fleet. He was a big, thick-set man with bulging eyes, a good head and an engaging manner. He looked like a sea dog. When the ladies withdrew, the Admiral moved up to sit by Bill Astor and I sat next to him. We got him to speak of two things, General MacArthur and the atom bomb on Hiroshima. It was evident that the Admiral was no admirer of MacArthur. He said: 'At the beginning of the Pacific war on Japan I was captain of a warship. Later I was a member of the Chiefs of Staff Committee in Washington. MacArthur was no strategist. His idea was a campaign where we laboriously moved forward 400 miles at a time (the range of our bombers) and he took a lot of persuading before he agreed to the leapfrog strategy of Wake Island. We told him in Australia—"We can capture Wake straight away." But he was stupidly cautious. Finally we had to order him to take it.'

In the matter of the Hiroshima atom bomb, he said: 'It was not a decision taken at the last moment. We had tried the thing out (the device without the full explosion) some time before. The question was whether it would be necessary to use the bomb. In fact, Japan was finished, but it was not known that this was so. It was believed that the bomb was necessary. Otherwise the invasion of Japan, with all the casualties and destruction entailed, would be necessary. An invasion was actually mounted in case Japan, even after the bomb, did not surrender. Moreover, it was not certain that the bomb would explode. That was the reason why the Japanese were not told it would be used if they did not surrender. If it failed to go off, it would greatly strengthen Japanese morale. Hence, it was dropped, in the confident hope that it would explode, that the explosion would finish the Japanese, and the invasion be not required. Had we known that the Japanese were about to surrender anyhow, we would not have dropped it.'

After dinner I was taken aside by Martineau.* He said that he was one of the trustees under the Stanley Spencer will. Another was Dudley Tooth.† Till Tooth returned from his holiday, no decision about the biography could be taken. He was in favour of my doing it.

* Friend and patron of Stanley Spencer.
† Spencer's London dealer.

There were large boxes of papers. Some of the drawings left by Spencer were very indecent. The trustees would have to decide what papers should be entrusted to the biographer. There was also the question of Lady Spencer; she was a difficult person. Mr Martineau talked at tedious length. I began to feel that, if I was selected as the biographer, he would be one of the difficulties.

I have forgotten to note that Stanley's brother Gilbert was also at dinner. I had rarely met him before. He is a very pleasant nice man. Martineau now suggested that I should have a word with him. Gilbert Spencer told me that he had written a 60,000 word memoir of his brother* and that it was in the hands of a publisher, though nothing had been definitely settled about its publication. I assured him that his memoir, published or not, would be most valuable for a biographer and advised him to go ahead and get what money he could.

I left feeling that everybody wanted me to write the biography— Lord Astor, Martineau, Irene Stirling, Collins and Gilbert Spencer. Tooth's concurrence had to be obtained, but as he had already asked me to do it, he was unlikely to object. The only question was whether Collins would offer sufficiently good terms. It will be a big undertaking and require much care and thought. Will such a biography sell sufficiently to make it feasible for me to undertake it?

*21 April 1960*

London. At 6 p.m. there was a party given by Fabers for authors on their list, whose books were about to appear. My *Nancy Astor* appears in a week. They had invited Lady Astor to the party, but she sent an excuse and did not come. This was a relief to me; one could not know what she might have said if there. During the party I had a talk with T. S. Eliot. Though he had been my publisher for twenty-five years, I had never spoken to him before. He is now much bent and lined, an old man, without the look of an old man, whose intellect is still in full vigour. His young wife was with him, a beautiful woman of about 37, somewhat Venetian renaissance front face and Pre-Raphael-ite side face. He spoke of his wedding and how he managed to elude the press reporters. He was not caught at the wedding or on the

* Although called *Stanley Spencer* (published 1961), this memoir is mainly about Gilbert.

honeymoon in the south of France until the last day. I told him that once when I was in du Sautoy's* room he popped his head in dressed up as Father Christmas—a long time ago now. He had no recollection of ever having dressed up as Father Christmas. When talking some minutes later to Jean Kennerley, with whom and Morley Kennerley* he had recently gone on holiday to Africa and missed by a few days being mixed up in the Agadir earthquake, she said that she did not think he would write more. He was occupied in putting his papers in order. During the African tour, she said, he was up and down in spirits and rather fussy about his health. He leant much on his wife, who looked after him with devoted care. I noticed that when he talked to me his eye was very kind. He is gentle and apparently worn out.

### 26 April 1960

London. I went by appointment for a short chat with Sir John Rothenstein about Stanley Spencer. Rothenstein was exceptionally polite. He came down to the hall to meet me and took me into his room. He said that he first made the acquaintance of Spencer in 1923. In 1938, soon after he had been appointed Director of the Tate and while he was living at Swiss Cottage, Spencer came up from Cookham to see him and his wife Elizabeth. It got late and Elizabeth asked him to stay the night. In the event he stayed six weeks. It was the moment of his greatest destitution and the year after the brutal disillusion of his second marriage. He had just been turned out of his house, Lindworth, by his second wife, to whom imprudently he had conveyed the house. During his stay with Rothenstein he made a confidante of Elizabeth Rothenstein and told her in intimate detail all about his relations with his first wife, Hilda, and second wife, Patricia. Elizabeth took down during the six weeks all he said. 'When war broke out and the bombing began,' Rothenstein told me, 'Elizabeth was afraid that this highly indiscreet record might conceivably fall into other hands and carefully burnt all she had written.' I assured Rothenstein that one need not regret this, because I had found among his papers, written by him, a very full account of these same misadventures. 'We might have known,' said Rothenstein, 'that we were not his only confidants.' I replied that I did not say he had

* Directors of Faber & Faber.

other confidants, but that he had written down what he told Elizabeth.

I asked Rothenstein whether he thought there was anything to be said for Patricia. He replied immediately, 'Nothing whatever.'

It was arranged that what letters they have, and the correspondence between Spencer and the Tate, would be sent to me. He and Elizabeth would call in at Maidenhead one day when driving up to their house in Oxford.

## 30 April 1960

My *Nancy Astor* was published yesterday and I was glad to accept Bill Astor's invitation to dinner at Cliveden tonight. Besides I wanted to talk to him about Stanley Spencer. As he has been away in New York, it is a couple of months or more since I had seen him. As I am much attached to him, I missed him badly.

I found Bill mixing cocktails. I asked him what was his mother's reaction to the book, now that it was out. He said that she had made three objections. If she had wanted a biography written, she would have arranged for it herself; she did not like it being dedicated to persons she had never heard of;* she had dipped into the book and found it dull. I said: 'That is very mild. I am getting off lightly.' He said she was staying the weekend and would be appearing any minute. Meanwhile I was introduced to Sir John Wolfenden, Vice-Chancellor of Reading University, the author of the Wolfenden report on prostitution and homosexuality. Next appear Dr Ward, the osteopath, Bill's great friend, and a most friendly charming man, who besides being a Harley Street specialist, is an amateur artist of talent. Finally the old lady herself, dressed in pale silk. She shook hands with me gently. I was careful to say nothing about the book, but the subject was immediately raised by those about me. Then she said what Bill told me she had said—that if she had wanted a biography she would have seen to it herself. I replied apologetically: 'We can't help admiring you and saying so.' She remained silent a moment and then said: 'That's subtle.' And taking my arm drew me aside and in a voice lowered so much (as if not to be overheard) that I found it impossible to be sure what she said, asked me apparently about Bill's plans for a third marriage. I said that I knew nothing about it. (The

* It is dedicated to a director of Fabers, Morley Kennerley, and his wife.

rumour that he intends to marry Miss Pugh, the model, is very strong. Michael Westropp, the vicar of Cookham, mentioned it to me when I dropped into the churchyard to see the daffodils. He spoke as if it was certain and deplored it, feeling that Miss Pugh was much too young, a disparity that is alleged to have bedevilled the second marriage.)

I was able to entertain the top end of the table with unknown items from Stanley Spencer's papers. Bill was surprised to learn, for instance, that the great *Christ preaching at Cookham Regatta* which he bought and which is unfinished, was only part of a vast never-painted series of *Regatta* pictures. He cried: 'I offered him all the money he wanted for the rest of his life if he would concentrate on his imaginative figure compositions, but he kept on saying that he must do this landscape or that, these roses or those cabbages, for old persons in the village.' I also said something about the connection between Spencer's ideas and the orgiastic side of various religions—for instance in Tantric Buddhism.

After dinner Bill put on a few amusing records—one of them a Bengali visiting Bernard Shaw's house, as caricatured by some English comedian. The copy of the Bengali accent was marvellous. One was convulsed with laughter. Dr Ward showed me his drawing of Stanley Spencer, owned by Bill and hung in one of the principal bathrooms upstairs.

Later in the hall the old lady talked to me pleasantly. 'I still play twelve holes a day,' she said. 'I remember,' said I, 'that your handicap was fifteen.' 'I got it down to twelve,' she corrected me. She looked round wistfully: 'How I wish I was still living at Cliveden,' she said. She began to ascend the grand staircase. I called a compliment after her. 'Shut up,' she said.

*5 May 1960*

I went to bring Sir Gerald Kelly, P.P.R.A.* a piece of Burmese silk which he had asked me for, when I met him at the Royal Academy private view. He had then said, as we stood under the Stanley Spencer pictures, that Spencer was 'a silly ass but a good artist'. One of my objects in seeing him today was to talk about Spencer, whom in 1950 he had induced to return to the Academy. I rang and Sir Gerald

* Past President of the Royal Academy.

132

opened the door. We went through into his studio. Nothing was changed in this big house; it was as I knew it years ago when I used to dine there.

When we had sat down, he told me a secret about Stanley Spencer. Munnings had tried to ruin him. The story was as follows: In 1952, when Kelly was P.R.A., Munnings was P.P.R.A. and Spencer R.A., having been re-elected in 1950, much to Munnings's annoyance, because he hated both him and his work. Kelly returned from a visit to America to find that Munnings was trying to get the law officers of the Crown, particularly the Attorney General, to institute a prosecution against Stanley Spencer for selling obscene pictures painted by him. Apparently some of these pictures were in the hands of a dealer, who was offering them to amateurs of pornography. Munnings heard of this and saw his chance to revenge himself (as he candidly admitted to Kelly) on Spencer. By a subterfuge he managed to obtain a view of the pictures and had them photographed. These photographs he showed to some members of the police force and, fortified by their opinion that a prosecution was practicable, approached the law officers. He also sought the support of the Church, for he showed the photographs to the Dean of Westminster in, said Kelly, the United Services Club. Kelly told me that he was profoundly angered by this. For many reasons he thought Munnings was acting disgracefully. The pictures, no doubt, were obscene. He was shown at least one of the photographs. He went to the Attorney General; as a result of their talk, any idea of a prosecution was given up.

### 13 May 1960

It occurred to me today that the early Stanley Spencer, always thought of as haunted by Christian visions, the painter of *The Nativity, Zacharias, The Visitation*, etc. never had specifically Christian visions as a youth. His feeling that the divine resided everywhere was, like Wordsworth's, a pagan vision. He merely used a Christian nomenclature under the pictures; used stories from the Bible to hang his pantheism on. Therefore there was no break later, no falling away from Christian ideals. He simply developed like the pagan he was. His painting became more overtly pagan as he grew older. His vision was always of the Golden Age, when everybody could do what they liked, when love was free, there was no death, no suffering, no judgment, no condemnation, no division of the good from the bad, no sin, no sinners, and where the animals too shared or were part of a universal divinity.

*14 June 1960*

Met Henry Rushbury at the Royal Academy to talk about Stanley Spencer. He spoke of how S.S. conducted his instructional classes in the Academy. He said that it was very unorthodox. He was very vague and didn't really get down to telling the students anything. In short, it was the eternal monologue again, the revelation of how he himself painted and the meaning he attributed to what he did. But, said Rushbury, the students themselves were very thrilled; they liked it more than the usual instruction or lecture, they thought he was a prophet.

I then asked Rushbury how he would advise me to treat Munnings's attempt to blacken S.S.'s reputation on account of certain erotic drawings in the hands of a dealer. He said he thought it should be regarded as a brawl. Munnings, he said, was always brawling. He, Rushbury, knew Munnings very well. His usual form of conversation was shouting and abuse; that was the way he spoke normally. Rushbury recounted several amusing anecdotes about Munnings including one connected with a Norwich exhibition of his pictures. He and Rushbury went up and were the guests of some important local personage. There was to be a big dinner in the evening with Munnings the guest of honour. After tea their host placed a car at their disposal and they drove round the country looking at churches and views. When it was time to go back, Munnings saw a horse in a field and shouted 'That horse is starving', and told the chauffeur to stop. He got out with Rushbury and they climbed into the field. Yes, said Munnings, the horse is starving, and he insisted on walking up to a farm house half a mile away, knocking at the door and demanding hay. This they carried back to the horse. By this time it was very late and when they arrived back at their host's house the guests had already assembled for dinner and he was waiting on the steps. Munnings emerged from the car in a rage. Pointing at his host he accused him in the most abusive way of starving horses, although it was by no means clear that the horse was his or even that it was hungry, as it seems to have been in a good field. He then refused to come to dinner and it was only with great difficulty that Rushbury got him into his evening clothes and brought him down. That was typical of the man.

It seemed to me, however, that in this case with S.S. it was more than a brawl. He was opposed to artists who differed from him. That perhaps would have been normal, but why in this case did he attempt to expose S.S. and harm him? Rushbury said that Munnings could not bear another artist in the R.A. getting more public acclaim than he; S.S. was getting more at that time; hence the enmity.

*21 July 1960*

Went to Cookham at 3 p.m. to see Westropp, the vicar, and talk about Stanley Spencer. When he was at the Canadian Hospital at Cliveden during his last illness, Westropp and also his wife Rachel visited him nearly every day. He was worn to a skeleton and found it increasingly difficult to speak. But he liked visitors and used to write his replies on pads. As all his life he had written his thoughts on pads this was no strain. Westropp gave me five pads of notes and I must try to decipher them. I asked what appeared to be Stanley's attitude to Christianity. Rachel Westropp was sure that he believed in the divinity of Christ. Westropp said, however, that he did not ask for any of the ministrations of the Church nor did he ever speak about what might be his fate after death, though he had an inclination to believe in Paradise and to reject any idea of punishment before or after a Last Judgment. Westropp's habit of reciting a Blessing before he left each night pleased S.S. because, said Westropp, he liked the beauty of the words, for the Blessing was the great one, from Numbers 6–25: 'The Lord bless you and keep you. The Lord make his face to shine upon you and be gracious unto you. The Lord lift up the light of his countenance upon you and give you peace, now and forever more.' Stanley was excited to feel that this great Blessing had come all the way from Aaron, its beauty having made it indestructible and endowed it with a potency which remained unabated, so that now in Cliveden hospital, thousands of years later, it spread its peace as it had in Aaron's day.

On the night of Stanley's death, Rachel Westropp was with him at 7 p.m. When his supper was brought in he had some difficulty in raising the food to his lips. It was prunes and he struggled with his fork and spoon to get the stone from the prune. 'Let me feed you,' said she. She had fed him on previous visits sometimes. But he was obstinate that night. 'I can do it,' he said, and he got the stones out and managed to lift the spoon to his mouth. He also lifted up his tumbler of water. 'But,' said she to me, 'after taking a sip he seemed to forget the tumbler and let it rest against his mouth a long time. He did not seem fully conscious of his surroundings and had his eyes raised and a smile on his lips. After silence for a while he spoke of the colour of the nurse's cloak, saying it was beautiful. Then he said to me: "I do not want to speak any more. But sit there so that I may look at you." And he gazed at me for a long time. It was as if he knew that he would never see me again. When it was time to go I wished him farewell.' Such was Rachel Westropp's statement to me.

Westropp then said that he went to the hospital soon after—about 9 p.m.—and sat with Stanley, who sometimes spoke and sometimes wrote remarks on a pad. After half an hour or so he thought he should go as Stanley seemed tired. He said: 'I think you are getting weary, Stanley, shall I leave you?' S.S. wrote on the pad quickly in answer: 'I most certainly am not (two words illegible) I am never weary, never bored. Why should you think I am? If you think I am that, you can go somewhere else. Sadness and sorrow are not me.' Westropp continued to me: 'So I stayed on as he wanted. Presently the nurse came and gave him his injection for the night. "Beautifully done," he said to her in thanks, for some of the sisters were rather clumsy. Those were his last words, for very soon afterwards he turned his head away to the right and stretched out his left arm. He had hardly done this when, as I looked, I saw that he was gone. It was hard to believe. He was gone so suddenly. Neither he nor I had any idea that he was on the brink of death. I had not given him the Blessing.'

I told Westropp of some of the contents of the Spencer papers. In this connection he asked me whether I had seen S.S.'s picture of Hilda* and himself which he kept hidden under the bed in the spare-room. It was with Tooth, he said. Tooth had it hidden somewhere. It depicted Hilda in the nude on a bed and the nude Stanley approaching her with an erection. It was beautifully painted, said Westropp.

* The first Mrs Spencer.

Stanley, who had been thoroughly alarmed by the Munnings affair of 1952, was careful not to let it be seen, even hanging on his own walls, though he was very fond of the picture.

### 17 August 1960

Met Ffrançon Davies, the pianist, and took him for a drink at the Bel and the Dragon bar in Cookham. In a conversation lasting two hours he said a number of interesting things about Stanley Spencer whom he knew from about 1947 onwards. Davies is an easy and agreeable man to talk to; he is intelligent, thinks and reads, and gives clear answers. His testimony is valuable.

I was pleased to find that he confirmed a view which I had gradually formed from reading the Spencer papers. Stanley, he said, was *au fond* a man of monkish temperament, whose inclination was to sublimate sex and who never ran after women. The four women in his life he liked better on paper than in the physical reality. His writings to them were consummation, which he enjoyed better than the real thing. They were both imaginative consummation and consummation by proxy, for sometimes he accompanied the writing of them by masturbation and emissions.

One of the difficulties with Hilda was that she was first and foremost a member of a clan, the Carlines. She was always more Miss Carline than Mrs Spencer. Stanley was treated by her mother, Mrs Carline, a regular matriarch, as a hanger on, the last person in the house to be considered. Hilda was a remarkable woman in some ways, but she was not a mother or wife. She was too absorbed in her own thoughts, too prone to a kind of meditation which was extremely self-centred. She was so much more interested in herself than in Stanley that he was unable to integrate her in his artistic life. Moreover, she was always retreating from him into the Carline clan. She was never quite sane. 'Just my luck to have married a lunatic,' Stanley once said to Davies.

From this intense strange personality it was a relief to Stanley to turn to Patricia,\* who was worldly in comparison. She gave him many things which Hilda could not.

Davies then spoke of Stanley's enigmatical character. 'He was truly an extraordinary man. There was something so vital about his face

\* Patricia Preece, later Spencer's second wife.

137

and expression, the carriage of his head. He was a true musician, for he had the power of hearing music inside himself, music which he actually heard, not merely thought of, music which was as loud as if it was being played, the same gift as the deaf Beethoven's. He knew every note of all the Bach fugues. His playing, too, was that of a musician, the rapt mood of a musician. He could have been a musician instead of a painter. Once when I asked him which, he thought awhile and then said, a painter. To know intimately as I did, he was most strange and a little mad. Seen in his long shabby coat, with his package under his arm, his curious gaze, his rodent-like scurry, he was an arresting figure in Cookham High Street. As he passed the shop girls would titter.'

In Davies's view, Stanley derived his main ideas from his own cogitations. His ideas are related to certain oriental religious systems, but he knew nothing of such Indian and Chinese philosophers. He had nothing of their intelligence as philosophers, but his mind some-how carried him to their conclusions. 'There was something cosmic about him.'

Davies continued that as an artist he integrated with himself every-thing which he saw and experienced. 'He crawled over things like an ant. That was why everything seemed extraordinary to him. He was like a midget looking at a giant, as in a Gulliver story.' And he remarked: 'It was impossible for him, wrapped up as he was in the mystery of his being, to have friends in the ordinary sense.'

Davies further said: 'His monologues were his method of releasing thoughts, so that he could use them in his art. Hence he had no ordinary conversation. In fact, when speaking, he was not conversing, but was reflecting out loud. He expected from those close to him an undeviating interest and attendance on himself. He was put out if they ceased ministering to him for a moment. I have heard him call it a disloyalty when I went out to post a letter without telling him.'

The last thing Davies said was: 'Stanley did not wash. He had some theory of natural oils, which a wash drained uselessly away. But, though he and his clothes were dirty, he did not smell. It was as if he had some strange kind of natural fragrance.'

Davies made another observation which I have omitted. He said: 'Stanley did not go back into the past in the sense of founding his paintings on early recollections, but he brought the past into the present. His pictures contain a quantity of references to former events or impressions, but were now constructions of his imagination. He lived in what was both past and present; his pictures were a subtle amalgam of the two.'

*9 October 1960*

Dine at Cliveden. On entering the hall Mr Lee, the butler, told me that Sir Alun and Lady Pugh, Bronwen's parents, were in the drawing room. That immediately suggested to me that the long expected engagement between Bill Astor and Bronwen was about to be announced. I went in and made their acquaintance. It appeared that Bronwen's sisters were expected for dinner and were staying the night. The likelihood of something definite about the marriage emerging was increased. There were very few guests, but Nancy, Lady Astor was present.

After dinner there was not much chance of conversation because an Eton master, one of the guests, gave a sort of music-hall turn at the piano. At the close of it Bronwen came up and asked me to sign the application for a new passport—the usual certificate that I knew her and that she was a suitable person. I did so and took it to mean that she would soon need a passport for a honeymoon. She gave no hint, however. It was just that her old passport had run out.

Old Lady Astor had kept fairly quiet, though she was heard at one point to say that she thought Bronwen 'the best of the bunch'. In the hall, when I was saying goodnight, she came out with a story which I had not heard her tell—A man, whose wife is ill, hurries to the doctor's house and rings. The maid opens. 'Is the doctor at home?' 'No,' says the maid. 'Is the doctor's wife at home?' 'No,' says the maid, and beckoning, says, 'Come in!'—the old lady told the story with that air of immense drollery and enjoyment which is character-istic of her. As she beckoned, the expression in her eyes was very funny indeed.

'Do you know, Mama,' said Bill, 'that if Mr Collis had put into the book all he might have about you, he'd have made a lot more money. I should say you have impoverished him to the extent of £2,000.' 'I know,' she said with a solemnity which you could take any way you liked. The old joke about not knowing my name is still on. Bill said laughing: 'The other day we were talking about a Mr

Collins, a rather unpleasant sort of dago type, and she said, "Ah, that's the man who wrote my life!"'

### 13 October 1960

Miss Thom, the secretary at Cliveden, rang up this morning to ask me to come up tomorrow and drink a glass of champagne with Lord Astor at 12. I said to her, 'What is the occasion?' She said, 'I am not allowed to say.' 'Well, I have guessed it.' 'Don't tell anybody.' However, I had not really guessed it for I did not know whether the occasion was to announce the engagement between Bill Astor and Bronwen Pugh or whether it was to be the marriage itself. But the more I thought of it, the more likely I considered it that it would be the marriage and I thought that the registrar would someway or other be asked to come to the house. As the wedding supposition was the more likely of the two, I looked for a little present which would be suitable and came on one of the mother-of-pearl plates which I had had made for me in Mergui* from oysters of exceptionally large size, the plates having the added attraction that, when put up to the light, a scene, not unlike a scene in the Mergui archipelago, was disclosed in colour.

### 14 October 1960

At noon I presented myself at Cliveden with my plate which I left in the car, till I knew what was going to happen. It was then that I learned that the marriage had already taken place in the registrar's office at Hampstead that morning between 9 and 10, and that they had motored down to Cliveden afterwards. The chapel ceremony was merely a homily and blessing. As soon as the bride and bridegroom returned from the chapel I went in and shook hands and said that I had no idea that the wedding was that day but that nevertheless I had brought a present.

At the lunch there were some attempts at speeches, old Lady Astor making one of them, and of course when she speaks it is always a success. She rolled off her stories. Photographs of the bride and bridegroom were handed round. It appeared that a reporter had managed to take a photograph outside the Pughs' house in Hampstead

* In Burma.

at the moment when Astor and his bride were leaving for the registrar's office.

## 1 December 1960

Today I went by appointment to Moor Thatch* to see Dorothy Hepworth. She had written to say that she was willing to talk to me, but that Patricia, Lady Spencer, was too ill to see anyone. I went in some trepidation, for Moor Thatch had taken on in my mind a rather sinister shape. No one I had seen had a good word for Patricia and Dorothy. The general story was that they were Lesbians who had tricked S.S. into marriage with the former in order to get his money. All the people who said this were friends of Stanley's. The allegations, however, were not borne out by the contemporary papers in the Spencer boxes. It was a story which took form later. It was essential, therefore, to hear what was said by the women themselves. I was only going to see one of them, but that would be some evidence.

The wooden gate of Moor Thatch garden was difficult to open. By pushing, however, I got into the overgrown garden. The path was covered by heavy grass. When I rang the hall door bell, Dorothy Hepworth opened it. I recognised her at once as a woman I have seen from time to time for many years, on the Maidenhead platform, in art galleries and quite recently in Bond Street. But though I knew her so well by sight I had never ascertained who she was. Now I knew. She is a smallish woman with white hair parted on one side and with a round plump face. Her smile was agreeable but in repose her features and eyes had rather a startling look, which was a little disconcerting.

I began by explaining the genesis of the book and then said that I would like what information she cared to give about Patricia and Stanley. She replied that she could give me no information directly about Patricia, who when well enough would speak for herself, but that she would give her own feelings about Stanley.

She then explained that she was a very old friend of Patricia whom she had met at the Slade just after the 1914–18 war and they had lived together ever since. They first met S.S. in 1929. From the very first she had not liked him. His habits were rather disgusting, scratching his hair and picking his nose at meals and never washing, even his

* The Cookham home of Lady Spencer, Stanley's second wife, and of her friend, Dorothy Hepworth.

hands. While he was deferential to people of position and got on well with Cookham people by whom he wanted to be liked, he had a bullying way with women. His temper was short and he would shout at them. Though it was her house she could not prevent him frequently calling to see Patricia. She had suffered a long time from his endless monologues which she found meaningless and very boring. She considered him a little mad.

Her view on his art was that in his early work there was a natural and genuine poetic expression, but that later on it became forced and theatrical. He wanted to draw attention to himself by shocking. No one could claim that he had any sense of quality in paint. As for his writings, she had never been able to read his pads and considered his pretensions as a writer ridiculous.

It was at this point that she came out with the big surprise of the interview. She said: 'The reason that I can only feel dislike for S.S. is that he spread the story after the breakdown of the marriage that Patricia and I were lesbians. This was a complete fabrication. But it was believed in some quarters, and has done us a great deal of harm in the village. When we heard about the slander there was nothing we could do. If I had had a brother I would have asked him to go and give Spencer a thrashing. To have brought an action for slander would have been an appalling course with all the horrible publicity it would have involved.'

She said all this with great earnestness. I reflected that though Spencer makes the charge in his papers, the charge does not appear till after he had quarrelled with Patricia. During the five years 1933 to 1937 when he knew her intimately, seeing her every day, painting her in the nude, spending money on her, begging her to marry him, a period when if she was a lesbian he must have known it, there is no allegation to that effect. Nor does, if I remember rightly, the charge occur in his draft autobiography.

She convinced me that she was speaking the truth.

28 February 1961

I went to see Dudley Tooth.* He had returned from his American tour and had read the same amount of the Spencer book as Astor. Though he was not pained in the same way as Astor was, he was

* Spencer's dealer and one of his executors.

surprised and also rather angry that he had been taken in so much and had believed everything Stanley told him.* In his capacity as executor, he accepted the truth of what was there, and did not suggest that I should do more than modify some of my expressions here and there. I told him that I was quite ready to do that, and that it had been understood from the beginning that I would at first put down more than was likely to be actually printed.

After an hour's talk with him, the other two executors, Jack Martineau and Mr Sheil, appeared. They had not read the book and were told that it was likely to surprise them when they got it. Tooth's idea was that I should make the amendments and send them both the present text and the amendments so as to show them first of all what the full truth was and then how far I had already gone to modify or soften it. He thought that if I did that, they were less likely to make objections than if they saw only the revised text without the other.

Tooth was very excited about the book. I told him one of Astor's objections was that he, Dudley Tooth, was its hero; he was not displeased with this.

### 5 March 1961

Finished the Spencer book today. It has taken me just four months to write and it is almost exactly a year since I received the papers. I think there will be less objection taken to the concluding part and when the amendments have been made it will probably pass.

### 13 March 1961

Tooth's Augustus John party. There was a large gathering. Dudley Tooth had sent his Bentley to Augustus John's house in the country and brought him up. There was an idea that at eighty-three he would be too tired to stand at a cocktail party and talk to everybody, and Tooth had thought of giving him a chair in an alcove and only letting two people speak to him at once. This was unnecessary, for he insisted on standing and talking like anyone else. He looked very old and unkempt. He had a noble and rather disapproving look on his face, the sort of look that a great dog sometimes has, the disapproval being mellow and as it were disillusioned, and in some degree droll. There were two rooms full of his paintings, which Dudley Tooth is reputed

* Chiefly the fictitious story of his second marriage.

to have dug out of his cellar. There were sketches or works which he had abandoned long ago. And there were a number of drawings. They were lively with an assured brush stroke. Perhaps their main interest was that they were by Augustus John.

### 4 April 1961

I called on William Collins at his office to enquire his opinion of the book, for he had been reading it for the first time during the weekend, and to find out what line he intended to take at the executors' meeting in the afternoon at Tooth's. He told me at once that he thought the book very well done, that it was skilfully balanced, and that the art side was clearly integrated with the private life. There seemed nothing objectionable about it and he did not see how the executors could find fault. I warned him that Martineau and Shiel were likely to do so and that we should be prepared. He advocated saying little and if they refused their sanction, to retire and consult his solicitors. But to feel our way and not use threats. Mrs Villiers, the head of the Harvill side of Collins, would accompany him.

At 4.30 we three were ushered in. Dudley Tooth as usual was very pleasant in manner, but the other two looked glum. The proceedings were opened by Martineau asking Collins to give his opinion of the book. He repeated what he had said to me in the morning. This seemed to surprise them a little, as if they had expected Collins to be lukewarm. On learning that on the contrary he was warmly in support, they stated categorically, Tooth backing them up, that they thought the book defamatory to Spencer and were opposed to its publication. Mrs Villiers then asked them to state more particularly what parts of it they objected to, so that amendments could be discussed. Martineau declared that he objected to it all and that he did not think it could be satisfactorily amended. It would have to be entirely rewritten. Pressed further by Mrs Villiers to be more definite, he cited some trivial matters, that, for instance, no mention was made in the book of S.S.'s pencil and oil portraits, that certain indecent words were quoted, that there was too much about sex. Martineau seemed very much upset. Shiel, old and small, remained quiet though he made it clear that he agreed that the book should not be published. It seemed a blank negative; they refused to agree that we should attempt to amend those passages in the book which, if amended, might meet their objections; the book should be rejected out of hand.

I had said little or nothing hitherto, but now intervened. I pointed out that if my book was not published, some other person would publish a book which might be purely sensational. There were publishers ready to offer a lot of money for such a book. The papers under their control were not essential; a writer of a sensational book could manage without them, as so much was common knowledge and also because there were other papers.

Dudley Tooth then said that, as executors, they could not be blamed for what some future writer might say, but that they would be blamed in my case, because they would be sponsoring the book.

I replied that I well understood their desire to protect themselves, but in doing so they should beware of exposing S.S.'s memory to the danger of a book over which they could exercise no control. Here they had, in my case, a book which they could control. I had always from the start made it clear that I would be guided by the executors' wishes and in submitting the book had understood that it would be subject to their amendment. I strongly advised them to take the opportunity of the controlled book now offered to them. I also drew their attention to the matter of Patricia, Lady Spencer, declaring that as a man of honour I could not leave her in the lurch. Shiel remarked that he did not suppose she would wish such a book as mine to be published; I assured him that on the contrary she now counted on my vindication.

Then suddenly and unexpectedly the executors abandoned their negative attitude. They agreed to study the text and note in the margin those places where they desired cuts or additions. In short, they agreed to do what was the only reasonable thing. Dudley Tooth seemed very pleased that Martineau and Shiel had withdrawn their embargo.

I then remarked that the amendments would entail extra work for me; that the publication would have to be postponed until after Christmas, as what they proposed would take time; that the serial rights and American advance on which I had been counting for my livelihood this year, would not come in till next year and might be affected detrimentally by the delay. They replied warmly that they recognised that and would compensate me for the extra work and delay.

As we left, Dudley Tooth asked me privately not to forget to let him have a copy of the original unexpurgated text for his private record. He seemed delighted at the result. 'It will be a good book,' he assured me. As I walked down Bruton Street with Collins and Mrs Villiers, they could not make out how it happened that the executors had so suddenly given in. It seems to have been that Shiel saw the sense of my arguments and that Tooth realised this and quickly suggested they should all work on the book.

*21 April 1961*

At a party in Cookham I was able to have a word with Unity Spencer, S.S.'s younger daughter. She wanted, of course, to know whether she could read the book before publication and I said that she would have to arrange that with the executors. She then went on to ask me what it was the executors wished to cut out. I replied that I did not know, but that I didn't think there was anything that should be cut out. The book seemed to me to be a clear, objective and reasonable account of her father's life, with an interpretation of his pictures that was quite original; if anything was cut it would be to the detriment of the argument. She rather surprised me by her attitude because she then said she didn't think anything should be cut out, and hoped that nothing would be, and asked me whether she might be allowed, if anything was deleted, to read the original unexpurgated edition.

Nevertheless, I think it would not be safe to trust her because she has shown herself in the past to be too influenced by other persons. If she was to read the book, then her sister Shirin would have to read it too. This would greatly increase my work and in the end would amount to very little. These people have nothing to add for the very simple reason that they have not read the papers. In my conversation with Unity I pointed this out to her. She said that while it was true she had never read a word of the papers, in the later years of her father's life he had told her a good deal. I asked whether he had ever told her the interpretation of the *Hilda Apotheosis*, the culminating work of his life. I said that in the papers there was a letter to her which had never been sent where he gave a rather limited interpretation of that picture. She replied that it was true that her knowledge of the picture was confined to the fact that she had actually seen it hanging in his studio for a long time, that is, seen the canvas with the drawing. She understood that it had to do with her mother and Hampstead Heath, but had no idea what it meant.* It was of course impossible to make out the work from the pencil drawing on the canvas, as I myself experienced when I saw it in Tooth's gallery. Even a photograph yielded no results. So that Unity is not to be blamed for her ignorance; but she had heard of his idea to have some sort of memorial chapel with four rooms dedicated to the women in his life.

*22 April 1961*

Dined at Cliveden. It seemed extraordinary to see Lord Alexander there at the table, sitting so quietly and unassumingly. He is a smaller man than I imagined, and hasn't a large head. He is now seventy and has suffered recently from heart attacks and so looks a little shaky. His manner was very charming to the people beside him at the table. After dinner he came up to me and began at once to discuss the Dufy which was on one of the easels there, a scene of the Doge's Palace in Venice. From what he said it was clear that he had a very good grasp of modern art and understood the drift of Dufy; and I remembered, of course, that he himself paints and sometimes even has exhibited in the Academy. Everything he said about the Dufy was true and refreshing. 'He has imposed himself on us; once you have seen his work you never forget it. Why I could see that was a Dufy from the other end of the room.' We then looked at the Stanley Spencer portrait of Bill Astor which was close by. His criticism here was that the background was given the same value as the figure, and that he would have preferred to have thrown a wash over it to make it a little less distinct; but that of course was not the way Stanley painted his landscape backgrounds. He never muted passages in the distance. Astor himself was with us at this moment. It has always been thought that this portrait was unlike him, and I myself had thought so, but curiously enough about a week before, when I was speaking to him alone about the Spencer book, he turned his face and I saw the exact likeness which is in the portrait. I said so now to Lord Alexander,

---

* It represented her mother having an orgasm on Hampstead Heath.

who felt that the likeness was not good, but Astor was impressed by what I had seen. No one had ever seen any likeness before.

Having in this way broken the ice by talking with this very famous soldier about these examples of modern art, I then said to him something about the Burma campaign. He replied, 'Why, that was a disgraceful defeat; all I did was to extricate the army.' I said, 'But you extricated it with marvellous sangfroid.' Then we came to the question of the famous block at Taukkyan on the Prome road.* He said, 'I have had some bad moments in my life but that was the worst. But the Japanese would never have got me even if they had attacked, or if we had failed to get through the block. I would have gone into the jungle by myself or with a few of my officers and we would somehow or other have got to Tharrawaddy.'† (It was wonderful the way he remembered the Burmese names.) And he gave me his explanation of how the road block came to be there and why it was suddenly removed, and no attack made on the British forces. This was the same as that in my book *Last and First in Burma* and in General Kirby's official history of the same episode. The Japanese thought Alexander and his men were no more than a small force sent to threaten their flank. They had no conception that it was the whole British army escaping. Needless to say, they had no idea that they were letting loose the future victor in North Africa and Italy, the man in fact who turned the tide and made the defeat of the Germans in 1945 possible.

Lord Alexander spoke in detail of that week in 1942. How Wavell briefed him on Calcutta airfield on 4 March, saying he must hold on. How he arrived in Burma on 5 March and how Hutton‡ had told him: 'It is unsafe to stay, we should leave at once.' But he said to me, 'How could I leave straight away like that, how could any general on the very first day of his command start bolting without even trying to retrieve the situation? I couldn't do it, I had to try something. Hutton had his troops, some at Pegu and some a hundred miles north. The Japanese infiltration had been between them and the obvious thing to do was to try and close the gap and I gave the order. But of course it was too late and nothing could be done. I saw that im-

---

* The only escape from Rangoon.
† On the road some miles north of the block.
‡ Lt General Sir Thomas Hutton, K.C.I.E., C.B., M.C.

mediately and ordered the evacuation of Rangoon to start at dawn. And he went on then to say how they were blocked but, he said, 'I was only a day later than Hutton suggested. For all we know the block would have been there if I had left when Hutton wanted. I think it was almost certainly there. We were fated to meet that block. But,' he continued (we were standing all this time behind Bronwen's chair in the little space between that and the portrait), 'I felt that all would be well. I felt that something would happen to get me through.' I said: 'It was your own private genius speaking to you; there was nothing else that could tell you.' He said, 'Yes; in something I wrote the other day I said that it was my angel.'

It was at this point that Lady Alexander came up saying, 'Alex, it is time to go home, it is very late.' It was in fact twenty minutes to midnight. They had driven over from Windsor. 'I don't want to go,' he said, 'I'm having a very exciting conversation.' She said, 'We have to go.' So he was dragged off by his wife and that was the end of the party.

*14 July 1961*

London. The final consultation with Tooth, representing the Spencer executors, took place today. I first went to the Harvill Press in Lower Belgrave Street to pick up Irene Stirling. Gathering up the papers, which included two typescript copies of the book, we set out to find a taxi. We were hardly in the road before a taxi rounded the corner. In an effort to stop it, Irene dropped her copy of the book which fell on to the street. The pages were not secured and the wind scattered them in all directions. With the help of passers-by they were all recovered before the traffic had run over them. Bundling into the taxi with the loose pages stuffed in after us we set out and managed to rearrange them in order before we reached Tooth's gallery. 'In the East,' I said, 'this would be taken as some sort of an omen, perhaps a good one.' 'Yes, and I'm very superstitious too. But it is clearly a good omen. That we have recovered the book in its entirety surely must mean that the executors will now pass it as it stands.'

We went into Tooth's sanctum. He was very amenable. He took the responsibility of sanctioning everything except in three cases, in which he said that he must get the concurrence of the other two executors. This was a great relief. On saying goodbye Tooth assured me how glad he was that the matter had been amicably settled. He would recommend that the three outstanding points should be passed in the sense which we recommended.

*22 July 1961*

Dined at Cliveden. I had a little chat with Bronwen on the sofa. She said that when Bill had returned from lunching at the Hongkong Bank one day he said to her that he had mentioned my name in connection with their book. I expect he did, but I know he doesn't claim that he got me the commission. In fact, it could not have been that because the suggestion was made from Hong Kong and not from London. Bronwen spoke also about Stephen Ward,\* who had been in the drawing room before dinner for a moment. She agreed entirely with me that he was no more than a versatile draughtsman who was able to get a likeness of sorts very quickly. We remarked how fortunate he was because it seems that he was recently commissioned by one of the newspapers to go to Israel and make drawings of Eichmann, and also to Moscow to draw Khrushchev. *The Illustrated London News* is bringing out a series of his portrait drawings. She said that his sudden transfer from being a Harley Street specialist and osteopath to an artist in the news had made him feel that he really was an artist and he was inclined to speak of giving up the medical profession. We agreed that that might be very risky for him.

*8 September 1961*

I dropped into the London Library for a short time and on leaving walked straight into Francis Rose. When he saw me he took hold of both my hands and said 'Did you get my autobiography safely?' I said no. He said, 'How extraordinary! I sent it to you. You were first on the list to receive a complimentary copy. The Queen Mother was only the second on the list. I had a dedication for you and there was also a drawing in it. I feel very angry with the publishers. Let's get into a taxi and go round there so that I can get you a copy straight away.' I said 'Francis, I am in a great hurry; I'm afraid I can't come with you now, but you just tell the publishers and I am sure it will be all right.' With that he began a long monologue saying among other things that he had dined with the Queen Mother the previous day (as

\* Principal actor in the future Profumo–Keeler scandal.

far as I know she is in Scotland but that is neither here nor there with Francis). He expressed a wish to give me one of his owl pictures. I managed with great difficulty to get away from him.

21 November 1961

On my way home I called on Noel Whiting. I asked him about the time that he was a prisoner of the Japanese in Burma. He described how at first he was thrown into the common lock-up in Kalaw (the town where he lived), the place where persons arrested for crimes were normally detained pending trial. After a time the Japanese Commandant of Police, when inspecting the lock-up, felt that it was wrong for a civil prisoner to be detained in that way and took him out, and made him his butler. It was his duty to serve at meals. He said that this man was a gentleman and that he was very pleasant in many ways; that after 6.0 he ceased to have to act as an official, and Whiting was invited to sit in his room and talk to him. He didn't, however, actually dine with him, I think, but the commandant was very liberal with his saki and Whiting was able to finish off whatever there was in the glasses or the decanters. This happy period did not last long because orders came from Tokyo that all European civil prisoners were to be confined in Tavoy to a special jail there. He was sent down to this other place, which was less agreeable. He much preferred being butler to the commandant.

Before I left the house Whiting said, 'There is one thing I have been meaning to show you. I have got a bird bath in the garden. It belonged to my aunt and has been there for fifteen years.' And he ran out to bring it in. I heard him in the kitchen washing it, and found him getting the mud off a huge platter in the sink. 'But,' I said with astonishment, 'that is a Ming celadon dish.' He was excited and removing the rest of the mud brought it in. 'I will keep it indoors from this on,' he said.

6 February 1962

I went to see Mervyn and Maeve Peake. I had not seen him for some time but knew that he had not recovered from the mental breakdown which he had had. Maeve opened the front door and I was pleased to see in the hall and on the stairway as we went up a quantity of Mervyn's best drawings nicely framed. On entering the drawing room I saw him seated in a chair. There were two other persons in the room, a man and a woman. I had brought him a present of a bottle of vodka, and came forward at once saying that I had brought him this and suggesting it should be opened straight away and that his friends should join in a drink. He seemed very pleased at this. On getting to his feet, however, it was clear that he found it difficult to stand and could only take a few short steps. He had rather a fixed expression but seemed largely conscious of what was said. He went across to the sofa and Maeve opened the vodka and began pouring it out.

Knowing they were very hard up, one of the ideas that I had in my mind was that Mervyn's manuscripts might bring them in something in the American market. When I mentioned this, Maeve said she had already thought of it. She then showed me the original manuscripts of *Ghormenghast* and *Titus Groan*. These are far more interesting than I supposed because in the text were a quantity of pen drawings to illustrate it, which had never been reproduced. I remember now how disappointed Mervyn was at the time when the publishers refused to include them, on the ground of expense. The manuscripts were much neater than mine, being written on smaller pages in his tidy hand-writing without a great deal of correction, and strongly bound with some boards that almost looked like leather. All his manuscripts were there on a shelf. Maeve also showed me some early manuscripts—things he had written when only fourteen, and very early drawings with rhymes. She said they also had a large collection of letters from famous people, Augustus John, Dylan Thomas, Matthew Smith, etc.

During all this conversation with Maeve about his books, Mervyn looked on and occasionally made some remark. Sometimes he was not able to follow what was said but when Maeve explained it to him he understood. Before I left we went downstairs to look through a great collection of drawings he had there, probably about a thousand. He came down with us and seemed very pleased that I was making these various suggestions, and said it was a great occasion. There was no doubt, however, that he was only partially aware of what was going on. Maeve said that his condition had been diagnosed as some kind of definite disease of the brain and there was no cure for it. I naturally did not ask her whether there was danger that he might lapse into complete unconsciousness. He has, of course, had to give up

13 Mervyn Peake

14 Nancy Astor in 1957

15 Maurice Collis sorting the Stanley Spencer papers

16 Feliks Topolski, Louise Collis and Maurice Collis at the National Book League, 1972

his appointment at the Central School of Art.

Mervyn apparently works in the lower room, or pretends to work. Maeve showed me some of his present drawings, which were not in any way confused but just simply lacking the style associated with him. She also showed me some writings of his, perhaps verse; it was hard to read the writing and it appeared, as she indeed told me, that it didn't make sense.

*14 March 1962*

I drove to the Hongkong Bank where I lunched.* Mr G. O. W. Stewart† and the rest were there, including a person called Meredith. It was a pleasant lunch. I kept them up-to-date on what was happening. Meredith's contribution was the statement that before the fall of Hong Kong he was put on special duty by the government to lay in provisions for the island in case it was besieged by the Japanese for six months before it could be relieved from home. This was on the supposition that the Japanese could be held off by the fortifications. He described how he laid in quantities of rice and soya beans. He then said that of course the moment the Japanese cut the water off at the reservoir north of Kowloon, which they did almost at once, the capture of the island of Hong Kong followed inevitably. They were dependent for more than three-quarters of their supply on that pipeline. All the supplies of rice and beans laid in for the garrison and islanders then fell into the hands of the Japanese. Meredith was not inclined to say that the Japanese starved them too much; they had regular rations which were certainly very short, but the Chinese on the island who had no rations were starving. They all felt much better to begin with, at least for the first six months, by being on a short diet. It was only later that their strength began to give way.

*20 March 1962*

Irene Stirling rang up to say that Humphrey Brooke, the Secretary of the R.A., received Unity Spencer and for an hour and a half sought to convince her that my book, far from hurting the reputation of her father, would greatly enhance it. He said that he had never understood S.S.'s art till he read it. It seems that he succeeded to some extent in

* He had been commissioned to write the Bank's centenary history.

† The London manager.

calming her and that on going she said that if everyone thought as he did, she would be quite happy.

### 2 April 1962

Attended Dudley Tooth's gallery party. I asked Dudley what I should write to Lord Astor to explain my absence at the opening of the Spencer Gallery at Cookham on the 7th. He replied that I should say that the executors were anxious to avoid exasperating the Spencer girls at a moment when they were doing their utmost to calm them down and therefore thought it would be best for me to keep out of their sight. I am doing this. He also said that the executors had had a meeting with the solicitor engaged by the girls and that this solicitor had described the girls' attempt to stop the book as a lot of bally-hoo. When I told him of Humphrey Brooke's attempt to pacify Unity, he remarked what a really good chap he was.

### 6 April 1962

I had written Astor a letter to tell him that the executors asked me not to attend the opening by him of the Spencer Gallery at Cookham tomorrow. He rang up this afternoon, having only just arrived at Cliveden from his annual trip to America, and said that if I was unpopular in Cookham I was very popular in the United Nations; he had been talking only yesterday to U Thant, the Secretary General of the U.N. U Thant expressed great admiration for me, not only as a writer, but as a man, on account of what I had done during my service in Burma. It seems that he expressed a particular liking for my *She was a Queen* and Astor suggested that I should send him a copy with a dedication.

### 7 April 1962

After the opening of the Spencer Gallery at Cookham, Anthony Rubinstein and his wife called in. As Collins' legal adviser about my Spencer book, Rubinstein would not have received an invitation, but he got one from Shiel on a ticket in his wife's name (Dent), he being described as 'and friend'. He reported that the occasion passed off uneventfully. The Spencer girls made no scene; Sir John Rothenstein made his address in the church after the audience (or congregation) had knelt to thank God for sending Stanley Spencer to Cookham.

(He might have sent him to Taplow,* for instance, where he sent Walter de la Mare.) As Rothenstein had a sore throat and no microphone, he was inaudible except to those in the front pews where Lord Astor sat with Bronwen in the vicinity of the two girls. In consequence, his speech seemed very long, as much as twenty minutes, but was actually about ten. After the church service and a view of the new gallery, which Astor declared open, the gathering adjourned to the Odney Sports Club, where tea—described as very bad—was provided.

### 28 May 1962

At 5.30 we went to a party at Tooth's. As soon as we entered the room Dudley Tooth rushed over to us, enquiring how I had stood up to the windy weather of the publication of the Spencer book. I assured him that I had not received a single abusive letter. He replied, 'Well, I have!' and taking us into his killing room,† brought out a large portfolio labelled 'Stanley Spencer biography', containing all the very numerous reviews and printed letters about the book. But what he wanted to show us was a long letter from Shirin Spencer. It was like the letters which her father used to write Tooth, but which he had the sense not to post. In the course of it she declared that her sister Unity was sinking under the terrible shock of the book and that she would hold Dudley responsible for whatever might happen. Of the three executors he was by far the most culpable, for the other two had tried to stop the book. Mr Shiel, too, she said, had been reduced almost to a nervous wreck by Dudley's behaviour. She had also some blame to lay on Astor's shoulders. At the end, her rage rising in a crescendo, she declared that nothing would induce her to touch a penny of what monies might be coming to her from the profits of my book.‡ Dudley, I am glad to say, did not seem in the slightest put out by this hysterical rigmarole and read us his reply, in which he said that no doubt it was a good thing to get such feelings off one's chest and that he believed she would take a very different view in a few

* Five miles from Cookham.

† Trade name for a dealer's comfortably appointed office where rich people are sold expensive pictures and given drinks, etc.

‡ It had been arranged that the Spencer sisters should have a share of the royalties.

months' time, when she had calmed down.

Dudley then read us correspondence which he had had with Gollancz, in which the latter reproached him in bitter terms for depriving him of the opportunity of publishing a biography of S.S. by Mr Middleton, editor of the *Maidenhead Advertiser*, in accordance with the dying wishes of Spencer. To this rubbish Tooth had replied that he was totally unaware of any understanding between S.S. and Gollancz. I was able to inform him that Middleton had taken the trouble some months ago to ring me up and declare that the rumours going about that he had at some time intended to write S.S.'s biography were without foundation.

### 9 June 1962

The Duchess of Roxburghe telephoned me yesterday asking me to come over to lunch. The party was outside on an open verandah, a small party consisting of Lord Alexander and his wife and two others to whom I was introduced though I never discovered exactly who they were. I was very pleased to see Lord Alexander again because I took a great liking to him when I met him at Cliveden. He began talking to me about his garden and his birds. He had bought some Korean doves which first he had had in a cage; then he built a dovecot which was covered with wire; and finally when they seemed quite tame he took the wire off. The doves were tame but they would not nest in the dovecot; they perched in the trees all round and when he came into the garden perched on him. He could not induce them ever to go back to the dovecot, which became a white elephant. He talked a good deal more about dogs and horses and the worlds they live in.

The conversation inevitably came round to the Stanley Spencer book and I was obliged to say something about that. I noticed that when I did speak of it everyone else stopped talking as if it was a subject of considerable interest to them. The Duchess did not say very much; she seemed a little bit shy. She had a magnificent cook who produced a French menu of the highest class.

On saying goodbye to Lord Alexander I was much struck by the expression in his eyes. He seemed to look into mine in a curious way, a look which I have never seen before in anyone's face; he is a very extraordinary man, so quiet. His face was suddenly illuminated; one was taken for a second into the privacy of his thought.

*27 June 1962*

Went to the Academy to see the Egyptian exhibition there, and met Henry Rushbury, the vice president. He asked me how things were going about the book and I said that all was well except for the altercation in the *Times Literary Supplement* with John Rothenstein. I feel that the truth of the matter is that Rothenstein is profoundly upset because my book shows that his and his wife's writings on Stanley Spencer are founded on misapprehensions. He also still clings to the view that Patricia some way or other wronged S.S., though he does not want to be associated with the fact that Stanley complained of these wrongs. He will not accept my view that Stanley's complaint against Patricia was duplicated many times in his life by complaints against all the women and most of the men he had to deal with. He required for his peace of mind the position of a victim. This point, which is one of the fundamental themes of my book, Rothenstein cannot bring himself to accept.

Before I left, Rushbury told me an amusing story about how he and S.S. were demobilised on the same day and that when they marched away from the headquarters in Reading, still in their uniform, they met a general whom they did not salute. The general called them to a halt and asked for their names and numbers, rebuking them and as punishment told them to crank up his car which was standing by. Neither of them had the slightest idea of how to do such a thing.

*27 October 1962*

Dined at Cliveden. Bronwen rang me up in the morning. I knew that they had been to Jura and Jerusalem. As I was entering the small drawing room Bill came from the direction of his study. He was just back from Hong Kong where he had been examining the refugee problem. As Bronwen introduced me all round I knocked over a small table.

Bronwen said that they asked King Hussein of Jordan for an audience, which was granted. She was much struck by the diminutive size of the King and by his shyness. He had no ease of manner whatever and did not look at her during the audience. Bill addressed the King as Sir and the King addressed him as Sir. There was no sign of his Queen, the English girl. Afterwards they went to Nazareth in the north and in the church there Bill crossed himself whenever the priests or others conducting them did so, to show, she said, his respect for their sacred things. She had evidently found this slightly bizarre, but at the same time winning.

After dinner I had a talk with Bill about Hong Kong. He said that he had stayed with the Governor, Sir Robert Black. 'I talked to Saunders, the Hongkong Bank's Chief Manager, about you,' he said. 'They would all much like you to come out and would give you a wonderful reception.' I asked whether the Hongkong people were quite happy at the idea of my writing their centenary volume. He replied that whenever he mentioned my name, there were smiles, and he unconsciously imitated the smiles, including Chinese smiles, for he is an amusing mimic, a gift he has inherited from his mother. 'The only reservation they made was that the book should not have so derogatory a title as *Foreign Mud*.'\* He told them, apparently, that the book would be more about dramatic scenes in the Asiatic background than about banking; this, they declared, was good news as they were far from wanting an economic treatise or a disquisition on finance and silver.†

Bill went on to tell me some interesting facts about the refugees at Hong Kong, still arriving at the rate of 7,000 a month. Water and housing were the problems. Water when he was there was only turned on four hours out of the twenty-four. Huge blocks of flats were going up, but not fast enough to cope with the influx. I asked why they could not be put on Lantao island, which is empty and larger than Hong Kong. He said that the only way the refugees could be supported was by putting them into industry, and that could only be done on Hong Kong island; to create a huge new city on Lantao like Kowloon would take time and a huge expenditure. Ultimately the solution rested on the maintenance of Hong Kong's exports. If they could be steadily increased, the refugees could be supported. If not, no refugee society could provide funds for them. But for Hong Kong to continue to increase its exports of manufactured goods depended on world trade in general.

*12 January 1963*

At Cliveden. After dinner I fell into conversation with Bronwen

\* Maurice's history of the opium wars, published 1946.
† They later changed their minds.

as she sat near the fire working on a piece of tapestry, the design being a peacock's tail. 'It will take me five years to finish it,' she said. She seems to get it out only on these occasions, when there are guests staying and after dinner. I said, it was as if she retreated into it as a protection. 'Ah,' she said, 'you know me too well.' She went on to speak of a prophecy made to her before her marriage—that she would one day be a very rich woman and would in later life be poor. When I protested that that seemed impossible, she said that perhaps the tax people might make it impossible for them to draw their American income. Look what had happened to Lord Astor of Hever.* I do not know exactly how Bill manages to have as much as he has in view of the income tax scale which eliminates very large incomes, but supposed it is managed by capital gains, not treated as income.

There was an episode during the time when we were at table which was a little out of the ordinary. Bronwen suddenly said: 'Where's Bill gone?' I looked and saw he was not in his place at the top of the table and supposed that he had been called away, as sometimes happens, to the telephone. But from what was being said by the women on his right and left it became clear that he had got under the table. He emerged soon afterwards by Bronwen's feet, having crawled the length of the table. The butler and footmen looked on with the expression of people laughing in rather a shamefaced way. Bill said when he got up from the floor that one of the two women by him had betted that he wouldn't do it. I thought that on the whole it did not go down too well.

*22 May 1963*

To lunch at the Hongkong & Shanghai Bank. As soon as I saw Stewart† on my way up to the lunch room, I perceived that he viewed our talk about my introductory chapters with some apprehension. After the usual pleasant good lunch I went to his room and a discussion began. I had never seen him in such an emotional state. It was evident that Morse‡ had told him that the chapters were unsuitable and my plan for the book not one which the Bank liked. He asked me to write an introductory chapter of some twenty-five pages instead

---

* He had to go and live in the south of France.

† G. O. W. Stewart, the London manager.

‡ Sir Arthur Morse, the Chairman.

of the two hundred I had written, and to confine it strictly to the circumstances leading directly to the founding of the Bank in 1865. 'A Bank book,' he said, 'is bound to be dull, because banking is dull.' This was such a new point of view that I was rather taken aback, but replied at once that my book must be made acceptable to the Bank.

*25 May 1963*

Dine at Cliveden. On entering the salon I found Bill Astor mixing a queer-looking cocktail. 'This comes from the Collis country,' he announced to the company. It was a Mexican cocktail. My connection with Mexico was *Cortés and Montezuma*, the book I dedicated to him. Very soon Tony* and Mary Keswick came in, Tony looking more huge than ever. He asked me about the Bank book and I sat down on a sofa with him.

At dinner I was seated next to Lady de Zulueta, the wife of the Prime Minister's private secretary. Opposite was old Nancy Astor, now very confused and tiresome. However, she gave me in the drawing room a gracious smile, though she did not know who I was. During dinner Lady de Zulueta said that a guard with police dogs was now patrolling round Cliveden every night. She ascribed this precaution to the increasing value of Bill's collection of pictures which includes Renoir, Matisse, Derain, etc. I did not remark that the connection was otherwise. It is bound up with the Ward affair,†—Ward's house on the Cliveden estate was entered and the furniture broken up, Bill's London house was entered and letters of some kind were allegedly read, these events following the attack made by a West Indian negro on a tart when she was in Ward's flat in London (during his absence in Harley Street), and the sentencing of the said negro to seven years' imprisonment. The tart was subpoenaed at his trial, but Ward sent her to Spain, for he was afraid what might come out if she were cross-examined in the box. The tart was either the mistress of the negro or he was living on her earnings when Ward took her up. The attack by the negro was probably less actuated by jealousy than by annoyance that Ward had not paid him. Ward went to the further

* Sir William Keswick, director of Jardine & Matheson, a company trading in China.

† On 7 June 1963 Dr Stephen Ward was arrested for living on immoral earnings.

imprudence of inviting the tart to his parties in his Cliveden estate house and actually bringing her to Astor's out-of-door swimming bath. Thus Astor was (to a degree unknown) mixed up in a big scandal.

After dinner I sat with Tony Keswick on a seat in the hall. He said: 'You will think me mad, I know, when I tell you that I keep a private balloon at the Hague. I balloon round Europe according to the wind. The views from a balloon are marvellous. I am going to Moscow this year for a conference of amateur balloonists. We shall all be in the sky together. I want an artist to come with me and do some sketches, say ten. I'd pay £300. Do you know a man?' I said Topolski might do. He also asked my opinion of his Henry Moore sculptures. 'Will Moore last?' he enquired. I replied that Moore's *King and Queen* would certainly last.

## 14 June 1963

Wrote a line to Bill Astor to assure him of my friendship at this moment when he is involved in the Profumo and Ward scandals. I feel that he has innocently become entangled in a drama with which he has nothing to do. By bad luck he made a friend of Stephen Ward. By bad luck Miss Keeler, Ward's girl, met Profumo, the Minister for War, in the Cliveden swimming pool and takes up with him. From that all the huge and hideous scandal arose. With Ward's arrest for keeping a brothel, disclosures affecting many prominent people are likely. Bill will be lucky if he emerges unscathed from what is coming.

## 2 July 1963

London. At 6 p.m. I went to Feliks Topolski's studio under an arch of Hungerford Bridge on the south bank by the concert hall. It is some time since I have seen him, I cannot say for certain how long, but maybe a year, though through having so many of his paintings and drawings hanging on my walls he is always present. When I rang and he opened the door, there he was with his charm, the same as ever. He pretended that I looked the same, protesting that, after an interval, on seeing people again one noticed how they had aged (which is true enough) but that I looked less old, so much so that he was disappointed I failed to grow into his portrait of me as an ancient dissolute character.

When we were seated over a vodka we got talking, as was inevitable, on the Ward case, which literally has set the whole world buzzing, as it has all the elements of a popular shocker, as presented by the press, with spying and leakage of vital secrets to Russia, orgies, a broken Minister, prostitution, organised vice, flagellation, voyeurism, the threatened fall of the Conservative government, all with the sauce that a noble lord, very rich, owner of race horses, a great mansion, a wife famous formerly as a model, and a name which for a generation or more has been news on account of his mother's wit and eccentricities, has been mixed up in the imbroglio. I said to Topolski: 'What about Ward himself? Can he be convicted on the evidence before the magistrate when he is tried in the Old Bailey?' Topolski's view was that the case was not genuine; his was not a real case of living on immoral earnings, arranging abortions, maintaining a brothel. When the laws were framed they had not in view men like Ward, but of real underworld racketeers. You could no doubt stretch the various enactments to catch Ward, but that would be going beyond the intention of their framers. Ward, of course, had to do with women, he himself had in his possession a drawing of him having intercourse with a woman; he even took money on occasion from prostitutes staying in his house, because he had a streak of meanness in his nature and could not refuse the offer of a ten-pound note. He had an obsession that he was poor, despite his good practice as an osteopath. Feliks's view was that the police might succeed in getting him convicted on some of the several charges, but if so he would be wrongfully convicted. He did arrange orgies in his house for acquaintances, but for all that he was not a real underworld person. He said that during a recent visit to Paris he had seen in *Paris Soir* photos of the women Ward was supposed to have started in life by training them how to secure rich husbands. Among the girls was Bronwen. I said that Ward's hand in the Astor–Bronwen Pugh marriage was nil. I had seen its genesis and development with my own eyes.

*6 July 1963*

After lunch I received a telephone message from the Astors asking me to dinner this evening. I told the butler to say I was delighted to accept. At 8 p.m. I rang the bell at Cliveden's hall door. Bill Astor came to let me in. He said; 'You ought not to ring, you should just come in.' As I looked at his face, while we stood a moment in the outer hall, I was moved by the expression of suffering I saw there. There was a softness, even sweetness, in his eyes, a look of gentle appeal, which in all the years I had never seen before. I had a sudden inclination to embrace him, but only pressed his arm. I said, 'I know what a horrible time you and Bronwen have been going through.' He half closed his eyes and sighed: 'Yes, yes, the only thing is to keep up one's dignity, go on as before and not engage in any public slanging match with these women. After all, my way of life is well known. Hundreds of people know exactly how I live, what my interests are, how I occupy my time, what I try to do in the public service, what my private life consists of. I have to bear all this scandal without an opportunity of replying. Anyhow it is so difficult to prove a negative, prove there is nothing, nothing in all the stories invented about me by goodness knows whom. We are being pestered by the press, spied on. The helicopters are the worst, hovering over the house. My best course will be to wait till the Ward case is over. Then when all the facts are out and adjudicated upon, it might be the moment for a letter to the press. What do you think? Could you do it then?' I assured him that I could and would whenever he thought the opportunity right.

Soon after we moved to go into the dining room. I entered last and, looking for my place, heard Bronwen say, 'Here, you are sitting beside me.' At once we began talking about what was uppermost in all minds. Among the things she said were: 'People think that because Ward's weekend cottage was on the estate we must have known what was going on there. But it's out of sight and people going to it use the lower park entrance and don't pass near the house.' I remarked that it was as far off as a house in the next street in London. 'Two streets away,' she said. And so it is, several minutes' walk and down below in trees. Besides, Ward was only there at weekends and then mostly in the summer. At weekends there were always large house parties at Cliveden. How could one possibly know what was going on at the cottage and who Ward's guests were, or what they were doing? He did not bring them up to Cliveden, though he had a general permission to use the swimming pool. Hence the fortuitous and fatal meeting between Profumo and the woman Keeler. Bronwen went on to say that all this had been a test of friends. Some when asked to dinner or lunch had made excuses. But, she added laughing, 'There were some old friends who complained, saying—we have been coming to you all these years, but you have never once invited us to an orgy!' A remark which showed that she was keeping up her spirits somehow. 'After all, I've been married to Bill since October 1960, before all this began. Surely I would have noticed something if he had been living the way the scandal would have it. It was a great shock to him when some of the people he thought his oldest and best friends deserted him or went against him in the crisis.'

After dinner I sat on the sofa in the little salon between Bill and Bronwen. He said that he thought his slanderers had overreached themselves and that was just as well, for they wouldn't be believed long. 'The most monstrous accusations have been made. I was accused of having paid £100 for a seat by the famous mirror fixed to give a view of what happened in a bedroom of Ward's flat in the mews, when Prince Philip was performing.'

The general view was that the case against Ward was rather weak. Sir Alun Pugh, Bronwen's father, said that the magistrate had no option but to send him for trial to the Old Bailey, as some sort of a *prima facie* case had been made out, but his granting bail was a hopeful sign.

### 23 July 1963

Lunched with Noel Whiting at Le Petit Club Français in St James Place. Penrose* and Herbert Read were sitting at the next table with some foreign-looking woman. Read gave his usual mysterious impression; his well-known conspirator's look was full on. Actually he is not conspiring about anything, it is just his way of talking. I think it has helped him a lot in his life because it gives an impression that he is the depository of immense secrets. It makes people all round stare and wish they were being favoured like the person to whom he is addressing what are probably quite ordinary remarks.

### 31 July 1963

In the newspapers this morning it was announced that Ward was in a coma through having taken an overdose of sleeping pills. He left

* Sir Roland Penrose, director of the Institute of Contemporary Art.

a letter stating that he feared from the tone of the judge's summing up that the verdict would go against him and he preferred to take his life. The judge continued his summing up during the day, holding that Ward's presence was unnecessary. Later the jury brought in a verdict of guilty on the charges alleging that Ward had lived in part on the earnings of the Keeler and Davies women.

*20 September 1963*

London with Louise. At 5.30 we reached the Portobello Road where Mervyn Peake's exhibition was to be opened at 6 p.m. We found Maeve and Mervyn there. The proprietor was present. He had had enough drink to make him a little incoherent. The room looked well, though Maeve said that she had had to come and sweep it out. I brought to help the party go three bottles of whisky. Quite a number of people arrived, including Tony Keswick and Julian Huxley's son, Francis, the anthropologist. It turned out an un-expectedly gay occasion. Maeve was in amusing high spirits. Mervyn moved about with the quiet abstracted expression he had, not all there, but able to follow something of what was happening. He shuffled back and forth, always as if surprised at what he heard. It was very strange to think of him as the artist who had made the drawings on the walls. Tony Keswick bought three; several others were sold in the course of the evening.

I asked Tony Keswick how he had got on with his ballooning, reminding him of what he had told me at Cliveden. He said that he had been swept into the North Sea from Holland by an unexpected change of wind, and came down in the sea and had to be rescued. 'Weren't you frightened?' I asked. 'Yes I was,' he said. I told him that in the Bank book I was nearly at his attempted assassination by Hayashi in Shanghai in 1939–40 when he was chairman of the Shanghai municipal council. He seemed pleased and smiled in a way which I have always found delightful.

Seated near me was a woman who said that she had seen Astor and Bronwen at Salzburg recently. They were pointed out as personages in the Ward drama and people were staring. 'Don't stare, dears,' she told her daughters, but they would stare. She did not know the Astors personally. She went on to declare that she thought nothing about the stories that Astor had joined in Ward's debaucheries, but considered it disgraceful that at Ward's trial Astor had not come forward to defend him. I pointed out that he had no knowledge which could have helped Ward. The charge was living on immoral earnings. As Astor had never come to close quarters with that side of Ward's alleged misdeeds, he could have had nothing relevant to testify. But the woman (whoever she was) went off still insisting that he should have come to the rescue of his old friend. She was rather drunk.

*3 November 1963*

Dined at Cliveden. Bronwen told me that the late scandal had ruined Bill as far as any public employ was concerned. The Government would never commission him to head an enquiry, represent the Crown or the like. They would have to fall back on private activities and charities and be happy with the children and the house. She said: 'During all this business I was bursting to speak out, but we were advised to say as little as possible. Bill has been blamed for not going into the witness box on behalf of Ward, but he was not asked to. Neither side asked him to give evidence. Anyhow there was nothing important he could have said. He really knew very little about Ward's private life. Would you believe it, that dreadful girl Mandy Rice-Davies, through her agent or lawyer, asked Bill if he would collaborate with her in a book she is writing about the scandal, or getting written. They offered Bill a sum of money. Can you imagine it? We wonder what will be in the book, if it really comes out. There was an occasion when she came to the house. Ward came up one evening in his usual way to give one of the guests a message and brought the girl with him. She stayed in the hall while he was messaging and was offered a drink. Bill saw her there and spoke to her. It never crossed his mind that she was a prostitute. The whole story of his having an affair with her was built up on that meeting in the hall and the drink.'

*5 February 1964*

Went to the Princess Zeid's to look at my portrait.* Found her having tea with her sister, Madame Berger. The Princess amused us at tea by telling us anecdotes about her former butler, Hooper, who died shortly after the Iraqi revolution and the end of the Prince's

* Painted by the Princess.

tenure of the Ambassadorship. Hooper continued to butler for the Republican embassy and one day fell down dead in the boiler house. He was a remarkable character, very well known in London as the Prince entertained lavishly, gave perhaps the best receptions in London. Hooper was wonderfully attentive and confidential with guests, though he had invariably taken a good deal to drink. The Princess treated him as general adviser and factotum. He would be told to take out the Prince and buy him an overcoat. Madame Berger recalled with merriment how he strove to prevent her from drinking more than he thought she should and also how, when she was to go out with the Princess, he would be anxious that she should not keep the Princess waiting. 'He would come to my room, knock and call "Her Royal Highness is nearly ready," and return again to say, "Her Royal Highness is putting on her hat"—and finally in an urgent voice, "Her Royal Highness has got her hat on and is about to come downstairs".' Hooper was just the right sort of servant for the Princess. She liked him immensely, despite his drinking and familiarities. But she was angry with him for taking service with the representatives of a regime which had murdered her relative, the King of Iraq, and his family. When he came to call on her at Brown's Hotel, whither they had gone after vacating the Embassy, she said, 'I'm not going to shake hands with a republican!' Nevertheless, when shortly after she heard that he was ill in hospital with his heart, she sent him kind messages and a present of money. All these reminiscences the Princess now recounted as she sat on her sofa.

*17 March 1964*

There was a party at the New London Gallery on the occasion of a retrospective exhibition of John Piper's paintings. I expected to see John Betjeman, Piper's closest friend, but he had not come. The first time I met him was during the Second World War. I was over in Ireland to see my mother and was introduced to him by my brother Bob at the Shelbourne Hotel. At that time he was Press Attaché to Lord Rugby, and had published little or nothing and was quite unknown. He said, 'I suppose you can get anything you write published. I wish I could.' He was ambitious to distinguish himself or at least to be talked about, for it was said that he and his wife had set out to shock Dublin. She was the daughter of Field Marshal Lord Chetwode.

When talking to them at the Shelbourne Hotel, her parents came in. He was a big presence, but it was Lady Chetwode who was really formidable. Betjeman has come a long way since 1944.

*24 March 1964*

We drove to Gordon Square to have a look at the Percival David collection of Chinese porcelain which he has given to the University. I wanted to see the Yueh pieces. As we entered we were informed by the man at the door that Sir Percival was close by. I saw him then in his wheeled chair in the lowest gallery, which has Ch'ing pieces. He was talking to Miss Medley, the curator of the gallery. I went forward at once, and giving my name in case he forgot me (he seemed to remember me when I did so, though our last meeting was several years ago), I asked him about Yueh wares. One could see that for the great expert in ceramics that he is, the question was a little naive. His manner was gay and excited. He seized Louise's hand and kissed it, excusing himself for being so foreign. Then he directed Miss Medley to take us upstairs and show us what so-called Yueh wares were in the collection. As we went up in the lift to the Sung gallery, Miss Medley remarked on his excitability. Most of the time he is confined to his flat at the top of the building, a bath-chair existence as his lower limbs are paralysed. When he comes downstairs and looks at the collection and meets people he becomes very animated and high spirited. But she seemed to suggest that he paid for this afterwards, being overtired and depressed. She was clearly devoted to him, as well she might, for he remains at seventy-four a wonderful intelligence.

*3 June 1964*

To London with Louise. We went to a party given by the Lefevre gallery for L. S. Lowry. He was there, a man now of seventy-seven. It is nearly twenty years since I went up to Manchester on a visit to him and afterwards wrote the introduction to the book on his paintings brought out by the Lefevre Gallery. He looked quite unchanged, as unchanged as his paintings, which differ only in price from what they have always been, and the price is still rising. I had a short talk with him. He professed now to have outlived his melancholy and to have reached a final content. He could view things with less tension and had become aware of the comedy around him. This, indeed, was reflected in his pictures; not sufficiently to change them, but enough to give them a slightly happier mood.

While we were looking round Tony Keswick came up. He asked if we knew that he was interested in harps. I said I thought it was balloons. 'Harps too,' he said and went off to enquire the price of a Lowry picture of a man playing a harp. When told it was £750, he returned to tell us that figure was too high. He was in his usual high spirits. He wanted me to say whether I thought Lowry was really a great painter. I said that anyhow he was the only distinctively English painter alive today now that Stanley Spencer is dead. There is no doubt he enjoys a considerable celebrity in his old age. It may well be that this celebrity, together with the comfortable income he now has after a lifetime of poverty, is the chief reason why his mood is so much happier. Nevertheless, it would be a mistake to think that Lowry has really become a social person. He remains largely a recluse and lets few people, if any, into his inner thoughts. I recall that when I wrote the introduction to the book on his painting he did, as I talked to him in Manchester, unbosom himself to quite an extent. I reread a few days ago what I wrote, and must say I think it is still true.

14 July 1964

At 6 p.m. I went in to see Maeve Peake to enquire about Mervyn. We sat talking for a couple of hours. She said that he was now at Banstead hospital. She goes to see him weekly. He seems aware that it is she, but is not able to converse. His frame is shrunken, his head has fallen forward with the chin on to his chest, his eyes have become larger owing to the emaciation of his face, and look wild and tormented. Saliva dribbles from his mouth. He either sits in a general room speechless, surrounded by men like himself, or shambles in a garden.* She went on to say that the faces of the people around him are those of his more fantastic drawings, his own appearance corresponding to some principal actor in his compositions or in his prose—a very strange paradox, but which did not, in her opinion, indicate any prevision. From this account it is evident that there is no hope for Mervyn, a man who, in my opinion, was an incomparable draughtsman, his best drawings standing level with the best of men who have been more fortunate in securing public applause, such as

* He had Parkinson's Disease.

Augustus John in this country and Modigliani in France and the world. They are pervaded not only with the mood of hallucination which fits so well into his drawings illustrating *The Ancient Mariner* but with other moods, comic as in his illustrations of *Alice in Wonderland*, the grotesque as in many of his drawings illustrating his own verses or the unknown ones in the MSS of his *Titus Groan* and *Gormenghast*, a swashbuckling half mock-heroic mood as in his illustrations of *Treasure Island*, and his erotic mood in my *Quest for Sita*. Maeve said that, contrary to his manner, which was soft and polite, Mervyn was a powerful character. One knew him to be a notable man.

*3 November 1964*

In the course of the day I dropped in to the Brook Street Gallery and had a talk with the proprietor. One of the things he said was that present-day prices for fashionable works of art are so high that the purchaser is not really getting his money's worth. A picture of the French school, in his opinion, is just not worth 25 or 50 thousand pounds. He said, however, that the Americans do not seem to mind these prices—they just pay; they want to get names and they want to get work characteristic of those names. Thus, in the case of Henry Moore, they like to have reclining women with cavities in them. An American would pay 2 or 3 thousand pounds for a very small reclining woman of which perhaps there had been nine castings taken. When he got back to the States people were satisfied that he really had got a Henry Moore when they saw it was a reclining woman. The proprietor said that he had had in his gallery some little time back an extremely attractive Henry Moore of a novel design, but he had the greatest difficulty in disposing of it. Moore was now a wealthy man but his Russian wife still felt their finances were precarious and was very careful over expenditure. She apparently didn't believe the public would continue to buy reclining women indefinitely, or at least there was a risk they might not do so, and she was therefore careful to conserve their funds. My own view (and indeed that of the proprietor) was that if ever there was an artist whose financial position was sure, it was Henry Moore. He is over sixty now and certainly has enough work promised and contracted for at a high price to last him many years.

On the way home I dropped in for a moment at Noel Whiting's house to ask what arrangements he had made about lunch with Mme Ne Win, the wife of the Head of State in Burma, who calls himself Chairman of the Revolutionary Council. Whiting said that this was now fixed for Thursday next and the party would consist of Madam and her sister, together with the Burmese ambassador.

## 5 November 1964

I arrived at the restaurant at 1 p.m. and found Whiting there. The Burmese party arrived soon afterwards. Mme Ne Win, whom I have lunched with twice before, but at a date anterior to her husband's seizure of power in Burma, has a rather grander air than formerly, which was to be expected considering that she was the wife of the Burmese autocrat and in Burma must have a great deal of personal power herself. She is now a woman of about forty-five, very good looking and has an easy manner. She gives the impression that she is really glad to see you, which I always think is the mark of the best manners. The sister was a little shadowy woman, very slight and unassuming, who was not meant to talk but just be there. Why the ambassador desired to be present, I do not know; whether she commanded him to come, or whether General Ne Win said he was to attend—it was not possible to guess. The General himself, though invited to the lunch, had not been able to accept. When we sat down at the table it was clear from the conversation that I had with Mme Ne Win that he had come to London for a rest cure and was seeing nobody. She said that this was the first time she had been out to lunch since their arrival in London, about a month ago, except that they had lunched with the then prime minister, Sir Alec Douglas Home. 'The General is of course very tired. He is also suffering from sinus trouble, but I think it may be that that is partly nervous. We have tried psychiatrists but I think complete rest is worth a hundred psychiatrists.' She told me that she had kept correspondence away from him as far as possible. I said I would naturally have liked to see him, and she said that perhaps she might be able to arrange, before they left for Burma next week, for me to come to the house. I said I felt that would be too much of an intrusion and I would prefer to see him on his next visit to London. She asked me whether they could come down and call on me in Maidenhead, and I said I would be very delighted to see them.

I also asked her how it was that the General managed to leave Burma. She said there were now no parties in Burma and there was therefore no risk of a rival coup behind his back. People left in charge were loyal and reliable. It is, of course, true that all his political opponents are in jail. There is no suggestion that the former premier, U Nu, would ever get out of jail; he has never been brought to trial. It is a complete tyranny. Yet Madam spoke of their ambitions to revive the Burmese, to distribute wealth evenly, to get rid of corruption and also to develop the economy without the assistance of grants in aid from America or Russia. 'You must not think of us as being communists. We are not. We want to develop our own country as best we can, even if it takes longer than if we got grants in aid. We did at one time have some American money but found it very unsatisfactory. A horde of so-called experts arrived to see that the money was spent on (I think) a railway. The first thing they demanded before doing any work was that bungalows should be erected for them. Then they got their wives and children over from America and the wives were dissatisfied with the furniture and fittings. Some months passed and it seemed to us that quite a percentage of the grant was spent on the Americans before anything was done. The attitude of both them and their wives was very unpleasant. In the end, as you know, we terminated the arrangement.'

During the lunch, Mme Ne Win dominated the conversation (her sister said nothing at all and the ambassador hardly spoke except to agree with her) but her manner throughout was extremely polite and agreeable. She speaks English without any accent. She said the General came from a small village near Prome.* His rise to power was very sudden and spectacular. I asked whether he had solved the problem of the bandits or rebels. She said not entirely, there were a certain number of these people still in the jungle living in her words 'like Robin Hood', a happy sort of existence in the wild woods, occasionally coming out and looting a village. This of course was a way of excusing the state of unrest. She said that entirely to suppress banditry was perhaps impossible, or at least would be very expensive. It didn't, in her view, interfere too much with the regeneration of the country.

She said they now lived in the old Government House in Rangoon

* North of Rangoon.

though they had kept their own house (which is a far nicer one, though too small) on the lake about seven miles north of Rangoon. The old Government House is roomy though hideous. The General had his office in it and it was there that he received all kinds of personages during the day and also in the evening. But not in a formal manner, as far as I could gather from her. If the conversation went on late, food was handed round, a sort of informal supper. I asked whether the throne had been removed. (The throne of the Kings of Burma, which had been looted from Mandalay and taken to Calcutta, was sent back by the Indian government and placed in Government House in Rangoon.) She said they had been able to get rid of that, as it was a white elephant and it was now in the museum. Evidently the General wished to avoid any ignorant suggestions that he was planning to revive the kingship in his own person.

She also spoke to me of my books on Burma, which she said her children (now I suppose about fifteen and eighteen) liked very much and would come to her with passages they wanted her to read.

Mme Ne Win seemed to like the dishes she chose, but her sister got stuck with a fish dish where there was a good deal of sauce, with shrimps mixed up in it, and couldn't eat more than half. We adjourned afterwards to Whiting's house close by. I came in for a short time and then bade them goodbye.


*1 January 1965*

Dined at Cliveden. On entering the grand salon I found among others, Enid Starkie and Osbert Lancaster, also Lord Grantley and his wife. He is the brother of Bill Astor's first wife. Enid Starkie is and looks a downright woman, rather formidable. Her two biographies on Verlaine and Rimbaud have become classics, though the other books she has published are less known. She was extremely pleasant in her manner to me, referring to how she knew my brother in the old days in Ireland, speaking of her brother, the famous Walter, and of how she had not visited Ireland since her mother's death. She has a heavy profile, is stoutly built and is going bald on the top of her head.

William, Bill's son and heir, now aged nearly thirteen, was at dinner. I have not seen him for some time. He is a slight boy, with most exquisite manners, quite unbelievably composed for his age. At dinner he had occasion to stand up for some reason, and Lord Grantly called out in a voice loud enough to intimidate a child of his age, 'Speech, speech!' But William calmly put it aside. 'I never make a speech,' he said with an aplomb which was both final yet marvellously polite.

Though Osbert Lancaster has a look of Kitchener, the squareness of his face and the bushiness of his moustache adding to the resemblance, his eye is not fierce; indeed, it has something indulgent in its depth, and a certain nobility as one may observe in some kinds of large dogs, whose faces in repose are more noble than the generality of noblemen's.

Bronwen spoke in an amusing way of how the shadow of her late mother-in-law Nancy Astor pervaded the house and prompted her to behave in an authoritarian way. 'When I am late for dinner and come down the staircase to a group of guests waiting for me, I shout at them—"Come on now"—as if they had kept me waiting.'

### 5 February 1965

Went to see Fabers about a proposal that I write a biography of Raffles.* I then went on to see Tony Keswick at Boodles. He has been asked by the Hongkong & Shanghai Bank to make the main speech at their big centenary dinner at the Savoy on 3 March. The prospect of having to do this, and propose the toast of the Bank intimidated him, he said, though as Director of the Bank of England, etc, etc, he must have experience of after-dinner speeches. So he asked me to make up the speech for him. I said I was delighted, suggesting he should read my book on the Bank† (an early copy of which could be procured for him) and that we should meet and discuss the speech. He pressed that I should bring a draft speech, and offered me £25. I said I would bring the draft and do the job for nothing as we were old friends. Accordingly I presented myself at Boodles at 5.45. On my asking the porter to tell Mr Keswick that I had come, I was informed that he was not yet in. I took a seat in the reading room. Twenty-five minutes later, Tony rushed in looking very apologetic. I had supposed that some important affair had detained him in the City. No, he said, it was not that; he had gone home. His wife had

* Published 1966.

† *Wayfoong*, the centenary history of the Hongkong & Shanghai Banking Corporation, published on 3 March 1965.

said, 'What are you doing here, Tony? Maurice is waiting for you at Boodles.' He had jumped into his car. 'And now,' he said, 'a strong whisky each.' The page produced it in a moment. 'You read the speech,' he said to me. I read it. He listened intently and declared it very good. We then discussed including a tribute to Sir Arthur Morse, the chairman, for one thing. He asked me whether I would accept the present of a Chinnery drawing and I said I would.

### 8 February 1965

At the Hamilton Gallery the artist Josef Herman came up. I hadn't seen him for some little time. He told an amusing story of how he was engaged by some tycoon, American I think, to paint his portrait. The tycoon said he could only give him sittings between aeroplane flights; he was continually flying from one part of the world to another, and he sometimes had 45 minutes or so at London Airport, where Herman could get to work. Herman said that he tried to fall in with this as the sum offered was very good, but he found that dashing to catch this man and having to paint against time between flights got on his nerves and he couldn't get a likeness. (These were, of course, the preliminary sketches.) He tore them all up finally, he said, and then went back to his studio where he painted from memory. The man was quite satisfied and bought the picture. It then appeared why he wanted this portrait. In a certain city art gallery there was a picture by Herman. This tycoon had business in the city and calculated that if he could get a portrait of himself into that gallery, painted by a man whose work was already in the gallery, it would be good business. Accordingly on getting the portrait, he presented it to the gallery which, as they knew Herman's work, was prepared to accept it.

### 4 March 1965

This was the centenary day of the Hongkong & Shanghai Bank and it was celebrated by a big cocktail party at the Savoy. I enquired for Sir Arthur Morse. He was pointed out to me seated at a table and I joined him. His foot was no better* and he had recently had a severe appendix operation. I asked how Tony Keswick's speech of the previous night had been received. He said it was a good one.

I set out to find Tony and did so at one of the long tables which

* He had had a thrombosis.

were laden with drinks and such refreshments as smoked salmon and caviar. My first question was to ask about his speech. He seemed satisfied that it had gone off well, and declared that he had mentioned my name nine times, though this was perhaps a manner of speaking.

## 11 March 1965

London. At the Marlborough Gallery. Henry Moore came into view and I hastened to go up to him. Since the time when I used to drive over to see him at his studio near Much Hadham I have only met him occasionally, a space of years in which he has become not only the most celebrated British sculptor but perhaps admitted abroad into first place. An O.M. and immensely courted, his works selling for tens of thousands of pounds, one might have expected to see some sign of his huge success in his manner. This was not so. He was exactly as he used to be, natural, modest, matter of fact and pleasant. I said to him, 'Henry, how does it seem to have become so astounding a celebrity now?' He assured me (and it was clearly the truth) that being a celebrity was a thing he did not feel. It did not seem to make any difference to him. There was a huge and tiresome correspondence from all over the world. His secretary was only just able to deal with it. On the whole he was happier and able to concentrate better when he was just an artist making his way, though, of course, having no money worries was a relief.

Continuing our peregrination through the crowded room we perceived Barbara Hepworth, dressed in golden pyjamas, her hair dyed a bluish tinge. She is at the moment the most celebrated woman sculptor in England and her standing abroad is at the top. I have known her for a very long time, and paid her a visit years ago at her St Ives studio. By the time Louise and I went to speak with her the party had been going on for over an hour and the atmosphere was lively. Our talk with her was accordingly a little extravagant and we may have seemed to her more frivolous and familiar than we should have been.★ She has not Henry Moore's wonderful absence of vanity.

## 22 April 1965

Bill Astor telephoned, asking me to come up today for what he called a tray lunch in his bedroom. The butler had laid a little table

★ Maurice congratulated her on the size of her biceps.

and brought in the dishes, first shrimps in sauce, then mutton with potatoes, peas and salad, and then some kind of tart with cream. Bill had a good appetite. During lunch and afterwards on the sofa he made a number of interesting remarks, his manner being far easier and less reserved than I have ever seen it, a change which, as Bronwen told me later, is due to his having consulted a psychiatrist, who supplied him with an outlook which has greatly quieted his nerves, soothing his irritation and giving him calm and confidence.

Speaking of the Ward imbroglio he said (alluding to the charge that he had deserted Ward in his need): 'I paid for Ward's defence, and when it seemed possible that the jury might find him guilty, I took the best legal opinion and on being advised that Ward would be acquitted on appeal, I was on the point of writing to reassure him on this point and to promise to pay council for the appeal, when the news came that he had made an end of himself.' And he went on: 'The charge that Ward was living on the proceeds of prostitution was unsustainable. He was quite incapable of carrying on a business of that kind; he was a casual happy-go-lucky sort of chap.' This I myself know to be a true estimate of Ward's character. To live on prostitutes is a difficult and tiresome way of making money. Ward was totally unfitted for such a business. Indeed, he had no business sense.

*1 June 1965*
London. Went to see Feliks Topolski. I hadn't seen him for over a year. His hair was a bit more grey but otherwise he looked almost exactly the same. The studio was absolutely crammed to the ceiling with paintings, hardly any of which I had seen. They were inspired by his drawings, and by the sort of current events which are the subject matter of his Chronicle. For instance, there was Lord Denning, the judge who was put on by the government to enquire into the Ward case. Feliks explained this was to be a sort of triptych, containing generally his comments on the Ward case; Denning himself was finished, and there were also two panels below him representing two couples, evidently a detail from an orgy. A further type of picture was that of the Pope on his way to Jerusalem. The pictures themselves undoubtedly, if properly hung and perhaps given a little bit of further attention from his brush, would make a remarkable exhibition.

There was an American agent in the studio, who was typing part of the time a letter to the press describing how moved he was at seeing a taxi driver return unopened and unrobbed a suitcase belonging to an old woman who had left it in his taxi. The American said a thing like that couldn't possibly happen in New York. 'No woman, no matter what she was like, young or old, plain or beautiful, would ever have seen her case again,' and as he spoke he burst into tears. 'Excuse me,' he said, 'for crying like this but I feel this very much. Maybe I seem a trifle too Anglophil but I do admire this wonderful country.' Besides this American chap there was a youngish woman of about twenty-five in the studio who came in and made the coffee and sat down. She didn't seem to have any connection really with either the secretarial or the art side.

*6 July 1965*

In the course of the evening we went to a party given by Mrs Juda at her Hamilton Gallery for the Iranian ambassador. The exhibition was of a selection of Persian arts from earliest times. After having had a couple of drinks I looked up and saw a tall figure, very close, with his back to me, and young looking. I thought to myself, 'Can this be the Honourable Runce?'* He looked round—it was. Of course front face he doesn't look young as he must be nearly seventy though he only looks about sixty. As his name is so much before the public on account of his *Fall of Constantinople*, serialised in the Sunday papers, reviewed on all hands, I congratulated him straight off. 'How did you do it?' I said. 'It is the most exciting thing you ever wrote.' He said, 'Well, the story was so exciting, it told itself.' I was interrupting his conversation with a rather pretty woman. With a side glance at Louise and myself he glided off to speak to another pretty woman.

I had a conversation with Stevie Smith† (whom I haven't seen for a long time) who looks like some sort of extraordinary old insect now, very small, creeping about, and her eye sockets almost as large as saucers. She looks a hundred.

*24 August 1965*

Called at the Burmese ambassador's private residence. He was

* Hon. Sir Steven Runciman. He was actually sixty-two.
† Poet.

giving a very curious party. At the time when he had arranged with the British Government to return the Burmese regalia, he told me that he had heard that the tusks of a White Elephant which had belonged to King Mindon (predecessor of Thibaw, last King of Burma) were in Ireland, and that he was making efforts to get hold of them and return them also to Burma. The tusks were traced to the ownership of the Marquess of Waterford. It appears that the marquess's ancestor was at the taking of Mandalay in 1885. The city was looted and amongst the things he got were two tusks purporting to belong to a sacred White Elephant which had died during the time of Mindon, about 1870. It seems that the present marquess inherited these tusks but found it difficult to place them in his house, and thought that the Natural History Museum in Dublin was the very place. They were deposited there, and it was from there that the ambassador retrieved them. The party was to celebrate the occasion and to mark their despatch to Burma.

On entering the house we found that in a series of rooms was a display of Burmese objects of art. At the far end of the main room were displayed the tusks, which were the largest I have ever seen belonging to an Indian elephant. They much more resembled in size African elephant tusks. My theory is that perhaps as a White Elephant was treated as a sacred beast in which resided a future Buddha, he was not called upon to use his tusks as he would have been if he had been a working elephant, and that consequently they grew larger; but that may not be so. The fact remains that the tusks stood up seven feet high, or perhaps more. They were mounted on wood and were inscribed in Pali to the effect that they had belonged to Mindon's White Elephant and the title of the animal was given.

The ambassador was immensely pleased with the result of his negotiations and I warmly congratulated him, saying I hoped General Ne Win would reward him for his great services.

*29 January 1966*

Dined at Cliveden. I found Bill sitting on a sofa. He looked much the same, I thought. I asked him whether he had regained any weight, but he said, no, only a pound and a half from the start of his recovery. However, he was very cheerful, much more so than I had seen him for some time; in fact he was in high spirits. It may have been that he had had a little more to drink than his doctors permitted him as a rule.

After dinner we went into the little salon. I noticed the parrot, the disgraceful bird they had bought in New York, which records a conversation and then you press a button and in the most appalling voice, which is like a parrot's but also in some way American, it bawls out what you have said and is exceedingly funny. Bronwen immediately said: 'We must try the parrot; you come out, Maurice, into the hall and we will think of something for you to say in front of the parrot.' So we went out and she said, 'As you liked the pudding so much why not say something about that?' Having pressed the recording button, she began, 'I hope you enjoyed your dinner, Maurice.' I said, 'Yes, I was particularly pleased at the pudding,' and she said, 'Why was that?' and I replied, 'Because you didn't have the "Brigade of Guards" savoury that Bill is so fond of.' She pressed the other button just to see if it was working and in a most disgusting way it repeated the words, in rather a low voice with blazing eyes. She shook it a little and we returned to the salon with the creature and handed it to Bill so that he could let it off. He pressed the button and there was dead silence; the parrot refused to utter a word. However Bill, determined not to let his parrot down, and I suppose to amuse the company, pretended that it was speaking in a low voice to him, and he shouted out what he pretended the parrot said, which was, 'I am an Irishman and I want more whisky.' The amusing thing was that although the parrot couldn't speak, its eyes were lit up and it had exactly the appearance of having said these words. I think some of the guests really believed that it had spoken.

*8 March 1966*

I went to see Charles Monteith of Fabers about the book on Edith Somerville.* He expressed eagerness for the firm and its publication is settled. I can begin the study of the papers as soon as I have got them from Paddy Coghill† in April, as is proposed. An amusing biography seems possible.

Later Louise and I went to see Maeve Peake. On arrival she informed me that the newspapers reported the death of Bill Astor. This

* *Somerville and Ross*, published 1968.
† Sir Patrick Coghill, nephew of Edith Somerville.

was a great shock to me. He was one of my oldest friends. The Cliveden period is over. My life will be different. I have written this evening to Bronwen. It appears that on arrival at Nassau, where he went about a week ago, he was taken ill suddenly at dinner with some friends and expired soon after in hospital. It was his heart. I had said to Bronwen that I wondered whether it was safe for him to leave the quiet of Cliveden and go to Nassau. She assured me that he was much better, wanted to go and that the doctors agreed that he might.

*9 March 1966*

I went up to Cliveden this morning at 10 with the note I had written to Bronwen. In the paper today it was stated that Bill's body would be flown back from Nassau for burial in the mausoleum in the grounds of Cliveden. I remember when a few years ago we were in the mausoleum together, he pointed to a spot near his father, the second Viscount's, grave and said, 'That will be my grave one day.' That his life would be cut short at fifty-eight years was very far from both our thoughts.

*12 March 1966*

At 10 a.m. the Cliveden butler rang up. He said: 'Her Ladyship asks you to dine with her tonight.' I said, 'I will do it.' Bill's body was cremated in Nassau and the ashes have been brought over for burial in the mausoleum. I do not know what will be the nature of our meeting tonight. 8 p.m. On arrival at the hall door I heard voices on the stairs and saw descending Bronwen and the Countess of Ancaster.* On seeing me, Bronwen came to where I was with her arms spread and I kissed her. She was thinner, somewhat worn and moved to see me. Laying her hand on my arm, she began to speak of Bill's death. She said (and as she spoke she broke down a little and my tears came): 'While we were dining at Nassau with some friends (that was six days ago) Bill suddenly had a violent pain across the chest. We all thought this was a heart attack, for it seemed to have the same sort of symptoms as the several attacks he had endured in the past six months. A doctor was phoned for and came immediately. He too thought it was a heart attack and at once gave him an injection, which relieved the pain and soothed him. "He will be all right,"

* Bill Astor's sister.

said the doctor. But soon afterwards Bill said that he could not see me. He seemed to be completely blind. Kept on asking—Am I all right? What is happening? At moments he seemed to regain his sight. I had no idea that he was dying. If I had thought so I would have become hysterical. And then he lost consciousness. His pulse had ceased by 2 a.m. on Monday morning. It was only then that it became known that he had not died of heart failure, but of a burst aneurism near the heart.'

That was what Bronwen said of the death scene. His blood drained away. She said: 'It might have happened any day in the last few years. It was the result of his blood pressure, which was bad for a long time and gradually got worse. What he suffered from the shock of the Ward case lessened his resistance. He has been a dying man since last August when he had the relapse in New York, which made him an invalid ever since. It was curious that his long illness mellowed him. He became easier, gentler. The last days of his life were the happiest I had had with him.'

So she spoke and we went into the little salon. Almost at once the butler announced dinner. An ordinary conversation was kept up. On returning to the salon Bronwen said that Charles Snow, the writer, now Lord Snow, had written a character sketch of Bill, which David Astor proposed to publish in the *Observer* on Sunday 20 March. Would I read it and give my opinion. Snow was a friend of Bill's of some years' standing. Bill admired his writings. But what I now read was not what one might have expected him to write. It was supposed to be an objective portrait, putting in what Bill's detractors said of him, repeating such irrelevancies as that he was unpopular at his private school fifty years ago and referring to the Ward case. The article struck me as unsuitable for publication. I said emphatically that it should not be published; it was extraordinary that David Astor should think it suitable.

Bronwen then asked me to hand the typescript to Lady Ancaster for her opinion. She read it and in her rather abrupt downright way said, 'Throw it in the fire.' Bronwen fell in with this unanimous opinion. One could not ascribe malice to Snow, only ineptitude, and presumably he would not seek publication elsewhere. Bronwen then went on to say that it was apparently thought by him and perhaps others that a definite attack on Bill's character was imminent. The

Rice-Davies woman* might be at the back of such an attack. It might be better to take the offensive first. In my view the Rice-Davies woman, though she has the power to harm Bill's reputation, will do nothing unless she sees money in it. She will not suddenly publish anything. There is no reason to seek to forestall her until she declares herself, which may very well never happen.

Bronwen went on to give certain facts. She said that Ward had got thousands of pounds out of Bill, nominal loans which he was to repay by providing free osteopathic remedies and massage to Bill and any of his guests. She also said that she had taken the view from the first that Ward was an undesirable person and should not be invited, but that Bill, quoting a friendship to which he must be true, had not taken her advice and continued to invite him. But, she added, to do Ward justice, he had not lived wholly or in part on the earnings of the girls whom he provided for his friends. As we know, however, it was his fear that the jury would find him guilty of precisely this misdemeanour, which drove him to suicide.

The party broke up before eleven. In parting I said to Bronwen that I would like some souvenir of Bill, some trifle such as a silk handkerchief or tie. She said, 'Yes, remind me of this.' She added that she would have liked me to come to the funeral at the mausoleum next Monday but only members of the family could be asked as there was no room in the mausoleum for more.

### 25 March 1966

To London with Louise. At 6.30 we went to a reception at the Carlton Towers given by the Military Attaché of the Burmese Embassy. As the government of Burma under General Ne Win is a military dictatorship, the Military Attaché here is a more prominent and authoritative figure than a mere embassy attaché. On our being announced and while we were speaking to the Military Attaché, Thein Doke, and his wife as they stood at the door, I noticed that he made a sign to some persons behind me. I looked round and saw it was his photographers. He desired to be photographed with me and this was done.

Moving away I saw the Ambassador and went to speak to him. Not content with his success in arranging the return to Burma of its

* Mandy Rice-Davies; one of the two chief witnesses in the Ward case.

old regalia, taken by the British in 1885, and also the return of the tusks of the White Elephant, as recorded further back, he was now about to acquire the Golden Umbrella, which, he said, had under the monarchy been held over the White Elephant. Someone here had it. He also said that he was on the track of the figurehead belonging to the prow of the Royal Barge.

We talked with Dorothy Woodman of the *New Statesman* and Irwin of the Victoria & Albert, both of whom have recently returned from Burma, where they attended ceremonies connected with the regalia. Irwin was the guest of honour in as much as he had facilitated its restoration. Dorothy Woodman said that on one occasion when attending some entertainment on the old Kemendaing racecourse in Rangoon she came to some stall or other where there were large photographs of myself displayed, together with copies of my books. On the next stall were photographs of Tolstoy with copies of his books. This astonished me, and I was yet more astonished when informed by Irwin that in the course of tours to various parts of Burma the places where I had resided were pointed out to him. The people, he declared, spoke of me with feeling. Dorothy Woodman said that some sort of an exhibition of Burmese art was being arranged this summer in Marlow* and asked whether I would open the exhibition with a speech. I promised to do this. Her proposal that a bus-load of Burmese should be allowed to eat a sandwich lunch on the lawn of my house I could not agree to.

Irwin's summing up of the situation in Burma today was that General Ne Win should be regarded as a moderate; that the national shops (for all shops and industry have been taken over by the state) have nothing in them; and that the people long for modernity, everything pertaining to the modern world of the West.

### 31 March 1966

I had received an invitation some time back to dine with the Master of the Worshipful Company of Armourers and Brasiers to meet the Lord Mayor of London and today made my way there in tail coat and white tie. The reason for the invitation was that the Master, William Syer Bristowe, is an admirer of my books. Altogether seventy-eight men sat down to dinner. At the top of the two

* 5 miles from Maidenhead.

long tables was a low dais on which eight persons had their seats, four on each side of the Master. On his immediate right were the Lord Mayor and Sir Arthur Bryant, and on his immediate left H.S.H. Prince Pleing Nobadol Rabibhadana, Ambassador of Thailand, and myself. I had never in my life been entertained in this style before. The dinner was conducted in the ancient traditional manner of the City guilds. We sat down at 7 p.m. and did not rise till 10.15. There were five courses and coffee, and a great variety of wines. Such old customs were observed as the handing round of the Loving Cup full of sack, and of a large heavy solid silver salver at the close of dinner, on which was scented water to refresh the face. There were many speeches, none of them interesting, though Arthur Bryant's was good farce. Three hours at table is too long for enjoyment and I looked forward to the end of the function. The Master made himself very agreeable to me, referring in his speech for the toast of the guests to my *Siamese White* and *Foreign Mud* as special favourites of his. In return for his kindness I promised to send him an inscribed copy of my *The Hurling Time*, as it has so much to say about the London of the 14th century, when the Armourers and Brasiers were founded, and its illustrations from manuscripts of that period give many examples of the armour then worn.

The guests seemed to enjoy themselves, though it struck me that for a great metropolis like London, which offered every sort of evening entertainment, intellectual, cultural or convivial, the entertainment it offered, outside a good dinner and various wines, was humdrum. His Serene Highness whispered to me with some distaste, 'These stag parties, are they common in London?'

## 9 April 1966

Dinner at Cliveden. Bronwen, who was in an emotional state (or showed that side to me more than usually), said that she would never have married Bill, had it not been for a vision, like some sort of a prompting from heaven, which she experienced two years before the marriage took place. At the time, she said, she was a top model and earning about £2,000 a year. Bill was one among the men she met and lunched with in London; the Duke of Marlborough was another. She regarded these men simply as rich acquaintances who gave her from time to time a very good lunch. Then she had the vision, of the nature of a psychic experience, which enjoined her to marry Bill, not for her advantage, but for his. His mother was destroying him. She was the only person who was able to stand up to his mother and deliver him from her. Such was the duty laid upon her by heaven. She carried out its behest as well as she could. Soon overtook him the turmoil of the Ward case. His sufferings were extreme. He knew he would not survive it. They both knew he was dying some six months before that happened. But he was a changed man, a person transformed. That was the meaning of her vision. There remained, she said, one more undertaking. What its exact nature was, she did not know, but it was comparable to what she had achieved in the first. She had no one to sustain her except her father. But he the other day had had a heart attack and would be in bed for a month. In the matter of writing a vindication of Bill, some sort of a biographical book, she advised that the project be postponed, a long postponement perhaps, since the inner meaning of his last days was bound up with the vision, a searing frightening vision, she insisted.

*17 May 1966*

Louise and I had suggested to Maeve Peake that we would like to visit Mervyn at Roehampton where he now is. We drove her there. The institution (a private hospital) is a huge sprawling hideous turreted building of fanciful Victorian design, with a large garden of pleasant aspect. Maeve went in to fetch Mervyn as we waited in the garden. Presently they emerged, she supporting a fragile bent stumbling figure, emaciated, white haired, like some tired old man of eighty. Mervyn is actually not more than fifty-four. I saw him last at his exhibition at the Collectors Gallery, Portobello Road, three years ago. Since then his physical decline had been rapid.

We went up to him and greeted him in an easy and cheerful manner. Maeve, of course, had told him we had come to see him. He looked at us now from his deepset eyes, smiled and showed a moving pleasure at the sight of us. He took my arm and with Maeve supporting him on the other side we moved slowly across the smooth lawn towards the rhododendrons in flower. He spoke now and then in a low whisper, which I could not understand, but Maeve did. He was, as it were, hidden away in the shadow of himself. He looked very distinguished with his magnificent brow and noble nose. Presently he desired Louise to take his other arm and she changed places with Maeve. I kept up a little talk about old days, his drawings, his wonderful books. He continued smiling and now and then muttering a word. We turned and came to a seat. When he was sat down between Maeve and Louise, myself opposite on a chair, he said he would like me to continue talking but would not himself be able to talk. So I spoke on in a way I thought he would like. Suddenly got up and Maeve said she thought he would like to take a short turn by himself, as that was a thing he often fancied. But what he wanted was to take his coat off. The sun was blazing down. So we helped him out of his coat. We sat on a little bit, when he intimated vaguely that he would like to show us the garden. We got to our feet, he put his coat on again, and arm in arm with Louise and I, slowly walked a distance towards a tennis court. Maeve, though she gave us to understand that our visit had greatly enlivened him, was now afraid he would overdo himself and perhaps be unable to move or would sink down. She made us turn back towards the building. He, however, did not want to do this. He seemed to enjoy the stroll with us and made efforts to let us know that he did not want to go back, uttering little short sentences—'This way.' 'Round there.' 'Not back.' But Maeve gently guided him back. When we came near the door an attendant moved up and took charge of him. The parting with him was very poignant. Before entering the door he turned, raised his hand, looked at us with a yearning smile and said, more clearly than any words he had so far spoken, 'See you soon'. We promised to come and see him again.

### 28 May 1966

At Cliveden. Bronwen said that her father had stood by them valiantly during the Ward case. When Bill received the news that Ward had committed suicide, he told Bronwen that he could not face the dreadful scandal any longer and that he was leaving at once for America. She begged him not to flee the country. Despairing of convincing him that such a step would be disastrous for his reputation, she rang up her father. It was then 8.0 at night. Her parents immediately set out from London for Cliveden and arrived at 11 p.m. Their appearance at the hall door with their suitcases was a dramatic moment in the Ward imbroglio and one which remains unknown outside the family. Sir Alun wrestled with Bill and before the night was over persuaded him to stay on at Cliveden and face it out.

## 4 July 1966

The Duchess of St Albans who, with the Duke, runs the Upper Grosvenor Gallery, rang to ask if I would say a few words to open Mervyn Peake's exhibition at a party at 6 p.m. Louise and I arrived on time, to find a gathering crowd of people. I spoke to Lord Snow and his wife the novelist.* He reminded me of the occasions, never alas to recur, when we met at Cliveden. She said that after his excursion into politics, he was writing again with renewed zest. He himself, I thought, looked less prematurely aged than before, as if he had been invigorated by his experiences as a minister,† though it had ended too abruptly to be pleasant, and had learned a lesson which gave him a clearer estimate of his powers than he possessed before, a humbling and yet valuable hint.

The moment came when I had to make my little speech. A gong sounded and my name was mentioned. Maeve Peake was on my right, the Duchess on my left. I had prepared some remarks and held a couple of typed sheets in my hand. But when it came to the point, I made an extempore speech. I described Mervyn's present state, saying that, although he was in London and not far off, he was unaware and could not be made aware, of the big gathering come to see and admire his work. I spoke for five minutes; what else I said, I do not remember.

## 11 August 1966

On the way to lunch with General and Mme Ne Win I picked up Noel Whiting in the car. Mme Ne Win was outside when we arrived and brought us into the room where was the General. He came forward and welcomed us. Drinks were brought. I said to him that I had seen only an hour or two ago in the *Daily Mail* that U Thant was not standing again for a further period as Secretary General of the United Nations. He had not seen it, and a curious expression flitted over his face for an instant, as if the news was not altogether agreeable to him.

* Pamela Hansford Johnson.
† Not quite correct. He had been Parliamentary Secretary to the Ministry of Technology 1964–66.

We went in to lunch. I was placed on the General's right, the Burmese Ambassador on his left. On my right was Mme Ne Win's sister, a very charming young-looking woman. Madame presided at the other end of the table with Noel Whiting on her right. There were two other Burmese men at table, members of the General's staff. He was dressed in Burmese costume, though the other men were in English clothes, including the chauffeurs, the A.D.C.s and house servants, all of whom looked very smart and alert. Madame was dressed in a manner of her own invention, a long silk gown of a reddish colour, reminiscent of a Chinese fashion, but not strictly so.

The lunch was the Burmese cuisine, there being laid on the table a great number of dishes of a dry kind, to be eaten with rice, the only dish to be handed by a table servant, an Indian.

The General, who has the reputation of being very quiet and reserved, was not so on this occasion. I addressed most of my remarks to him, though sometimes spoke down the table to Madame. I said I hoped that he was amusing himself in London, and going about. He replied that he had come here to rest after the heavy duties which devolved on him in Burma as Head of State. He was taking it easy and already feeling the better for it, though the sinus, from which he has suffered for so many years, still afflicts him in some measure. He seems to have gone out little during the fortnight he has been here, though he was received by the Queen and had lunch with the Prime Minister, Mr Wilson. He and Madame had also visited the Victoria & Albert, and she spoke of a few theatres.

Among other things I said to the General that he was for people here somewhat of a mystery man; neither his character nor his policy was well understood. What, in a word, was his aim? He replied: 'I want to give the Burmese people back their country.' They had been given back the country in a political sense, but they could not use political freedom if the West held them in an economic and financial grip. His policy was to loosen that grip. The Burmese must get on without foreign aid, especially loans. They must work out their own salvation. Madame interjected: 'The difficulty is that the Burmese are lazy.' They have to be forced to reassume control of their destiny. The General's aim is to oblige them to become, as they once were, complete masters within their dominion. I said to him, 'Are you not shortly going to America?' He said that was so. I went on: 'The

Americans will want to tempt you again to take their money. The Burmese had a narrow shave some time back from becoming an American satellite. Had they fallen for that temptation they would soon have lost the political independence they had won.' The General did not deny this. Indeed, it was precisely his view. But he did not reveal what was his purpose in going to America. Will he be able to refuse the fortune they will certainly offer him?

I spoke of Chiang Kai-shek. His face clouded. 'The Taiwan people give us nothing but trouble.' He referred to trade and also the machinations of their agents on the border. The fact that they were exactly what he wanted to avoid, American puppets, a people who had taken up the American way of life, also disgusted him.

The General throughout adopted towards me an attitude of the utmost consideration, though he remained reserved, but for a moment, turning towards me more particularly, I noticed a certain ferocity or violent resolution on his mouth, and reflected that here was the man who had seized power in Burma and was driving its people in a manner which he conceived to be essential for their salvation, if hardly what they conceived as essential, for they were, as Madame said, too lackadaisical. For an instant he looked as formidable as I believe him to be. Yet there are those who contend that he is governed by the wishes of his military junta, whose major desire is to remain in power. I was unable to come to a clear view in my mind.

At the conclusion of lunch, when we rose from the table and were in the hall, he wished me goodbye and ascended the stairs to his study, leaving me with Madame and the Ambassador. As he left I said to him that I would record the occasion in my diary. It is always an interesting thing to meet a remarkable personality. General Ne Win is an historical figure. Whether he succeeds in his task or is overthrown, he remains part of Burmese history. What English opinion finds it hardest to accept at the moment, is his imprisonment of U Nu, the former Prime Minister, a man who had many friends in Europe and America, an imprisonment without trial and possibly for life. U Nu had, no doubt, become a rather foolish creature, not strong enough to prevent the country from dissolving into anarchy. Such a man must be prevented from doing more harm, and detention was the only safe way to effect this. But this view is too extreme for our English notions of liberty of the individual and the rule of law.

*6 November 1966*

Went to dine with Bronwen. Among the things of interest she said was that Ward's cottage, which is now inhabited by some man or other, is haunted. The man complains of thumping on the windows and footsteps coming upstairs in the middle of the night. The man before him either committed suicide or had heart failure and fell into the sink and was drowned. This man seems to be on the same route. When I mentioned to her the curious Edith Somerville and Violet Martin* psychic communications, she said that she had received from a psychic friend a communication purporting to be from Bill. She hadn't credited it, however, because the message was merely that she should use her influence to persuade the Cabinet to take a different view on some point of foreign policy. As she said, surely he would have sent her a more personal message than that. However, she said that she was now consumed with a curious compulsion to write letters to Bill. She knew about Stanley Spencer's extraordinary correspondence with the dead Hilda,† and she said that the same compulsion had taken hold of her and she didn't know whether to give way to it or not. In this connection of communications with the dead, she put forward the view that the reason spirits rarely give information about themselves, particularly their surroundings, is because their surroundings are ineffable and there are no words to describe them. I mention this to show her present state of mind.

Just before I was going she spoke of the fearful rows that occurred between Bill's father, the second Viscount, and mother, Nancy Astor, towards the end of their lives. She got on his nerves to such an extent that he didn't allow her into his room except for half an hour once a week. That side of Nancy Astor's character was of course not emphasised in my biography, at Bill's request; indeed, he hardly spoke to me at all of it, only hinted that something of the kind existed towards the end of his father's life.

*15 January 1967*

Dined with Bronwen. Part of the time we spoke of Ward. One of the questions I asked her was, 'Did Bill never realise the danger he was in by associating with persons who were really crooks?' She

* He was writing *Somerville and Ross* at this time.

† The first Mrs Spencer.

replied that it never crossed his mind. He never thought he was in any danger.

She also said there was no telephone at Ward's cottage. When sometimes Bill wanted Ward to come up for one reason or another, a message had to be sent down, and that if it so happened that she was going for a walk in the park with the dogs, Bill would say, 'Just drop in for a moment and tell Stephen to come up before dinner.' That meant, she said, that (though it didn't happen very often) she would walk over to Ward's cottage with the result that she might well have been seen going there by herself, which gave rise later on during the bust-up to every sort of surmise and was one of the reasons why she was so mixed up in this business. She said she had again and again warned Bill against Ward, when she had got to know things a little better, but he paid no attention to her, and after all she had then only been married to him for about six or eight months, and she was the third of his wives and naturally, taking over charge like that, he wasn't prepared to listen to anything to start with. It was not until later that she managed to exercise some influence over him and it was then of course too late.

*6 March 1967*

At 7 a.m. my wife, Eleanor, came into my room and said she was suffering a violent pain in the stomach. I jumped out of bed at once, hurried to Louise's room, woke her up and rang our doctor. An ambulance arrived at 8.30 and Eleanor was carried to it, in very severe pain in the abdomen. She was taken to a private room and soon afterwards the surgeon informed us that an immediate operation was necessary if her life was to be saved. The operation took place before noon. During the afternoon the surgeon telephoned that the operation had been successful from a surgical point of view. He gave no details. It was evident, however, that the pain had been due to a severe peritonitis.

*7 March 1967*

Louise and I arrived at the hospital about 3 p.m. and found Eleanor looking remarkably well, good colour, clear in the head, no pain. In speaking to the surgeon, however, it was clear that the operation was a most severe one. She was having continuous blood transfusion.

However the surgeon and matron declared she would be out of hospital in a month. We went home reassured.

## 8 March 1967

We got an early telephone message to say that Eleanor had had a heart attack and was dangerously ill, and hastened to the hospital. Eleanor was flushed, wandering in mind and barely conscious of our presence. By this time David and Bryan* had come. The surgeon now informed us that though the operation had been surgically successful, her heart had been put to too much strain by it. Her heart was, in his view, not as strong as it should normally have been, though she had never actually had a heart attack or any disturbance in the heart which could have warned her. She had perhaps only survived by reason of the very quiet life she had led for some years. We asked him what was her present chance of surviving? Could the heart sustain the shock? His reply was that there was still a ten per cent chance.

As nothing further could be done at the moment we returned home, though David remained. During the day Eleanor got weaker. Warned by telephone we went back to the hospital about 6 p.m. She was no longer conscious. Her eyes were staring, very wide open and rather horrified, though she was not conscious of her state. She was clearly dying and death might come at any moment. Her breathing was more rapid. Louise, I, David, Bryan and his wife Carol, stood round the bed, a nurse being in attendance. As we watched she suddenly rolled her head to the right and stopped breathing. She was gone. I closed her left eye, the nurse her right eye, and laid her on the pillows. We withdrew, all weeping.

## 13 June 1967

I had been asked by the Central Office of Information to write a sketch on Lowry and so went to the Lefevre. On entering the gallery, I saw Lowry sitting on a sofa giving an interview to a journalist. I told him of this commission to write an article on him. He seemed very happy that I should do so. The next day there was a picture in *The Times* of Lowry talking to the Postmaster General in the Lefevre Gallery. It is a good likeness, with the curious stare and smiling look that he has. He complained to me of his poverty, as usual, which is a

* Her sons.

kind of fiction. The walls contained thousands of pounds of Lowrys on sale (many of them already sold). He had invented an ingenious way of making a little money, he told me. The G.P.O. next month are bringing out a 1s. 6d. stamp on which will be one of Lowry's pictures, a very signal recognition that I had never heard of before for an artist. Lowry's idea now is to have 500 postcard sized reproductions of the picture on the stamp, and to sell them himself from his house at 2s. 6d. a time with his autograph, to persons who come bothering him. If he sells his 500 that would net him about £60 minus costs, a modest sum one might think for a man who commands £3,000 even for a small picture. However he is like that, as indeed he has always been.

### 8 July 1967

Feliks Topolski rang up this morning to say that he was in a difficulty with the Duke of Edinburgh over the price of the equestrian portrait which he had done of him two years back, and now hangs in the Palace, but is not yet paid for. Apparently at the time of the commission no price was named, as Feliks and the Prince were old friends. Things have got to a point now, said Feliks, that the price he asked was considered too high by the Prince, and it seemed a matter for arbitration; would I act as arbitrator? I said I would. He said, in that case he would suggest my name to Prince Philip, giving him some biographical details to show that I was the right person. No doubt I shall hear more of this in due course.

### 9 July 1967

Lunch with Bronwen at her new house, Tuesley Manor, near Godalming. I told her about this request by Topolski to arbitrate over the Prince's picture. She knows Topolski quite well, because he did a portrait of her, the portrait which Bill Astor wouldn't allow to be hung in the Carlton Tower Hotel. Her first reaction was to say I ought to refuse because it would only involve me in goodness knows what. But when I assured her that I didn't care what it involved me in because I wasn't out to get anything for myself, and what did I care what was said by anyone connected in the matter, because they couldn't touch me; and indeed, as all I was to do was to suggest a reasonable price, that was hardly ground for a quarrel. She agreed I should go on. I asked her if she knew the Prince. 'I have met him, of course,' she said, 'and he is very tough.' Then she went on to talk of luncheons, or a luncheon, in Buckingham Palace. She said that the royal party had very little conversation, their interests were narrow, and it was almost impossible to interest them except on certain specified subjects. The Queen, she said, was aware the conversation at the table was inclined to halt, and she had a man there whose duty it was to suggest some subject when the conversation languished; she also had on the table little curios, or bits of silver, in the form of pheasants, or the like, to which she could draw people's attention and so have a little subject for conversation.

But I wouldn't have thought that this description applied to Prince Philip, who must have plenty of things to talk about.

### 14 July 1967

At 5.0 we went to Topolski's studio. He said there were some things connected with the Duke of Edinburgh that he wanted to tell me and which he did not wish to say before women, including Louise and his secretary. They therefore retired to the other arch* and he then proceeded to talk to me. Characteristically, nothing that he had to say had to do with any matter which could conceivably be regarded as indelicate or what you like. In fact what he wanted to tell me really was all about the correspondence that he had had with the Duke. He got out the Duke's letters and showed them to me. He explained the circumstances from the very beginning. Several years ago the Duke had in the first instance said that some public body or other wanted a portrait of him on a horse, this body presumably being endowed with sufficient funds to pay for such a portrait. However this body, whatever it was, seems to have disappeared—whether when they saw the picture or not, I don't know. Two years ago the picture was finished and delivered to Windsor Castle. The Queen saw it and did not like the background, and asked for it to be changed. Feliks refused to tamper with what he rightly considered was his own creation and informed the Duke accordingly. There was then a rather awkward pause of a year or so. The Duke had taken delivery of the portrait but nothing at all had ever been said about the price. A point was then reached when Feliks sent in a bill for what he considered a

* He had two arches under Hungerford Bridge.

reasonable sum, considering that the picture was 15ft × 10ft, and was a commission. He had been paid similar sums both in America and, I believe, for his pictures of the Coronation procession hanging in Buckingham Palace. He showed me the Duke's reply to this demand for payment in which he said, 'We were all thunderstruck' by this demand. The Duke went on to say that he had taken the opinion of some experts and they had suggested a very different figure. He didn't say who they were, and he suggested in this letter to Feliks that an arbitrator might be called in. The tone of the Duke's letters was very cordial throughout; he always addressed Feliks by his Christian name, signed himself Philip and the letters were always in his own hand-writing. His proposal for arbitration was not immediately acceptable to Feliks. However, in the end he wrote to the Duke saying he would be willing to have an arbitrator and would the Duke sanction this. To which the Duke replied in a letter shown me that he agreed as he wished to keep the picture, but he did not want to bind himself in advance to agree to the arbitrator's findings as to the price.

As already related, Feliks asked me whether I would act as arbitrator and I agreed to do so. He then wrote to the Duke saying he would like to appoint me. He has not yet heard from the Duke, which is not unnatural because he only sent his letter three days ago, and the Duke is always flying about here and there. I intend to do nothing until I have had it in writing from Windsor, when I will naturally try to do my best.

### 10 August 1967

London. Met Kathleen Raine, the poetess. She was going next day to Sligo to give a lecture on Yeats. I told her how I had attended his funeral at Sligo with the poet MacNeice, who declared that the body, exhumed in France and brought to Sligo, was not Yeats's body. She had heard this story before.

### 21 August 1967

The visit by General Ne Win to this house.* General Ne Win, the Head of State, Burma, who is over in this country to consult his doctor, rang up to say that he would like to call today on his way back from lunching with his doctor near Newbury, as he would be passing my door. It was actually Mme Ne Win who was on the

* In Maidenhead, Berks.

phone. I said how glad Louise and I would be to receive them. At 4 p.m. the Burmese Ambassador, U Hla Maung, arrived from London and half an hour later the General and his party reached us. They were in two cars, himself and his wife and a companion in one and his bodyguard in the other. While waiting we had taken our seats in the drawing room, much against the Ambassador's inclination, for he felt that the General should find him waiting on the gravel in front of the house. However, we caught sight of them alighting from their car at the gate and hastened out in time to welcome them on the gravel.

We entered the house, after the General had ordered his bodyguard to go off in the cars and come back in about an hour. We had arranged a buffet tea, so that we avoided the formality of all having to sit down to table. After tea I took them over the house. I showed them in particular my books, including the Burmese translations by Ma A Ma of Mandalay; my pictures, including the one on the Burmese handmade paper on which Mme Ne Win had once written to me. Madame had a natural feeling for art and had evidently picked up something during her travels. The General said that in Burma they were excavating the site of the old capital at Taungdwingyi (where I was subdivisional officer in 1915) and asked me to come out and advise on the archaeological plans. I replied that within four months I would be entering my eightieth year and was too old to come east. He seemed surprised I was as old as that.

At about 5.30 the bodyguard returned and drew the cars up at the front door. Mme Ne Win declared they must leave. The visit had been very pleasant. Among other things I had said to the General that he ought to have his portrait painted while in London. Topolski was the very man for the job; he required few sittings. But the General declared roundly that he intended to have no portrait painted of himself. I said to Mme: 'The Burmese people will insist on having a portrait of the General, and one would not like a poor likeness of him, without force of character, to be handed down to posterity.' She agreed but the General would not hear of it. So ended the visit.

Nothing was said about politics, the condition of Burma, the General's policy. The tone of the conversation was easy, casual and warm. No attempt was made to lead the General into making any statement whatever about his own affairs. All reference to persons or international events was avoided. Nothing could have been more informal than the talk. On our bidding them farewell, as we saw them to their car, their manner showed how frankly they had enjoyed the occasion. I, of course, was very gratified by their visit.

*8 September 1967*

Our visit to Windsor Castle to view the Topolski portrait of the Duke of Edinburgh. At the main gate the police on duty instructed us to drive into the courtyard up to the Superintendent's office, where we were expected. There we found looking out for us a man of the messenger type who had been deputed to conduct us. He led us down subterranean passages, humming as he went, and reminding us of a character out of *Alice in Wonderland*. After a time we reached a vast lumber room containing piles of armour, weapons and the like, in which we saw the Topolski picture, propped against the wall but on its side, so that the horse's nose was on the ground. On our protesting to our amiable guide that the picture could not be judged unless the right way up, he at first declared that it was beyond his power to move it, but on our showing how light was even a large canvas and easy to shift, he summoned a workman and the picture was moved. It was then revealed as a slight and rapid sketch, a thin wash of colour over the outline. Many passages were left quite unresolved, such as the horse's legs, of which a double version was given. The background in some places suggested the presence of other men and horses; in other places nothing in particular except indeterminate lines. I was placed in an awkward position; with the best will in the world it was impossible to support Topolski's price, and I have been obliged to report this opinion. How Topolski will take it I do not know. The valuations of the other two assessors have still to be sent in. They are likely, I suspect, to be less than mine. It is the average of the three valuations that the Duke proposes to pay Topolski.

*26 September 1967*

To London with Louise. Bernard Leach's private view of a new series of his pots was on at the Crane Kalman gallery. When we went in we saw Leach sitting on a bench. He is now eighty and looked very shaky. We have been acquainted for twenty-five years and he, of course, knew who I was but could not recall my name. 'I had a stroke lately,' he said by way of excuse, 'and find it impossible now to remember names.' I sympathised with him, saying that as one grew older one remembered names less well. He said he had neither seen nor heard of me lately; what had happened to me? I said that I had continued as usual with my literary work and mentioned my Somerville and Ross book, due to appear next spring. His reply was that he never read anything, but at the same time drew my attention to the book he had just published on Kensan, the Japanese potter. It was on the seat beside him. This caused me to mention that I had signed Kensan a bowl. 'Probably a copy by a follower or a fake for the foreign market,' he announced. 'Japan is full of such things.' Leach has never been a man, in my experience, who allowed that anyone but himself knew about pots. When I replied that I had bought it at Sotheby's twenty-four years ago and that it came from a well known private collection, he became less certain it must be a fake and myself an ignoramus. Taking up his book I pointed to an illustration. 'It is similar to that,' I said. But he had lost interest. To begin with he had shown pity for my lack of expertise and gladness that he could correct me; it only bored him now to perceive that I probably had a genuine Kensan. It is not to be supposed that he was suffering from senility, though his stroke had not improved his mental faculties. He was the same as he always was. 'I am leaving next week for Japan again,' he said and left the gallery.

A couple of days ago in the press was an account of how Sir Francis Rose, Bart, had appeared as complainant in a magistrates' court, accusing his wife's son (by a previous marriage) of assaulting him. He declared under oath to the court that having had a difference with his newly-wed wife he retired, as had in the past been his practice at moments of stress, to a Catholic monastic institution. There he heard that his wife and her son were committing incest. At this he left the monastic retreat and returned to his wife's house in Park Lane. There was no one at home. Accordingly he cooked himself something and went to bed with a bottle of wine. His wife's son came in after a while and an altercation began, ending in his stepson setting on him and violently assaulting him. His Honour declared, after taking what evidence was produced by both sides, that he did not believe Francis's story, dismissed the case and ordered Francis to pay costs.

*20 February 1968*

Having heard that Topolski proposed to hold an exhibition of his

199

paintings and drawings at the Grosvenor Gallery, Davies Street, we went there to enquire and were told that such an exhibition was to be opened by the Duke of Edinburgh on 27 February. I have heard nothing from him about the Duke's equestrian portrait since I saw it at Windsor Castle and wrote in giving my estimate of its value. It seems, however, as if that has all been arranged with the Duke, as he is opening the exhibition. We were told a party is to be given at 5.30 p.m. on the 27th for which an invitation is necessary. I accordingly wrote to Topolski asking for an invitation, and saying how glad I was that he was having the exhibition under the aegis of the Duke, a course which I had urged him to take over a year ago.

### 27 February 1968

The Topolski party at the Grosvenor Gallery. We arrived wondering what the last scene of the comedy of the Duke's portrait would be like. Though we were on time, the gallery was already crowded. The Duke's huge Rolls was drawn up at the door. There were policemen about and a small crowd of people watching. We presented our invitations to some sort of sergeant and began threading our way down the immense room. Soon we saw Feliks in converse with the Duke. I did not think it proper to go straight up to him, and we hovered in his vicinity until he caught sight of us. He and the Duke then came up. The Duke shook hands, saying: 'You were one of the assessors, weren't you?' Feliks's collar had broken loose, his tie was under his ear. To make it all seem like a laughing matter I rallied Feliks on his untidy neck. 'Oh!' said the Duke, 'My son's collar is just as bad.' With that he moved off to speak to others in the crowd. So the drama ended. Nothing more was said. How the affair was settled I do not know and probably never will.

### 20 August 1968

London. Lunch with Herman Schrijver. It was some ten years since we last met. He is now very well off, having made quite a big reputation as an interior decorator and moved in interesting circles. In fact, he knows most people in the arts and has a store of anecdotes which he relates in an amusing style. He has long been a friend of Ivy Compton-Burnett, whom I often met at his luncheon table. She used to boast of the fact that she knew no language except English. Herman now reminded me of this eccentricity of hers and recalled how on one occasion, when he had remarked that he had the fluent use of four languages, that she declared it only showed how common he was. A vulgar trait, she called it. She is now over ninety, and is still writing, though slowly. She is, I would say, the top woman novelist of today.

Herman went on to describe a ridiculous occasion when he had invited Sir Francis Rose to luncheon. He was expected at 1.0 but there was no sign of him. At 1.45 the bell rang, and Herman, accompanied by one of the guests, went to the hall door. On his opening it, there was Rose who, on the instant, fell flat on the ground. He was dead drunk. He had been in the act of taking a pinch of snuff and his snuff box was open when he fell, and the snuff went up in a cloud. Herman and his companion began sneezing violently. 'It was like a scene out of a comic opera,' he declared.

### 17 September 1968

Louise and I in London. At 4.15 we went to tea with Julian and Juliette Huxley. I had not been there for several years. We found Julian in better form than we expected. Though eighty-two and rather feeble, he retains his interest in life. He said that at one period in his life, the thirties, he made a study of psychical phenomena with mediums etc, but never got further than perceiving that the occult was a subject which one could neither accept as presented nor reject as a total delusion. There was something there, but what precisely? The subject came up in connection with an entry in Edith Somerville's diary about the Flower Medium, which mentions the Huxleys and the strange materialisation of violets in Juliette's hand after the séance when in their car in Hammersmith Broadway. In Edith Somerville's diary no mention is made of the presence of the Flower Medium in the car, but Juliette says she was in the car and could have slipped violets surreptitiously into her hand. I then recounted the circumstances under which I saw two ghosts in Burma, the one at Mrauk-U in 1926, an alleged guardian ghost of the treasure of the Kings of Arakan, and the other in my house as Deputy Commissioner of Mergui in 1933. Julian showed the greatest interest in these two appearances, which are described fully in the last chapter of my *Into Hidden Burma*.

### 22 October 1968

Drove up to Cliveden and had a look at the house which has had such a place in my life. One could peep in through the windows of the dining room and the big salon. The table was laid in the former. But what a fall from its former elegance. The cloth was soiled and hung down in a slovenly manner. An effort had been made to lay the forks and spoons; but we noticed that tablespoons were set out, which of course was incorrect, for the guests never required them, as the dishes were always handed round by the butler and footmen. Flowers were in bowls in the centre, but common flowers, not the splendid greenhouse blooms that used to grace the table. It was a distressing sight. Looking into the big salon was even more saddening. The books and pictures were no longer there. One saw only a few bits of furniture, none of which was there in the old days. A few visitors wandered about. The entrance cost 2s, too high a figure for what was now to be seen.

### 10 November 1968

As Louise and I were walking along the towpath of the Thames we met Geoffrey Baker, once our milkman, who became an artist, exhibited at the Academy, taught at an art school in High Wycombe, came under the influence of the Beatles' mentor, the Maharishi Mahesh Yogi, and joined him in the foothills of the Himalaya, where his academy is situated. Baker has just returned thence. He has a luxuriant beard, so bushy that I did not recognise him at first. He told us how he had become one of the Maharishi's missionary preachers and was shortly going to South America to spread his master's tenets. He begged us to go forthwith to India and stay at the Maharishi's Himalayan institute. 'You will have a lovely room with a vast view towards the eternal snows.' And he gave us samples of the Maharishi's sayings and intoned over the river some of his catchwords, such as, 'Wait on, wait on.'

It was very interesting to see to what a milkman might come, and come quickly.

### 31 December 1968

London. Went to see Julian and Juliette Huxley. He was in better health and spirits than when last we saw him. He told an amusing story: Some years ago he was asked by one of the newspapers to write something about the séances held in London at that date. One séance he attended was where a medium undertook to bring back from the beyond the spirits of dead dogs, pets much missed by the owners. The light was, of course, very dim and he could see nothing, but he heard one pet dog's spirit wagging his tail on the floor, a swishing or dusting sound. In fact he detected it *was* a duster swished adroitly by the medium or her adjutant. Julian told this anecdote in a droll manner, as if he had much enjoyed the occasion and felt indulgent to the grieving owners who had so hopefully paid their money to the ingenious medium. It entertained me very much, as so many of the séances at Drishane★ were to commune with dear deceased dogs, as very fully described in my *Somerville and Ross*.

It was a pleasant call. At the end I gave Julian and Juliette a copy of my *The Hurling Time* as they had not read it. I wrote a dedication in the hall as I was leaving—so hurriedly that I spelt Julian's name with a 'y' and also got into difficulties with the form of the sentence.

★ The Somerville family's house.

# FINIS

The last entry in the Diaries reads: '*20 February 1969* heavy fall of snow'. The rest of the pages in the new foolscap book he had bought are blank. The flow of anecdote and observation stops as if smothered. He was eighty and old age had suddenly invaded him, like a plague or hostile army of some sort. He who had been scornful of all weakness, especially in the head, began to grow forgetful and easily confused. The ferocious independence of character he had possessed changed into a habit of never taking any steps in even the smallest matter without asking my advice. He clung to me tighter and tighter and tighter: death was treading on his heels. As he was not daft in the ordinary sense, he was aware of these mutations of his personality.

Yet still he loved a party, a new book or exhibition. When not otherwise engaged, we would spend the evenings talking gaily on all manner of subjects with a bottle of whisky between us. He got drunk a little sooner than heretofore, but not much. Though writing had become a labour rather than a happiness, he painted with enthusiasm, dozens of fantastic landscapes in the colours of paradise. There was nothing decrepit about them. They were like the poetic visions of a young man newly arrived in the tropics.

As 1969 went on, I became increasingly worried by the failure of his strength. I would find him at all hours in a collapsed sleep in his study chair, his book fallen on the floor, his head sideways on his shoulder, his glasses half off, his teeth askew in his open mouth. Or I would come on him somewhere in the house, just standing. He looked like an apparition.

I began to have bad dreams, a disease I am not subject to, in general. Nor do I have a compulsion to write down everyday doings, but I sometimes make notes. The following is one of them:

*22 October 1969*
My dream early this morning just before waking: I was in bed

and could hear classical music coming from the next room, also the voices of neighbours in their garden. I was curious about the music (Mozart and Beethoven) and got up and pushed the door slightly and peeped in. The room was full of people. They did not notice me. I understood them to be ghosts. I shut the door at once, conscious that I had done a very dangerous thing in looking at them.

I am dressed and in a room which perhaps is my bedroom still. Maurice comes in. He says to a small woman, something like Mother, 'Why you're only a ghost! Look at the gap between your shoulders!' He strikes her shoulder and a large split appears in the centre of her back. She is plainly a phantom. I am filled with terror for him, saying: 'You fool! You oughtn't to have done that.'

All the ghosts come out of the room where they were. They pass me in a crowd and vanish. They have taken him with them. I am left sitting on the ground beside a toast rack which I understand to be his mortal remains. I woke with an indescribable feeling of anguish and horror.

Shortly afterwards there was an incident that showed his heart had begun to weaken, though neither of us recognised it at the time. I had previously noticed that his ankles were swollen, but at my remarking on this he had replied: 'No, they're not.' So I hadn't pursued the matter. However on 16 November 1969, he had a crisis in the night. I wrote:

He came into my room in the small hours saying he felt very ill. He was pale, his breath rasping, but didn't seem to me as bad as he thought. He was quite steady on his feet. He said he felt very sick and couldn't breath, might suffocate at any moment. I invited him to sit on my bed. He said he couldn't decide what medicine to take. Could I advise? He went off and got two packets and a tin. I suggested something out of the tin. He asked if he might sit on my sofa for a bit, and flung himself on to it heavily, mentioning his mother on whose last days he is now inclined to brood. He asked me to mix him a dose from the tin. In spite of his fears, he was obliged to admit the attack was passing off. He began to feel cold and to think tea would be nice. I suggested he go downstairs and poke up his fire while I made tea. He assented to this. I left him in his study at 6.15 drinking tea in front of a roaring fire. He was wearing an assortment of underclothes, socks, pyjamas, ragged dressing-gown, his best coat, worst scarf, a rug. He took up Oscar Wilde's *Salome*, he tells me, and slept peacefully until 9.0 in the chair.

By the spring he was finding the journey to London, the day of exhibitions and drinks with friends, too much for him. As he now could not bear to be alone in the house, it was clear that we would both shortly be buried alive in Maidenhead, a place where we had lived for thirty-five years without taking the smallest interest in local people or affairs, for we were Londoners by nature.

We had been talking of moving since 1967 when my mother died, but he had always put forward objections, such as the impossible amount of packing that would have to be done, and the necessity of having a garden large enough to grow one's own vegetables; also that it would be melancholy not to be able to walk in woods when one felt like it; and finally that the expense would be prohibitive. These arguments were at last seen to be fallacious. During the autumn of 1970 we settled in a suitable London flat.

Our life was outwardly gayer than before. Five days a week either we went out in the evening, or people came to us, and the odd two days we drank happily together. But how is Time to be deflected? Only God knows. Though he was writing slowly and reading and painting a lot, he was steadily disintegrating, body and soul. The groundswell of unreason which was an essential part of his nature became more difficult to control, and scenes occurred such as we had not had in twenty years. They would blow up suddenly, unpredictably, intensely, to be followed by tears of remorse; not that I minded the things he said in these transports, or even thought of replying to them. Again, he would fall into a gentle, tender mood and a smile of the most piercing sweetness would transform the ruins of his face.

He was still alert and interested in the world around him. As we drove to parties, museums, art galleries, he would sit contentedly beside me reading the advertisements on the back of buses and vans. 'What a splendid achievement it would be in one's life to have invented Bisto,' he said. 'Or to have painted that picture of the two kids sniffing Bisto fumes. It is a famous picture and more widely known than the *Mona Lisa* or *The Virgin on the Rocks*.'

Car number plates fascinated him, for the letters on them often formed Burmese words, which set him off on a chain of recollection so vivid that he would seem to be motoring up winding creeks overhung by the tumbled foliage of a tropical forest towards a small village, perched on stilts, with monkeys chattering on the roofs.

Sometimes his reflections were linguistic: 'What a number of excellent words there are that aren't made use of,' he remarked one day as we sat in a cloud of diesel smoke in the middle of Piccadilly. 'Imagine saying to a person, "You TUS you!" Or, "I'll TUS you, you FOT."' Occasionally he disapproved, 'If my name was Drinkwater,' he stated as we drew up behind a lorry with this legend painted on its tail, 'I wouldn't advertise it like that. I'd give up the ghost.'

We were haunted by ghosts from the past and by the fact that he was himself becoming a ghost. If we could have halted the ordered progression of the weeks and months that flowed through our consciousness, each taking with it another piece of his strength. If the elixir which was sent him in a Horlicks bottle by a Burmese admirer had not been made of coloured sand. '24 July 1971, 9.30 p.m.' I noted: 'He said: "I shall be leaving you soon. I'm sinking." Only this afternoon I looked back as he followed me out of the Institute of Contemporary Arts (in the Mall). As he came into the light he seemed like a walking corpse. "Don't let's go home yet," he said. So we crossed into St James's Park. But after fifty yards he was tired. We slowly climbed the Duke of York's steps to the car and went to the London Library.'

Yet, in spite of exhaustion and the occasional fits of depression that went with it, he remained cheerful for the most part, especially in company: for then he could temporarily forget that he was a man without a future. He had not believed in the hereafter since early manhood when the tenets of the Church of Ireland seemed, all at once, preposterous. And if you could not accept the possibility of God as laid down by one religion, how could any other overthrow your intellect? Though he never was converted to a recognised faith, now, on the brink of the void, he felt the idea of dust to dust, ashes to ashes, too cold and harsh to contemplate. He began to entertain fancies of floating about among the galaxies in some kind of a timeless, bodiless ether where the personality remained essentially unchanged.

'I will be waiting for you in the outer galaxies,' he said to me eagerly. 'It won't be long. What's thirty years or so among the

207

stars? Then we will be together again for ever and ever.' Thus he comforted himself in the face of dissolution.

So long as he could keep his feet under him, his enjoyment of parties never flagged. On 25 April 1972, we presented ourselves at Roland, Browse & Delbanco, the art gallery in Cork Street. The occasion was a centenary exhibition of Sir William Nicholson. We moved into the crowd, I noted at the time, 'and I passed a stout man who seemed to me to be Betjeman. He was saying: "That's Maurice Collis, but he doesn't know who I am." A little later, when Maurice was talking to James Laver, whose complexion gave the impression of heart trouble and whose hands shook, he came up and introduced himself. After some talk of old days in Dublin, he drifted off. He is a man of personality and charm, rather comical. He puts on no airs except a disinclination to talk to anyone for more than three minutes. He was closely accompanied by a tall clergyman with a red face. Betjeman introduced his wife, a short, rotund person in tweeds. She said she was just back from a bus tour in India, where she had been employed to lecture on the sights as they motored through them. She said the tourists were awful, except for Ann Yeats★ whom she got fond of. All the outings were arranged for the middle of the day.

'I began to feel stifled, and we went to stand on the pavement for a few minutes. Lady Betjeman came out shouting, "Where's John? We'll miss the blasted train." The clergyman followed shortly saying Betjeman was getting his coat. I said she was afraid of missing the blasted train. "We have missed the blasted train," says she. "We can take the next one," says the reverend soothingly. At last Betjeman appears in a navy coat, his face full of a vague joviality, but watchful, his legs thin and not too steady under his stout body. The three of them set off in the direction of Piccadilly.

'We went in for one more drink. Someone said to me: "Is that the prime minister?" It was Heath, accompanied only by a detective. All heads were turned in his direction. Miss Browse, one of the proprietors, began speaking to him of the exhibition. He took off his glasses, breathed on them, polished them, put them back on and bent attentively towards the nearest picture. He shook hands with a rich woman. Maurice stepped up. Heath turned at once, alert to the smallest movement near him. Maurice said: "I am Maurice Collis. I

★ Artist, daughter of W. B. Yeats.

have written thirty-five books, some of which were considered bolshy in their day, but I believe there is nothing in any of them that a modern conservative would object to." Heath listened with apparent interest. He shook Maurice's hand with an agreeable smile and turned to shake mine. His hand was warm and soft as a woman's. His eyes were a deep sea blue and profoundly agitated. We then left.'

During the summer and autumn of 1972 Maurice's decline accelerated to such an extent that it seemed to me he could not last more than a few months. He was crumbling. Every day his voice seemed fainter, his lips more purple, his eyes more sunk, his moods more capricious. He was no longer sure that what he wrote made sense, and never sent a letter without asking me to read it. His weariness was very great. But he still wished to be taken out every day, preferably to a drink. 'It's feet first for me if I don't make the effort,' he said, shuffling towards the car, leaning heavily on me. Then he might suddenly say: 'I know what's in your mind. You think I'm a burden. You're dying to be rid of me.' And he would work himself up into a rage which left him hardly breath to end his tirade with: 'Ah, if I didn't love you so much, I wouldn't care.'

Now he was afraid to let me out of his sight for a minute and would crawl after me from room to room and listen carefully to everything I said on the telephone in case of plots; and scrutinise the outside of my letters with suspicion, although he did not actually dare to open them. These things were trying, but it was not possible to object, for they originated in his powerful fear that I would find the load too heavy, would vanish, would ditch him and he would die thereupon.

In November 1972 he became very ill and the doctor could not say exactly what was the matter. I took him to hospital for tests to be done. We had not been there more than two hours before his weakness increased to such an extent that he could not stand. They told me all his organs were diseased and there was no hope. He was comatose.

At a certain point he had a feeling that he was in the Antipodes and said: 'What is the kangaroo for bread?' I replied, 'Bread.' 'Is that so?' said he. 'Bread?' He seemed to ruminate, to sleep, to think. Then almost immediately he rose up in his bed saying, 'What a dreary place New Zealand is! Surely there must be a museum with portraits of local worthies. Let us go there at once.' He struggled to get his feet on the floor. His temporary strength was such that I had difficulty in restraining him. He said many other interesting things, as I recollect, but they are not recorded. When I got home after the day's watch I was unable to take up my pen and write.

Against expectation, he began to rally after a month and in the new year I brought him back in a taxi. Then began the most horrific ten days I have ever experienced. He was not a human being any more. The degradations of extreme age have to be seen to be believed. His memory for everything had gone; he frequently talked gibberish; was incontinent, fell over, tottered restlessly about at night, sometimes turning on the gas and sometimes the taps. He complained of terrifying dreams. The worst thing was that he knew he was like this, a dreadful simulacrum haunting rooms of happy memory.

On the morning of 12 January 1973, I heard a disturbance and hurried down the passage. He was stretched absolutely stiff, half out of bed, a demented look on his face. 'The rats! The rats! I'm being eaten by rats!'

I took up a tin of baby powder, saying, 'This is the proper cure for rats.' I opened his pyjamas and sprinkled him liberally. He began to relax and to seem more normal, but all at once drew back and, pointing to a mark on the carpet, said, 'What's that? Is it a rat?'

I said, 'No. It is a feather out of the eiderdown.' He considered the matter for a short while and then said, 'What we want is a good strong cup of tea.' He got to his feet somehow and staggered towards the kitchen. On entering, he said with amazement, 'But who are all these people?'

'They have come to enquire after you,' I said. 'They are going now.' He sat down and I put a cup of tea in front of him which he did not touch.

For some reason that escapes me, it had been arranged that he should have a blood transfusion. He was, of course, far too weak and ill, but I did not cancel the nurse who had been engaged to supervise the operation as there was no more food or money in the flat and I wanted her to stay with him while I went out to the shops and the bank.

I left him in bed turning the pages of *The Times* which rattled in his shaking hands. Although his gaunt features were drawn into a fixed expression, he knew why I was going out and had even tried to sign a cheque for the household expenses, but could not manage to hold the pen.

I suppose I was gone about twenty-five minutes. On my return, I found that he had, on a sudden, dissolved into the elements and only his carcase was left on the bed. I felt as if I had been knocked over the head.

# INDEX

Abdul Hamid II, 98, 103
*Ape and Essence*, 16
*Apple Cart, The*, 98, 112
Alexander the Great, 74
Alexander, Field Marshal Earl, in Burma, 147–9; 156
Alexander, Margaret, Countess, 149
Alexandra, Queen, 109
*Alice in Wonderland*, 170, 198
Ancaster, Phyllis, Countess of, 181–2
*Ancient Mariner, The*, 170
Antrim, Randal John, 13th Earl of, 27
Arts Council, The, 46, 49, 78
Astor of Hever, 1st Baron, 159
Astor, Bronwen, Viscountess, 132; marriage, 139–41; 149, 150, 155; in the Holy Land, 157–9; 162–6, 174; her vision, 185–6; on Ward case, 180–3, 187–8, 191–2; 194
Astor, Hon David, 182
Astor, Nancy, Viscountess, 58–60, 69–72; her biography proposed, 87–8, 92–3, 95–7; recounts her life, 100–2, 106–13, 115–17; at Cliveden, 103–6, 118–20, *et passim*; her character, 107, 109–10, 113; opens exhibition, 122–4; her impersonations, 126–7; reactions to biography, 131–2; 139–40, 174, 186, 191
Astor, Philippa, Viscountess, 70, 71, 85, 87
Astor, Sarah, Viscountess, 30, 51–2
Astor, Waldorf, 2nd Viscount, 93, 98, 101, 107, 111, 112; his marriage, 116, 191
Astor, William, 4th Viscount, 173–4
Astor, William Waldorf, 3rd Viscount, 30, 51–2, 57–60, 65. 69–72, 74; second marriage, 85, 86–8, 92–3, 98, 103–6, 110; describes his mother, 115–16; 118–20, 121, 122–4; speech at Stanley Spencer's funeral, 124–5; charades, 126–7; 128; 3rd marriage, 131–2, 139–41; 142, 147, 150; opens Spencer Gallery, 154–5; on Hongkong, 157–9; on Ward case, 160–1, 162–6, 176–7, 187–8, 191–2; illness and death, 179–83; 173, 185–6, 194–5
Atholl, Katherine, Duchess of, 62–3, 109
Attlee, Rt Hon Clement, 66
Aung San, General, 27, 66, 68–9

Baker, Geoffrey, 202
Balfour, 1st Earl, 101
Barrie, James, 107
Bartlett, Vernon, 45
Beaverbrook, 1st Baron, 49
Bellini, Giovanni, 34

Berger, Mme, 166
Berlin, Sir Isiah, 71
Betjeman, Sir John, 83, 167–8, 208
Betjeman, Penelope, Lady, 167–8, 208
Bevan, Rt Hon Aneurin, 45
Birdwood, 2nd Baron, 62
Black, Sir Robert, 158
Blake, William, 24
Blunden, Edmund, 29
Booth, Evangeline, 111
Bottomley, Rt Hon Arthur, 66
Bristowe, William Syer, 184–5
Brooke, Humphrey, 153, 154
Browse, Lillian, 208
Bryant, Sir Arthur, 185
Buddhism, 3, 100, 132
Bullitt, William C., 96

Cadogan, Theodosia, Lady, 72
Calder, Alexander, 67
Carline, Mrs Richard, 137
*Castle, The*, 73
Cecil, Henry, 34
Cézanne, Paul, 22
Chadwick, Lynn, 89
Chamberlain, Rt Hon Neville, 116
Channon, Sir Henry (Chips), 84–5
Cheng Tien-Hsi, 18–19
Chetwode, Field Marshal Lord, 167–8
Chetwode, Lady, 168
Chiang Kai-shek, 27, 96, 190
*Chiaroscuro*, 44
Chopin, Frederick, 18
*Christ Preaching at Cookham Regatta*, 120, 125, 132
Churchill, Mrs Randolf, 87
Churchill, Sir Winston, 87, 88, 93, 115, 116
Clark, Baron, Kenneth, 49, 79
Clarence, Duke of, 108
Cliveden, *passim*; Cliveden set, 98; last view of, 201–2
Coghill, Sir Patrick, 180
Collins, William, 144–6
Collis and Ward, 1
Collis, Bryan, 193
Collis, Carol, 193
Collis, David, 193
Collis, Edith (M.C.'s mother), 1, 16; death of, 19–21, 40, 53–4, 167
Collis, Eleanor (M.C.'s wife), 4, 8–9, 13, 14; death of, 192–3; 205, 206

Collis, Joyce, 20, 21
Collis, Maurice, childhood, 1; in Burma, 2–13; begins literary career, 13–14; connection with Cliveden, 57–9, 69–192; last days, 204–10; death, 211. Writing: for films, 17, 25; *Cortés and Montezuma*, 52, 61; *Last and First in Burma*, 64–6, 68; *Nancy Astor*, 93–119; *Stanley Spencer*, 127, 130–56; *Wayfoong*, 153, 159–60; *Raffles*, 174; *Somerville and Ross*, 180. Painting: begins to paint, 84; his exhibition, 122–4. Observations: on literature, 16–17, 33, 36–7, 43–4, 73, 121; on art, 27–8, 37–8, 43, 46–7, 49–50, 64, 81, 94, 133–4, 169, 170, 199; on Burma, 40, 42, 68–9, 114, 148, 154, 172–3, 184, 188–90, 197–8; on antiquities, 12, 30–1, 59, 72, 168
Collis, William (M.C.'s father), 1, 21, 53–4
Collis, Dr W. R. F. (Bob), 16, 19–21
Compton-Burnett, Ivy, 200–1
Confucianism, 3
Confucius, 18
Contemporary Arts, Institute of, 29, 33, 48; exhibition of paintings by chimpanzees at, 94; 207
Coombe, Carol, 28–9
Corot, Camille, 30
*Cortés and Montezuma*, 52, 57, 61, 65, 72, 160
Craxton, John, 89
Cripps, Isobel, Lady, 63
Cripps, Rt Hon Sir Stafford, 63
Crowley, Aleister, 32
Curzon, 1st Marquess, 44, 93, 109

*Danse Macabre*, 33
Darnley, 9th Earl of, 18
David, Sir Percival, 168
Davies, Ffrançon, 121–2, 137–9
Dawson, Geoffrey, 107
de la Mare, Walter, 155
*Demoiselles d'Avignon, Les*, 23
Denning, Lord Justice, 177
Dennison, Robert, Admiral, 128
Derain, André, 160
*Descent of the God, The*, 31
Digby, Wingfield, 121
*Discovery of L. S. Lowry, The*, 37
Dobson, Frank, 39–40
Dorman-Smith, Rt Hon Sir Reginald, 63–5, 68–9, 74; cured of semi-blindness, 75–6
*Duchess of Malfi, The*, 91
Dufy, Raoul, 61, 147
du Sautoy, Peter, 130

Edinburgh, Duke of, 164; and Topolski, 194–6, 199–200
Egon, Nicholas, 41
Eisenhower, Dwight D., 96
Eliot, T. S., 84, 129–30
Eliot, Valerie, 129–30

Elizabeth, Queen Mother, 81, 150
Elizabeth II, Queen, 11, 189, 195
*Eminent Victorians*, 107
Empson, William, 48–9
Epstein, Sir Jacob, 40, 51

Faber, Sir Geoffrey, 5–6
Fagg, W. B., 54
*Fall of Constantinople, The*, 178
Feisal, King of Iraq, 15, 97, 167
Ferdinand, Archduke of Austria, 105
*First Holy One, The*, 18
Fitzgerald, Desmond, 42
Fon of Bum, The, 118
Ford, Sir Edward, 123
Ford, Henry, 108
*Foreign Mud*, 48, 158, 185
Forrester, C. S., 38
Freud, Lucien, 46

Gainsborough, Thomas, 34, 65
Gandi, Devadas, 38–9
Gandi, Mahatma, 6, 7, 39
Genghis Khan, 103, 121
George V, 108–9
Gibbon, Edward, 67
Giri, Prince, 103, 105
Giri, Princess, 104
Glass, Douglas, 55
*Glass-Blowers, The*, 30
*Glasgow Resurrection, The*, 24
Goering, Hermann, 45
Gogarty, Oliver, St John, 44
Gollancz, Victor, 156
*Gormenghast*, 30, 31, 36–7, 152, 170
Gowrie, Zara, Countess of, 103, 104
Graham, Howgrave, 83–4
Grantley, 7th Baron, 126, 173–4
Greene, Graham, 17
Grier, Dr Lynda, 67
Grierson, Sir George, 1
Grylls, R. Glynn, 29
Guedalla, Philip, 71
Gustav, King of Sweden, 57–60, 70–2

Hailey, 1st Baron, 57–60, 70–2
Hals, Frans, 34
Harrisson, Tom, 90
Hayward, John, 29, 32
*Heart of the Matter, The*, 17
Heath, Rt Hon Edward 208–9
Hendy, Kythe, Lady, 76, 77
Hendy, Sir Philip, 35, 76
Henriquez, Fiore de, 55
Hepworth, Dame Barbara, 27, 64, 81, 176
Hepworth, Dorothy, 141–2
Herman, Josef, 175
*Hilda Apotheosis, The*, 146–7
Hitler, Adolf, 110

Hla Maung, U., 178–9, 183–4, 189, 190, 197–8
Home, Sir Alec Douglas, 171
Hongkong and Shanghai Banking Corporation, The, 150, 153, 159, 174, 175
House of Commons, The, 85–6, 97, 101, 105, 107, 109, 110, 117
Hsiung, S. I., 28
Hurling Time, The, 75, 84, 90, 97, 185, 203
Hussein, King of Jordan, 157–9
Hutton, Lt General Sir Thomas, 148–9
Huxley, Aldous, 16
Huxley, Francis, 165
Huxley, Sir Julian, 73–4, 76; 70th birthday, 89–90; 91, 94, 165; on the occult, 201, 202–3
Huxley, Juliette, 91, 201, 202
Huxley, Michael, 76

Indigo Days, 89
Into Hidden Burma, 3, 4, 58, 71, 201
Irwin, J. C., 184

James Henry, 101, 105
James, Martin, 35
James, Philip, 46, 49
Jameson, Dr, 93, 101, 105
John, Augustus, 44, 55, 143–4, 152, 170
Johnson, Pamela Hansford, 188
Jones, Miss, 101, 110
Journey Outward, The, 2, 42, 62
Joyce, James, 1, 4, 44
Juda, Annely, 178

Ka Si, U, 42
Kafka, Franz, 73
Keeler, Christine, 160–1, 163, 165
Kelly, Sir Gerald, 32–3, 132–3
Kennerley, Jean, 130
Kennerley, Morley, 130
Kent, Duke of, 108
Kensan, 199
Kerr, Philip, 98, 107, 111
Keswick, Mary, Lady, 174–5
Keswick, Sir William (Tony), 67, 80–1, 160–1, 165, 169; his speech, 174–6
King and Queen, 80, 161
King's Peace, The, 67
Kipling, Rudyard, 93, 106–7
Kirby, Maj. Gen. S. Woodburn, 148
Kitchener, 1st Earl, 105, 174
Korda, Sir Alexander, 17, 25, 29
Korda, Zoltan, 17, 25
Kruschev, N., 150

Lancaster, Osbert, 105, 120, 173, 174
Last and First in Burma, 64, 68, 85, 148
Laver, James, 208
Lawrence, Lord Justice, 45
Lawrence, T. E., 111, 119, 120
Leach, Bernard, 198–9
Lenin, V. I., 111

Leon, Henry, see Cecil, Henry
Leonardo, 34
Literature, Royal Society of, 36
Livingstone, Dr, 95
Lloyd George, David, 1st Earl, 109
Lopokova, 4
Lothian, 11th Marquess of, see Kerr, Philip
Love on the Moor, 66
Lowry, L. S., 37–8, 41, 46, 55–6, 168–9, 193–4

Ma A Ma, 197
MacArthur, General Douglas, 128
Macaulay, Rose, 89, 90, 91–2
Mackenzie, Compton, 81
Macmillan, Rt Hon Harold, 86
MacNeice, Louis, 196
Maharishi Mahesh Yogi, 202
Maisky, I., 111
Mander, Rosalie Lady, 29
Mann, Thomas, 73
Mantegna, Andrea, 34
Margaret, Princess, 114
Marie, Queen of Romania, 93
Marlborough, 10th Duke of, 30, 185
Marshall, Gen. G. C., 96
Martineau, J., 128–9, 143, 144–6
Mary, Queen, 108, 119
Matisse, Henri, 22, 160
Maugham, W. Somerset, 40–1, 49
Medley, Margaret, 168
Menon, Krishna, 50
Meredith, 153
Middleton, 156
Millionairess, The, 112
Minney, R. J., 38
Modigliani, Amadeo, 170
Molotov, V. M., 111
Mona Lisa, The, 207
Monteith, Charles, 180
Montgomery, Field Marshal, Viscount, 111
Moore, Henry, 21–2, 56–7, 76; at home, 72–81, 89; 161, 170, 176
Morse, Sir Arthur, 159, 175
Motherly and Auspicious, The, 17, 28
Mountbatten, Earl, 27, 65, 68
Mumtaz Mahal, 17
Munnings, Sir Alfred, 133, 134–5
Murray, W. Staite, 59, 91–2, 93–4, 95, 100
Mystery of Dead Lovers, The, 25

Nancy Astor, 121, 129, 131
Nativity, The, 133
Neguib, Muhammad, 59
Nehru, Pandit, 50–1
Ne Win, Mme, describes Burma, 171–3; 188–90; visit to M.C., 196–8
Ne Win, General, 171–3, 179, 183, 184; his character and aims, 188–90; visit to M.C., 196–8

214

Nicholson, Sir William, 208
Nicolson, Sir Harold, 43–4
Nu, U., 65, 66, 172, 190

*Opium War Through Chinese Eyes, The*, 121

Palmer, 3rd Baron, 103, 105
Palmer, Baroness, 104
Pankhurst, Christobel, 109
Pankhurst, Sylvia, 109
Peake, Maeve, 151–3, 165–6, 169–70, 180, 186–7, 188
Peake, Mervyn, 29–30, 31, 36–7, 41, 86; his illness, 120–1, 151–3, 169–70, 186–7; exhibitions, 165–6, 188
Penrose, Sir Roland, 164
Phillips, Ewan, 118
Picabia, Francis, 22
Picasso, Pablo, 22–3
Piper, John, 69, 70, 71, 167
Pleing Nobadol Rabibhadana, Prince, 185
*Potato Seller, The*, 123
Pound, Ezra, 39–40
*Precious Stream, Lady*, 28
Priestley, J. B., 89, 90
Profumo, Rt Hon John, 161, 163
Pugh, Sir Alun, 139, 164, 186, 187–8
Pugh, Bronwen, *see* Astor, Bronwen, Viscountess
Pugh, Kathleen, Lady, 139, 187
*Pye Mr*, 43

*Quest For Sita*, 170

Raine, Kathleen, 196
*Raffles*, 174
Ramsay, Lady Patricia, 101
Raverat, Gwen, 63
Read, Sir Herbert, 35–6, 46, 48, 49, 79, 81, 164
Reith, 1st Baron, 57–60
Rembrandt, 34
Renoir, Pierre Auguste, 160
Reynolds, Sir Joshua, 30
Ribbentrop, Joachim von, 110
Rice-Davies, Mandy, 165, 166, 183
Rimbaud, Jean Arthur, 173
Rodd, Commander G. G. (Taffy), 26
Rose, Sir Francis, 22–3; in lunatic asylum, 81–3; 150–1, 199, 201
Rose, Frederica, Lady, 23, 81
Roosevelt, President Franklin D., 96
Rothenstein, Alice, Lady, 50
Rothenstein, Elizabeth, Lady, 130–1, 157
Rothenstein, Sir John, 33; Stanley Spencer confides in, 35, 130–1; 154–5, 157
Rothenstein, Michael, 50
Rothenstein, Sir William, 50
Roxburghe, Duchess of, 156
Rubens, Sir Peter Paul, 34

Rubinstein, Anthony, 154
Runciman, Hon Sir Steven, 90–1, 178
Rushbury, Henry, 134–5, 157
Rutland, Duchess of, 70, 87

St Albans, Duchess of, 188
St Albans, 12th Duke of, 188
St Davids, 2nd Viscount, 36
*Salome*, 206
Sargent, Sir John, 93
Saunders, J. A. H., 158
Sayadaw, The, 3, 4, 5, 6, 7, 9, 10, 12
Schrijver, Herman, 200–1
*Secret History of the Mongols, The*, 121
Sen Gupta, 6–7
Shah Jehan, 17
Shakir Pasha, General, 98
Shaw, George Bernard, 60, 98, 107, 111–12, 132
*She was a Queen*, 154
Shiel, G. G., 143, 144–6, 154, 155
Siam, King of, 11
*Siamese White*, 13, 33, 185
Simon, Sir John, 66
Sitwell, Edith, 29
Sitwell, Sir Osbert, 29
Skeaping, John, 47
Smith, Sir Matthew, 152
Smith, Stevie, 42, 178
Smyth, Sir John, 85
Snow, C. P., Baron, 182, 188
Snow, Lady, *see* Johnson, Pamela Hansford
*Somerville and Ross*, 180, 191, 199, 201, 203
Spencer, Gilbert, 26, 129
Spencer, Hilda, 130, 136, 137, 191
Spencer, Patricia, Lady, 129, 130–1, 137, 141–2, 145, 157
Spencer, Shirin, 127, 146, 154–5
Spencer, Sir Stanley, 23–4, 25, 29, 47, 65–6, 69–70, 74, 105; his illness, 119–20, 121–2; funeral, 124–5; death, 135–7; his biography, 122, 127, 128–9, 130–1, 132, 133, 134–5, 137–9, 141–3, 147, 149–50, 154–6, 157; 169, 191
Spencer, Unity, 127, 146–7, 153–5
Stalin, J., 59, 60, 111, 112
Stanley of Alderley, 6th Baron, 26
Stark, Freya, 51, 74–5
Starkie, Enid, 173
Starkie, Walter, 173
Stein, Gertrude, 22–3, 81
Stephens, James, 33
Stewart, G. O. W., 153, 159–60
Stirling, Irene, 127, 149, 153
Storrs, Sir Ronald, 62
Strachey, Lytton, 107
Strong, L. A. G., 81
Sutherland, Graham, 49–50
Sweeney, J. J., 53
Symonds, John, 32–3

Taj Mahal, 17, 25, 76
Thant, U, 154, 188
Thein Doke, 183
Thomas, Dylan, 152
Titian, 34
*Titus Alone*, 120
*Titus Groan*, 30, 121, 152, 170
*To the Lighthouse*, 73
Tolstoy, Leo, 184
Toklas, Alice, 22–3
Tooth, Dudley, 70, 128–9, 142–3, 144–6, 149–50, 154, 155
Topolski, Feliks, 18, 35–6, 38–9, 44–6, 51, 54, 117–18; on Ward, 161–2, 177–8; 197 ;and Duke of Edinburgh, 194–6, 198, 199–200
Topolski, Marion, 35, 48, 63
Toulouse-Lautrec, Henri de, 23
*Towers of Trebizond, The*, 89
Townsend, Peter, 114–15
*Transposed Heads*, 73
*Treasure Island*, 170
Trevelyan, Julian, 76, 89
Tzu Hsi, 126

*Ulysses*, 1, 4

Verlaine, Paul, 173
Villiers, M., 144–6
*Virgin of the Rocks, The*, 206
*Visitation, The*, 133

Waley, Arthur, 26, 40, 47, 77–8, 121
Wallace, Neville, 122
*Wandering Ecstatic, The*, 123, 124
Ward, Dr Stephen, 131, 132, 150, 160–6, 182–3, 186, 191–2
Warner, Frederick, 114–15

Watteau, Antoine, 82, 83
Wavell, Countess, 85
Wavell, Field Marshal Earl, 85, 148
*Wayfoong*, 174
Webster, John, 91
Wedgwood, Dame Veronica, 67–8, 77
Westminster, Dean of, 133
Westropp, Rev. Michael, 125, 132, 135–7
Westropp, Rachel, 135–6
White, Samuel, 11–12
Whiting, Noel, 151, 164, 171, 188, 189
Whyte, Margaret, Lady, 91
Wilde, Oscar, 206
Wilkinson, Ellen, 109
Wilson, Rt Hon Harold, 189
Wilson, Scottie, 28, 33
Wilson, President Woodrow, 96
*Wit to Woo, The*, 41, 86
Wolfenden, Sir John, 131
Woodman, Dorothy, 184
Woolf, Virginia, 73
Wordsworth, William, 133
Worsley, Joyce, Lady, 70

Yeats, Ann, 208
Yeats, Jack B., 52–3
Yeats, W. B., 52, 81, 196

*Zacharias*, 133
Zadkine, Ossip, 43
Zeid el Hussein, Prince, 15, 16, 97, 99–100, 166–7
Zeid el Hussein, Princess Fahrunissa, 15–16, 24–5, 61, 62, 88–9, 97–100, 102–3, 166–7
Zoete, Beryl de, 47, 77
Zulueta, Marie-Louise, Lady de, 160